COMMUNICATING FOR MANAGERIAL EFFECTIVENESS

THIRD EDITION

Phillip G. Clampitt

University of Wisconsin, Green Bay

SAGE Publications
Thousand Oaks ▪ London ▪ New Delhi

For information:

Sage Publications, Inc.
2455 Teller Road
Thousand Oaks, California 91320
E-mail: order@sagepub.com

Sage Publications Ltd.
1 Oliver's Yard
55 City Road
London EC1Y 1SP
United Kingdom

Sage Publications India Pvt. Ltd.
B-42, Panchsheel Enclave
Post Box 4109
New Delhi 110 017 India

Printed in the United States of America

Library of Congress Cataloging-in-Publication Data

Clampitt, Phillip G.
Communicating for managerial effectiveness / by Phillip G. Clampitt.—3rd ed.
   p. cm.
Includes bibliographical references and indexes.
ISBN 0-7619-3099-X (pbk.)
   1. Communication in management. I. Title.
HD30.3.C52 2005
658.4′5—dc22

                         2004003804

This book is printed on acid-free paper.

06   07   08   10 9 8 7 6 5 4 3

Acquisitions Editor:	Todd R. Armstrong
Editorial Assistant:	Deya Saoud
Production Editor:	Kristen Gibson
Copy Editor:	Annette Pagliaro
Typesetter:	C&M Digitals (P) Ltd.
Indexer:	David Luljak
Cover Designer:	Janet Foulger
Proofreader:	Tricia Lawrence

Contents

Foreword

The communication that takes place in an organization is an important influence in the success of that organization. Therefore, a good book on organizational communication can be a valuable resource for all kinds of students—managers who want to be effective communicators, as well as academic students who want to understand how organizations work. Phil Clampitt has written such a book.

Over the years, I have evaluated a number of manuscripts offered to various publishers, and many of them have good coverage of rather standard materials that are commonly covered about organizational communication. What Phil Clampitt has done, however, is to write a book that is original and interesting.

What strikes me most about his work is its freshness. The quotations that begin each chapter are not typical organizational literature; they demonstrate how well read Phil Clampitt is and how this breadth of resources have led him to think about organizational life in some innovative ways. He also demonstrates great originality in the way that he uses metaphor to explain how communication works. For example, although I love to dance, I would never have thought of using dance as a metaphor for the way organizational communication works. Yet, Clampitt does so in a convincing way. Furthermore, he is able to coin new phrases that are rich in explanatory power.

I also like the way Clampitt makes this book a statement of his theory about organizational communication. It is not merely a report on the research about a topic. He includes basic propositions and clarifies some of his basic assumptions. He also makes a major addition by describing some common problem areas and then telling his reader "what to do" about them. Finally, he adds some important areas that are often overlooked. His work with communication audits has prompted him to add chapters on facilitating boundary spanning and cultivating an innovative spirit.

One of the great rewards of being a university professor is being able to watch exceptional graduate students become major contributors to one's discipline. Phil Clampitt is doing this with his book. There are many gems in these chapters, and I am delighted to recommend it.

Cal Downs
University of Kansas

Preface

A new edition of a book provides opportunities to update material and fine-tune critical ideas. I seized these opportunities but I also wanted to do something more. My goals focused on making this edition more accessible, actionable, and thought-provoking.

- *Accessible:* Readers will notice that each chapter contains a "By the Numbers" feature. These sidebars underscore critical facts that highlight the chapter's communication challenge. This edition also includes more summary charts designed to underscore critical notions. I moved much of the background research to the book's Web site to better organize supplemental material. For example, the citations for "By the Numbers" are on the book's Web site (www.imetacomm.com/CME3).

- *Actionable:* Since the second edition of this book, I have consulted with numerous organizations about many of the communication issues discussed in the previous editions. I learned first-hand the difficulty many organizations experience translating seemingly simple and straightforward principles into action. For instance, after leading dozens of change efforts in the past few years, I have grown to appreciate the need for actionable tools based on sound theory and designed to assist with the planning process. This edition includes examples of those tools. In general, I emphasize how to successfully and quickly implement the principles discussed in each chapter.

- *Thought-provoking:* Scores of business and communication books are published every year that tell us what to do, but not how to structure our thinking. I've paid particular attention to this issue because I believe that although tactical decisions change with situations, a robust thinking routine can endure and be applicable to a wide range of situations. Thus, readers will note a renewed focus on core models designed to structure thinking about issues such as spanning organizational boundaries. Likewise, a new chapter (11) discusses in considerable depth the difficult question of measuring and judging communication effectiveness. Hopefully, readers will have a vision of the relationship between communication assessments, strategies, and tactics.

In short, every chapter has been revised in some major way. I have also been mindful of how the Internet continues to change the way organizations communicate. The "dot" is the most significant aspect of the dot.com evolution because dots can be easily connected. The ease of connecting employees, managers, and executives has not made organizational communication easier; it has only changed the nature of the challenge. This edition tackles this issue in a variety of ways. In fact, my consulting firm, Metacomm, developed a Web site for the book intended to improve the connection between motivated readers and the material (see www. imetacomm.com/CME3). The site contains chapter outlines, exercises, and case studies. I hope the book and Web site provide the wisdom, insight, and advice necessary to enhance your communication effectiveness.

Acknowledgments

C. S. Lewis once said, "Two heads are better than one, not because either is infallible, but because they are unlikely to go wrong in the same direction." Many wise minds steered me in the right direction. I'm profoundly grateful for the guidance of many friends and colleagues. First, I must thank my CME3 team headed by Laurey Berk and complemented by dedicated research assistants including Jerome Allen, Ryan Nodorft, Amanda Kaminski, and Kristine Polland. Todd Armstrong at Sage Publications provided wonderful guidance on the project and selected a number of insightful anonymous reviewers, who provided wonderful continuous improvement suggestions. My colleagues, Tim Meyer, Cliff Abbott, and Dan Spielmann at the University of Wisconsin-Green Bay, as well as two of my former professors, Lee Williams and Cal Downs, provided provocative and illuminating comments on many of the core ideas in this edition. I also had a "real-world" team of advisors who actually manage business communication on a daily basis. My thanks to John Rhodes, Dave Spencer, Bill VanDenBrandt, Rick Fantini, Tom Cashman, Bob Heimann, Dr. Barry Usow, and Bob DeKoch. The Sage editorial team, Deya Saoud, Kristen Gibson, and Annette Pagliaro, has been wonderful to work with. Finally, there is the unlisted co-author of this book. She refuses to let her name appear on the cover, despite the fact that she read countless drafts, reworked major sections, and clarified my sometimes garbled thoughts. While listening to Mozart's concerti in beautiful Door County, we reshaped the manuscript into a work that we hope resonates with many people. I cannot imagine anyone having a better partner. In fact, she is mine—for life.

Introduction

"The first principle is that you must not fool yourself...and you are the easiest person to fool," wrote the Nobel Laureate, Richard Feynman. Physicists are not the only ones who must guard against self-delusion—managers must, as well. And the temptation of self-deception proves almost irresistible when it comes to the elusive business of communication. The purpose of *Communicating for Managerial Effectiveness* is to enable managers to clearly view their communication abilities, dilemmas, and challenges.

This presents an unusual challenge for two reasons. First, our knowledge of the communication process continues to grow and change. New and exciting theories have recently appeared on the horizon that allow us to see communication in a light never before possible. Only in the past few years have we started to discern the implications of these ideas. For instance, some scholars have challenged the traditional assertion that "understanding" or "persuasion" should be the only goals of communication. Sometimes managers are purposefully ambiguous. What are the implications of this notion for managers? Can misunderstandings be useful in an organization? These are the types of questions entertained in these pages.

Second, there is what I call the "Everybody/Anybody Phenomena." Translation: Because everybody communicates, anyone can hold a seminar on the subject. Hence, what often gets passed off as training for "communication excellence" consists of nothing more than warmed-over platitudes or rehashed pop psychology. That is unfortunate not only because it misrepresents a rich field of scholarship but also because managers encounter a host of communication challenges that are not addressed by the "Everybody/Anybody" speakers. They treat ideas like they are cotton candy; something fluffy and sweet, but not the staples of organizational life. Nothing could be further from reality. Ideas have consequences. Bad ideas have bad consequences. When the communication system breaks down, tragedy is often the result. A case in point: the space shuttle Columbia tragedy, discussed in the culture chapter (Chapter 3).

The impetus for this manuscript came from research I conducted in over fifty organizations and from concerns revealed in numerous consulting engagements (see www.imetacomm.com/CME3). The methodology consisted of administering surveys and conducting interviews with employees. As I conducted communication assessments, often in conjunction with students, I discovered a group of concerns that emerged as common themes in these organizations. For instance, executives were often dismayed at the seeming impossibility of getting departments to communicate effectively with one another. Employees were often frustrated by the lack of useful feedback from their managers. Therefore, the manuscript took shape around these concerns.

The illustration below provides the framework for the book. At the hub of managerial effectiveness lies communication, corporate culture, and ethics. The first two chapters are devoted to explaining the complex process of communication. The third chapter concerns the core issue of corporate culture, which has a pervasive impact on the communication climate. Chapter 4 focuses on communication ethics. If managers are not deemed to be ethical communicators, then their lack of credibility undermines any attempt at effective communication. The spokes of the wheel represent six critical communication challenges most managers face. In each case, I begin by analyzing the challenge and close with practical recommendations based on actual cases. These six chapters discuss:

- Selecting and using communication technologies (Chapter 5)
- Managing data, information, knowledge, and action (Chapter 6)
- Providing performance feedback (Chapter 7)
- Communicating across organizational boundaries (Chapter 8)
- Communicating about organizational changes (Chapter 9)
- Cultivating an innovative spirit (Chapter 10)

The final chapter (Chapter 11) focuses on the complex issue of measuring and judging communication effectiveness. It suggests a way to analyze and think about an organization's communication system. It represents the rim of the wheel because it provides the macro-level viewpoint that holds the entire manuscript together. The wheel symbolizes wholeness as well as movement. I hope this book will provide a more complete picture of managerial communication effectiveness, while presenting an image of the ever-changing nature of that quest.

I use examples from the business world—many from my consulting experiences—as well as from a wide range of arenas including politics, history, science, and art. The rationale: Communication issues pervade every arena of life. Unless otherwise noted, I have changed the names and slightly altered the background in order to "protect the guilty." When particularly illuminating, I discuss the findings of key scholarly studies. However, I focus on the practical implementation of the research. I hope that executives, managers, potential managers, training personnel, and students of business communication will find in these pages a way to abide by Professor Feynman's "first principle."

SECTION 1

Foundation

1

How Managers Communicate

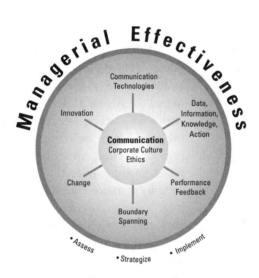

Human communication permeates the human condition. Human communication surrounds us and is an in-built aspect of everything human beings are and do. That makes any effort to explain, predict, or to some extent control human communication a pretty big order. How does one get a handle on the totality of human communication?

Frank Dance

If, by a wave of a magic wand, managers could communicate perfectly, how would organizations change? Would the company be more productive? Would employees be more satisfied? The magic wand presents an intriguing dilemma for the manager. On the one hand, managers know that their success is largely a function of their communication skills. On the other hand, they are often unclear about what constitutes "perfect" or effective communication. Some argue, for example, that if employees completely understood their managers, organizations would function smoothly. Yet, misunderstandings may prove useful as in the case of an employee who misinterprets a manager's sarcastic criticism as a legitimate suggestion. Such a misunderstanding may temporarily preserve "the peace." How managers might use this "magic wand" proves revealing. It creates the illusions and reality of their world. Typically, managers choose to wave the wand in one of three ways. The Arrow, Circuit, and Dance approaches are highlighted in the following sections.

The Arrow Approach

Chapter 1: By the Numbers

60%
of employees are satisfied with communication from their supervisor

55%
of managers are unfit for their job

20
Average number of people murdered at work each week in the United States

45%
of employees have confidence in the job being done by senior management

70%
of communication metaphors describe the communication process as a conduit

Mr. Taylor managed the information technology (IT) division in an organization. He almost perfectly, although unwittingly, articulated the Arrow philosophy during a meeting with a consultant. The consultant was presenting the IT division's results of a communication satisfaction survey to Mr. Taylor and his management team. Mr. Taylor asked the consultant numerous technical questions about how some survey data were analyzed. After each response, Mr. Taylor appeared increasingly uneasy and antagonistic. When the consultant suggested that his employees were less than satisfied with the communication system, Mr. Taylor's technical questions assumed an almost acidic quality. The tone of the conversation became increasingly combative. As frequently occurs, Mr. Taylor's technical questions masked his actual concern. Finally, he exploded with a fifteen-minute diatribe, with comments such as:

Why should I take *my* time to ensure that people understand? I send e-mails because then I know that I've communicated my message. Then I don't have to worry about it. They got my message. These meetings you propose may make people feel good but I just see them as a waste of my time and the company's time.

After this rather illuminating soliloquy an uncomfortable silence prevailed for a moment. Yet there was also a sense of relief because Mr. Taylor had laid all his cards on the table. His comments had some merit. He clearly pointed out one of the greatest challenges in organizational communication: providing efficient methods of communication. Yet, there were significant flaws in his thinking.

First, he assumed that messages sent via e-mail would be received at the proper time. But what about messages that are filtered out because they are inadvertently treated as spam? Second, Mr. Taylor assumed that if the message was received, it was read. With information overload being one of the facts of organizational life, this assumption may be suspect. Finally, he assumed that if the message was actually read, it also was understood in the way intended. This is probably the most tenuous of all his premises. Yet these are exactly the kinds of assumptions that all Arrow managers make.

Judging Effectiveness

Nowhere is this orientation more evident than when managers are asked about the meaning of effective communication. These are typical responses:

- "Being able to clearly and precisely put my thoughts into words."
- "Speaking with credibility and authority on topics I know about."
- "Getting the results I want by talking to my people."

Certainly managers should seek to speak clearly, concisely, and with credibility in order to achieve results. Yet, a re-examination of each of those statements in light of the underlying assumptions proves revealing (see Table 1.1).

Table 1.1   Arrow Manager's Assumptions about Communication Effectiveness

Communication Effectiveness	Underlying Assumptions
• Being able to clearly and precisely put thoughts into words.	• What is clear and precise to one person is clear and precise to another.
• Speaking with credibility and authority.	• Credibility is something the speaker possesses and not something given to the speaker by the audience.
• Getting the results desired by talking to employees.	• Communication is primarily a one-way activity.

In short, Arrow managers focus on accurately encoding their thoughts into language—much like selecting, aiming, and firing arrows at a target. They see communication as a one-way activity based primarily on the skills of the sender. Receivers of messages are viewed as passive information processors who react appropriately if the words are "on the mark." Thus, feedback is not only improbable, it is unnecessary.

Explaining Communication Breakdowns

Even with "proper" encoding, communication inevitably breaks down. Yet, many managers tenaciously hold to the Arrow approach with explanations such as:

- "Why didn't they just follow my instructions? If I told them once, I told them a thousand times."
- "How could this project get so fouled up? I told them exactly how to do it."

In each case the Arrow manager assumes the receiver errs. After all, the meaning of the words is self-evident and fixed; therefore, everyone should understand the message similarly. And certainly the workers heard what was said because management repeated it a "thousand times." This type of reasoning inevitably leads some managers to the conclusions that their employees are inherently ignorant, lazy, or subversive.

But what if the Arrow manager fails to understand someone? Curiously, the onus of fault shifts from the receiver to the sender. The Arrow manager's likely responses include: "I should have been notified." or "Why didn't you just say that?" In these cases the sender clearly failed to "hit the target" because the "proper" words were not uttered. In sum, communication breakdowns are always the fault of the sender or the receiver. Arrow managers never think that the problem, and hence the responsibility, might be mutual. They fail to recognize that effective communication is a shared commitment between senders and receivers.

Origins

Why would a manager adopt this orientation? It is probably not the result of a conscious decision. Rather, through countless individual experiences, an unconscious pattern forms that becomes the modus operandi. There are three major factors that appear to contribute to the process.

First, the technical training of many managers reinforces a stimulus/ response orientation. On a number of occasions I have talked with engineers who had recently assumed managerial responsibilities. Many experience special challenges in managing people. For years they have been trained to use precise formulas that exactly predict certain outcomes. If the design is developed according to standards, then it works and performs as expected. Transferring such logic to management is as natural as it is problematic. As managers, these engineers tend to view communication as another type of design problem. After all, like the design specifications, everyone should interpret the message in the same way. Choosing the right language, as in selecting the proper materials, should lead to effectiveness. Of course, people do not always react like they are "supposed to" and human beings are not passive objects like girders, cable, and concrete. It requires great intellectual dexterity to get rid of these conceptions, built up literally through years of training and countless daily experiences.

The second contributing factor, strangely enough, is the "speech teacher." The very term, "speech teacher," implies a one-way view of communication. Why not "speaking and listening teacher"? Or just "communication teacher"? Historically, teachers of public address have been profoundly influenced by Aristotle's remarkable work, *The Rhetoric,* which was one of the first truly systematic treatises on the spoken word.[1] He emphasized the speaker, or the orator, arranging an appropriate message in accordance with general principles. Audience members were seen as passive and reactive rather than active and interactive. In short, Aristotle primarily viewed communication as a one-way act of influence.

More recently, communication theorists have taken to model-building in an attempt to represent the communication process. Claude Shannon, an engineer at Bell Telephone Company, developed one of the classic and most influential models. This model, shown in Figure 1.1, was developed to help engineers decide how to most efficiently transmit electrical impulses from one place to another. Other models having a more social-psychological emphasis were developed based on Shannon and (his colleague) Weaver's basic premise.[2] These types of models represent communication as a one-way activity, not only visually but also conceptually.

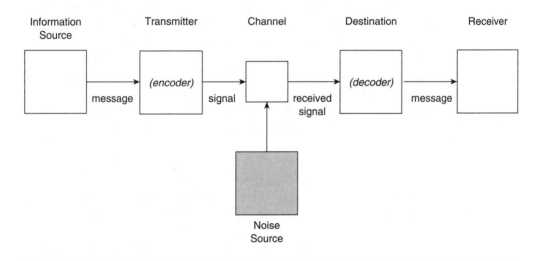

Figure 1.1   Shannon & Weaver Model

Finally, certain people may have personality predispositions to communicate in this way. Treating communication as a one-way event allows the Arrow manager to avoid the complexities, ambiguities, and paradoxes of human behavior, thereby creating the illusion of permanence and finality. Dynamic contexts, unique individuals, adjustable styles of discourse, and multileveled conversations can prove not only bewildering but also deeply troubling to those who tenaciously cling to a simplistic worldview. Arrow managers avoid all this, with seeming efficiency and total control. Their personal psychological makeup may make this some sort of functional necessity. After all, a world in which all elements are dynamic can be profoundly unsettling and deeply disturbing.

Evaluation

Arrow managers believe that:

Effective Expression = Effective Communication.

This belief simultaneously limits and expands our understanding in the following ways.

Arrow managers assume that receivers are passive information processors. This assumption trivializes the listener's role and limits our understanding of the communication process. Although some Arrow managers recognize the difficulty of transforming an idea into a code and transmitting it, they usually fail to appreciate the listener's or reader's challenge of accurately reconstructing the message from the sender's signals. In short, they incorrectly treat communication as an *event* instead of a *process*. Consequently their work units are often devoid of interpersonal warmth, sapped of the creative spirit, and soured by employee resentment. Taken to an extreme, this can be enormously debilitating. Consider, for example, the communication practices of top military leaders during the Vietnam War. Their Arrow style of communication prompted one distinguished pilot to remark:

> I didn't hate them because they were dumb, I didn't hate them because they had spilled our blood for nothing. I hated them because of their arrogance . . . because they had convinced themselves that they actually knew what they were doing and that we were too minor to understand the "Big Picture."[3]

He targets his anger and resentment at those "leaders" who would not treat fellow military personnel as thinking human beings. He implicitly recognized that effective leaders treat communication as an *active,* not passive, process fraught with potential points of breakdown.

Arrow managers inappropriately assume that words are containers of meaning. The language we use subtly works against us in this respect. The expressions we use every day convey the notion that we put meaning into words and the words act as carriers of meaning: "capturing ideas in words," "putting ideas into writing," or "I have difficulty putting my thoughts into words." In fact, linguistics professor M.J. Reddy has made extensive studies of the metaphors used to describe the communication process.[4] He conservatively estimates that about 70% of the English language is directly, visibly, or graphically based on metaphors that stress this perspective on communication. For example, when managers exclaim, "Just read my e-mail," or "Read my lips," they create the illusion that meaning resides in the words themselves. In reality, words act as useful, although usually imprecise, stimulators of meaning, more than they do as containers of meaning. We actively construct meanings within a unique vortex that includes the words used, the context of the utterance, and the people involved.

The Arrow approach encourages clear thinking, lucid expression, and organized speaking. Emphasizing the sender's skill benefits the entire organization. Corporate recruiters often complain that new college graduates lack basic communication skills, such as how to make presentations, write a memo, and develop a meeting agenda.[5] Arrow managers tend to excel at such communication tasks.

The Arrow approach appropriately links communication behavior and action. Arrow managers discourage idle chatter, discussions of personal problems, and unnecessary information sharing. The result is often higher productivity because potentially time-wasting communication activities are eliminated. Provided that subordinates do understand directives and management knows what's best, the Arrow approach may actually encourage maximum performance.

Circuit Approach

If the language of the Arrow manager involves "targeting an audience," "attacking arguments," and "firing a volley of commands," then the discourse of the Circuit manager involves "networking," "going with the flow," and "making connections." The Circuit approach represents an evolution from the arrow to the circle. Circuit managers stress feedback over response, relationship over content, connotations over denotations, and understanding over compliance. They view communication as a two-way process involving a dynamic interplay of an active sender and receiver.

Mark, a district sales manager for a national life insurance company, was the quintessential Circuit manager. His office visits to "touch base" with the sales agents in his district were met with eager anticipation. Why? Mark conducted his "meetings" in exciting off-site locations such as a golf course or ski village. The meeting agenda was equally stimulating because the team rarely talked about business, production goals, or skill development. Yet, Mark was a master at building rapport, camaraderie, and a team environment. He assumed that because the agents "felt good" about working for him, and hence the company, they would then be more motivated to produce. The result? A happy, cohesive team that improved their golf scores more than their selling skills or sales record. Everybody loved Mark but few respected his managerial abilities.

Judging Effectiveness

The effectiveness issue exposes the Circuit manager's ultimate aims:

- Communication effectiveness is actively listening to my workers, so I know what makes them happy.

- I'm effective as a manager when I am sensitive to employees' needs and concerns. Then I try to communicate that sensitivity by adapting my message to each individual.
- My communication is effective when my employees feel included and understood.

As seen in Table 1.2, Circuit managers reveal their implicit perspective about the communication process in these comments. They make conceptual leaps from communication behavior to job satisfaction to productivity. The research suggests that these leaps, particularly from job satisfaction to productivity, are dubious at best.[6] The odds are about the same as one athlete completing the high jump, the broad jump, and the pole vault in one bound.

Table 1.2   Circuit Managers' Assumptions About Communication Effectiveness

Communication Effectiveness	Underlying Assumptions
• Listening to employees in order to make them happy. • Showing sensitivity and openness to employees by adapting messages to each individual. • Make employees feel included and understood.	• Job satisfaction is the goal of organizational communication. • Messages are exclusively interpreted in the context of interpersonal relationships. • Openness is useful in all circumstances. • Understanding will lead to agreement. • Understanding is the primary goal and is always more acceptable than ambiguity.

Explaining Communication Breakdowns

The Circuit manager recognizes the certainty of communication breakdowns. According to this approach there are three primary reasons for breakdowns.

People just "don't connect." Circuit managers are fond of saying "meanings are in people, not in words," which suggests that everyone has a unique interpretation for each message. They also believe that employees' values, ideas, or feelings are often so dissimilar that they have difficulty in relating to one another. Thus Circuit managers invest vast amounts of time in "reaching an understanding" and "building relationships" instead of other task-oriented goals. Employees in these types of organizations often dread meetings because they perceive them to stifle creativity, suppress productivity, and squelch progress. Nevertheless, Circuit managers are hopeful that everyone can "get on the same page" because they believe that ultimately everyone shares the same basic needs and desires.

People are poor listeners. Circuit managers often encourage their employees to develop active listening skills such as paraphrasing others' remarks, giving feedback, and asking the appropriate probing questions. These skills help employees think about possible misinterpretations of their remarks as well as check for unintended messages. Therefore, employees involved in a misunderstanding are frequently reminded of the maxim, "You cannot not communicate."

People fail to develop the proper communication climate. The Circuit manager believes that communication relationships, like electrical circuits, can operate only under certain conditions. Specifically, a defensive as opposed to a supportive climate inhibits communication effectiveness. Spontaneity, equality, and adaptation promote supportive climates. Evaluative comments, a dogmatic demeanor, and an attitude of superiority produce defensive climates. Proper climates can also be disrupted by "hidden agendas," which occurs when employees hide their underlying goals or true feelings from one another. Circuit managers believe that trust will emerge once the hidden agendas are exposed.

Origins

Managers develop a Circuit orientation to communication for a variety of reasons, but three are particularly noteworthy.

The human relations school of management has influenced many leaders. The well-known Hawthorne studies often provide the key arguments used to build the human relations case. These studies began as an attempt to investigate the relationship between the levels of lighting in the workplace and worker productivity. Employees at Western Electric's Hawthorne plant increased their productivity in all instances: in the test group when lighting was improved as well as made more dim, and even in the control group where there were no changes in illumination. Therefore, researchers determined that factors other than lighting influenced performance. The mistaken interpretation of the research often passed down in folklore was that employees thought management was interested in them, so they continued to increase their production regardless of the physical conditions. Hence the axiom, "Satisfied Workers are Productive Workers." Yet researchers have discovered that a satisfied worker can also be a very lazy one.[7] In fact, those who believe the folklore make an inappropriate inference. The key reason for the productivity increases was not managers' behavior but the *interpretations* made by employees.

Some communication teachers encourage a Circuit orientation. Courses in Interpersonal Communication have been quite popular on campuses. Such courses typically focus on receiver listening skills, giving appropriate feedback, and relationship-building. Even the communication models used in these courses stress the circularity of the communication process. The Schramm model in Figure 1.2, considered a classic, looks like a circuit diagram.[8] It highlights the feedback concept and the interaction of communicators. Such models lend theoretical justification to the Circuit perspective of communication skills.

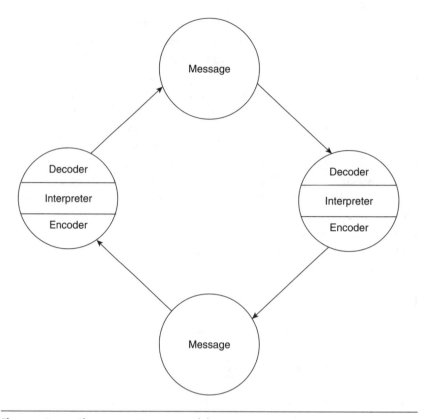

Figure 1.2   Shannon & Weaver Model

Some people have a natural affinity for the Circuit orientation. They tend to focus on people's feelings and interpersonal relationships. People are naturally attracted to those who are sensitive to their feelings. Circuit managers tend to avoid controversy, build self-esteem, and meet affiliation needs. Hence, the Circuit manager may have a deep need to keep peace and harmony.

Evaluation

Circuit managers believe that:

Understanding = Effective Communication.

This belief both detracts from and enhances our understanding of the communication process in the following ways:

Circuit managers incorrectly assume that understanding always leads to agreement. They believe that most "communication problems" occur because the parties do not understand one another. But the problem may be that they understand one another all too well, and they simply disagree. For example, an employee may well understand that the company needs for him to work overtime, but he refuses to do so because of family obligations. Unlike the Arrow manager, the Circuit manager acknowledges that people do not always understand a message in the same way. Therefore, it seems logical to assume that two people might not agree. Ironically, such thoughts are rarely entertained because Circuit Managers will spend endless hours trying to ensure that their messages are "really understood."

Circuit managers inappropriately assume that understanding should be the singular goal of communication. People communicate for a variety of reasons. Effective managers, like politicians, may equivocate in order to induce creativity or give themselves room to change. As two well-regarded scholars note, "Ambiguous missions and goals allow divergent interpretations to coexist and are more effective in allowing diverse groups to work together."[9] Moreover, there are instances in which a manager may not have time to explain, just as a physician gives orders during an emergency.

Accommodation strategies, although useful at times, do not guarantee solutions to difficult problems. Chris Argyris perceptively notes:

> The ability to get along with others is always an asset, right? Wrong. By adeptly avoiding conflict with co-workers, some executives eventually wreak havoc. And it's their very adeptness that's the problem. The explanation for this lies in what I call skilled incompetence, whereby managers use practiced routine behavior (skill) to produce what they do not intend (incompetence).[10]

Paradoxically, an organizational culture that emphasizes "understanding" often breeds a reticence to bring up areas of disagreement. Employees become afraid to clearly articulate their views for fear of exposing how deep the gulfs really are. Hence, differences—important and meaningful ones— are often glossed over in the name of "understanding."

Circuit orientation highlights some important communication skills. Building strong relationships and providing feedback generally enhances communication effectiveness. Research has shown that competent communicators do pay attention to these aspects of interaction.[11] And these are precisely the issues the Arrow manager ignores. The Arrow manager focuses on constructing the best possible message, but the Circuit manager looks at the meanings imposed by listeners. This shift in perspective is enlightening and useful. Even though the link between job satisfaction and productivity has proven tenuous at best, the Circuit approach has persuaded many that job satisfaction is an important variable in its own right.

We can learn much from the Arrow and Circuit approach. However, both are incomplete and limit our understanding. The lens of each perspective creates a somewhat distorted view of the communication process. There is a better point of view. I call it the Dance perspective of communication.

Communication as Dance

Some have argued that dance was the first form of communication. There are so many similarities between dance and communication that few people would disagree. Dance involves patterns, movement, and creativity. Participants as well as observers can enjoy it. There are as many styles as people. Tastes vary, styles change, and trends come and go, but dance will always be part of the human community. Once performed, a dance can never be recaptured in the same way again; it is unrepeatable and irreversible. Even the simplest of dances involves thousands of intricate and complex maneuvers. So, too, with communication. The list of similarities could be quite lengthy indeed. A few of the more important ones are highlighted here.

Communication Is Used for Multiple Purposes

People dance for a wide variety of reasons: to entertain, inform, persuade, incite, and even seduce. Some dance as a form of self-expression, whereas others dance for audiences. The same can be said of communication. The famous physicist and poet, Leo Szilard, once commented:

> When a scientist says something, his colleagues must ask themselves only whether it is true. When a politician says something, his colleagues must first of all ask, "Why does he say it?," later on they may or may not get around to asking whether it happens to be true. A politician is a man who thinks he is in possession of the truth and knows what needs to be done. Scientists rarely think they are in full possession of the truth, and a scientist's aim in a discussion with his colleagues is not to persuade but to clarify.[12]

Herein lies a problem. The scientist, politician, salesperson, philosopher, and preacher all use the same language but with different objectives in mind. So we can never be sure of a communicator's precise intentions. In fact, communicators often have multiple goals for a single message. The effective teacher seeks to enlighten and motivate, the salesperson to inform and persuade, and the philosopher to clarify and question. Effective managers, at one time or another, perform each of these roles.

Therefore, communication effectiveness cannot be limited to either the "results" or "understanding" criteria as characterized by the Arrow and Circuit perspectives, respectively. For instance, the Chairman of the Federal Reserve, Alan Greenspan, once "explained" to a Congressional committee how he made decisions regarding interest rates: "If I say something which you understand fully in this regard, I probably made a mistake."[13] Was he saying, "This is too difficult to explain"? Was he telling the committee,

"This is none of your business"? Was he merely equivocating? It remains unclear. But clearly, communicators can have any number of goals, including obfuscation, confusion, or deception. So no single measure of communication effectiveness exists, just as no one criterion should be used to evaluate all dancers.

Communication Involves the Coordination of Meanings

Dancers have to learn to coordinate their movements with one another regardless of the type of music. Communicators do as well. As long as communicators know how to respond in their roles or according to the "rules of the game," it may not be necessary or even desirable to totally share meanings. In fact, this notion provides the foundation for a theory of communication, called the Coordinated Management of Meaning. These theorists argue that:

> . . . Communication is the process by which persons cocreate, maintain, and alter patterns of social order, but . . . the coordination of talk through which patterns of order emerge is not necessarily based on mutual understanding or a shared social reality.[14]

Subordinates may not know why the boss asks, "How are things going?," but in time they learn how to respond. It may be interpreted as "intrusiveness" on the part of the subordinate and "concern" on the part of the boss. Despite the vastly different interpretations, they learn to maintain social order. Meanings are not necessarily shared but they are coordinated.

So what? This view of communication underscores how messages facilitate social order, maintain structure, and set up patterns. Dancers are evaluated, in part, on the degree to which their actions are coordinated with one another. Managers can use similar criteria to judge communication effectiveness. Organizations and dance studios do not reward clumsiness, whether self-inflicted or induced by others. So Dance managers focus on this question: How does communication help or hinder the process of coordination in our organization?

Communication Involves Co-Orientation

In order to coordinate actions, dancers must learn to co-orient. They must be able to sense one another's cues, anticipate their partner's possible actions, and know the appropriate responses. So, too, with communicators. When communication breaks down, people have failed to co-orient; they have no adequate predictive capacity. Effective communicators are able to forecast with some accuracy the actions of others, their responses, and interpretations. For example, the CEO of a paper manufacturing firm was bewildered by rampant rumors about layoffs and plant closings that circulated in the plant after his brief announcement about forthcoming pay freezes. In his speech he specifically noted that layoffs and plant closings were *not* viable alternatives to cope with an industry slowdown. When asked if he ever had a meeting like this before, he said, "I never had the need to." Even though he had personally hired most of these workers, he could not anticipate these possible reactions to his announcement. He did not effectively co-orient.

Professional dancers whirl, pirouette, and leap into one another's arms with seeming ease. Yet, their artistry only emerges after long and tedious hours of practice. Even when improvising they co-orient because they have learned how to respond to one another's subtle cues. If you are lost in a forest, you try to calculate your position in relation to some fixed location. Dancers do not have that luxury. Rather they must simultaneously orient with one another, even as their "locations" constantly change. Likewise, this complex and difficult challenge faces communicators, who must simultaneously orient to each other while both are constantly evolving.

Communication Is Rule-Governed

How can dancers cope with the tremendous range of possible movements? How can all the possibilities be mastered? Communicators, like dancers, develop rules-of-thumb to cope with the uncertainties. For every style of dance there are rules of some sort, whether written or unwritten. Joan Lawson, who for seventeen years taught at the Royal Ballet School, wrote, "Principles and rules should all be studied by aspiring dancers and choreographers if they are to create the style and qualities of movement necessary to communicate the mood, emotion, theme, and story of classical dance."[15] Years of experience are distilled in these rules.

Communicators, as well, develop a wide range of implicit rules that govern conversations, such as who has the right to initiate or terminate a conversation, what topics are appropriate to speak about, and under what conditions such topics may be discussed. These rules affect the conversation in much the same way that rules of dance constrain movement. Conversational rules, too, are a way to handle uncertainty and distill the essence of learning into a few easily manageable units. When employees enact these rules they coordinate their actions.

There are basically two types of rules at work in conversations: interpretation rules and regulative rules.[16] *Interpretation rules* are the communicator's rules for abstracting the meaning out of a message.[17] For example, during a meeting a manager might say to an employee, "Tell me more." The employee's interpretation: "I have a great idea; the manager wants the details." On the other hand, the same manager who says, "Tell me more," after an employee gives an unacceptable explanation for being late to work, communicates a very different message. The manager's message: "Shape up; this excuse is unacceptable." Even though the same words are used, the context has changed and different interpretation rules apply.

Regulative rules are those that regulate or guide the ongoing action of the communication event. Effective listeners, for example, often have these kinds of regulative rules:

- Initiate conversations with questions about unrisky topics.
- If a person's comments are unclear, then ask for clarification.
- Terminate conversations by summarizing the conversation.

Note that in each case these rules help guide the conversation in a particular direction.

Effective communicators learn the special rules that apply in different settings. They, of course, vary from person to person, department to department, and organization to organization. Yet, there are some common rules regardless of the situation, just as there are fundamental dance steps. The rules do not exist on some unseen tablet waiting to be discovered. Rather, people are actively engaged in negotiating the rules, particularly during the first stages of relationships. As a result, Dance managers pay particular attention to the orientation of new employees.

Communicators Develop a Repertoire of Skills That May Pass From the Level of Consciousness

Beginning dancers have to consciously think about each movement in executing a pirouette, for instance. Over time they become concerned less with body mechanics and more with artistry. The ease of execution comes from years of practice, as movements that were once conscious submerge into the subconscious. Communicators learn in much the same way. When we learn a foreign language we have to think more consciously about syntax and semantics. But over time, through trial and error, we learn the rules and can speak more naturally by relying on subconscious processes. Language skills are, in essence, the ability to utilize the right rules. The same can be said of pragmatic rules of conversation.

Frequently, communication problems are the result of an unconsciously used rule, long ago forgotten. For example, one manager told me that her employees often accused her of being a poor listener. She had difficulty understanding their perceptions. During a lull in a social conversation, I mentioned being involved in a minor car accident. Her response: "That reminds me. Did I tell you about *my* new car?" Clearly, such episodes might cause her employees to infer that she was uninterested in them and lead to the "poor listener" assessment. This manager apparently never learned the regulative rule: "When someone mentions an unusual event, probe for further information." Effective conversationalists utilize this rule all the time without any conscious thought of it. Instead, this manager's operative but unconscious rule was: "When someone mentions an unusual event, talk about something similar that happened to me." So I was not surprised when the manager was asked to step down and assume a lower paying job.

Most individuals' existing set of rules need to be refined to become better negotiators, speakers, or motivators. For example, skilled negotiators don't make concessions all at once; they use a more deliberate approach.[18] At first, they may consciously have to think about appropriate behaviors, but with practice over time, it becomes natural. Dance instructors use a similar technique when they point out a motion that should be consciously attended to in order to execute a graceful maneuver.

Communication Can Be Viewed as a Patterned Activity

Choreographers map out patterns for their dances, a kind of circuit diagram drawn with arrows. Even with improvisational dances, a map can be drawn of the dancer's movements. Likewise, there are patterns of interaction in a conversation. The patterns emerge from the interlocking of the communicator's rules of interaction.

Expert chess players who are familiar with an adversary's style of play (i.e., personal rules), are frequently able to sense deep but recurring patterns to their opponent's games—not move by move, but in a more general sense. Communicators, like amateur chess players, may not be aware of their own patterns but perceptive observers can see them. For example, a manager may jokingly insult an employee by saying, "Hey, Pat! Has your golf game improved yet? The employee may respond by placating: "I haven't been golf-ing lately." The manager could react to the placating with even harsher insults, to which the employee responds with more placating responses. The pattern repeats itself until either someone else steps in or the employee gets angry. The manager's regulative rule: "Respond to placating with playful insults." The employee's regulative rule is: "Respond to insults with a pla-cating reply." These rules interact to form a pattern in which the manager sees the employee as the problem and the employee feels the manager causes the problem (see Figure 1.3). Such problems, technically known as punctua-tion difficulties, occur when each party sees the other as the source of the conflict.[19] Neither the manager nor the employee sees the overall pattern resulting from these personal rules of interaction.

The patterns are not always counterproductive. In fact, exceptional com-municators identify and eliminate the destructive patterns while they establish and reinforce constructive ones. They often have an artistic appreciation for intricate patterns of coordination. The aesthetic thrill of an illuminating dis-cussion or a scintillating meeting may prove elusive and rare, but to the Dance manager there are few experiences more pleasing and fulfilling.

Manager's Interpretation (meaning rules)	Manager's Regulative Rules	Actual Conversation	Employee's Regulative Rules	Employee's Interpretation (meaning rules)
Greeting.	Initiate conversations with playful repartee.	**Manager:** *Hey, Pat, has your golf game improved yet?*		Insult. Manager doesn't care about my game or me.
Employee is ignoring me.		**Employee:** *I haven't been golfing lately.*	Respond to insults with placating reply.	Factual reply to a question.
Playful question.	Try to re-establish conversation with another playful comment.	**Manager:** *Well, how's that clunker of a car running?*		Another insult. What kind of game is the manager playing?
Employee is catching on, but still takes the conversation too seriously.		**Employee:** *I sold it.*	Respond to insults with a placating comment.	Another factual reply.
Joke.	Continue conversation with another playful insult.	**Manager:** *I hope you didn't buy another lemon.*		Another insult. Now the manager is questioning my decision-making ability.
What is the employee so upset about? I'm just trying to build some rapport. The employee is a poor conversationalist.		**Employee:** *Why don't you just get off my back and mind your own business!*	If placating doesn't work, then stand up for yourself.	My only alternative was to be assertive. The manager is insensitive and unprofessional.

Figure 1.3   Conversation Analysis

19

Conclusion

The anthropologist, Mary Catherine Bateson, said ". . . there are few things as toxic as a bad metaphor."[20] The Arrow and Circuit approaches mask the complexity of the communication process. Managers who view communication as a dance have a more vivid metaphor with which to analyze organizational situations. They see the complexities in the apparent simplicity of communication. They are concerned with patterns and unwritten rules. They look at the degree of co-orientation between employees as well as departments. They do not expect to be understood at all times and do not always see understanding as the goal of communication. Their communication style and choice of medium vary according to the goals and context. Unlike Circuit managers, they are not exclusively concerned with relationships. Unlike Arrow managers, they are not solely focused on immediate results, but seek deeper patterns of sustained success. They do not share the Arrow manager's belief that humans are basically lazy but neither do they believe that all humans are well intentioned. Finally, they take comfort in the fact that there appears to be no relationship between their ability to communicate and their ability to dance.

Notes

1. Aristotle. 1960. *The rhetoric of Aristotle.* (L. Cooper, Trans.). New York: Meredith.

2. See, for example, Lasswell, H. D. 1948. The structure and function of communications in society. In *The communication of ideas,* edited by L. Bryson (pp. 37–51). New York: Knopf.

Also see, Gerbner, G. 1956. Toward a general model of communication. *Audio-Visual Communication Review,* 4:171–199. Also see Shannon, C., & Weaver, W. (1949). *A mathematical theory of communication.* Urbana: University of Illinois Press.

3. Clancy, T., & Horner, C. 1999. *Every man a tiger.* New York: G.P. Putnam & Sons, p. 96.

4. Reddy, M. J. 1979. The conduct metaphor: A case of frame conflict in our language about language. In *Metaphor and thought,* edited by A. Ortony (pp. 284–324). Cambridge, MA: Cambridge University Press.

5. See, for example, Golen, S., Lynch, D., Smeltzer, L., Lord, W. J., Penrose, J. M., & Waltman, J. 1989. An empirically tested communication skills core module for MBA students, with implications for the AACSB. *Organizational Behavior Teaching Review* 13:45–57.

6. Locke, E. A. 1976. The nature and causes of job satisfaction. In *Handbook of industrial and organizational psychology,* edited by M. D. Dunnette (pp. 1292–1350). Chicago, IL: Rand-McNally.

7. Downs, C. W., & Pickett, T. 1977. An analysis of the effect of nine leadership-group compatibility contingencies upon productivity and member satisfaction. *Communication Monographs* 44:220–230.

8. Schramm, W. L. 1954. How communication works. In *The process and effects of mass communications*, edited by W. Schramm (pp. 3–26). Urbana: University of Illinois Press.

9. Eisenberg, E. M., & Witten, M. G. 1987. Reconsidering openness in organizational communication. *Academy of Management Review* 12 (3):418–426, p. 422.

10. Argyris, C. 1986. Skilled incompetence. *Harvard Business Review* 64 (5):74–79, p. 74.

11. See, for example, DiSalvo, V. S. 1980. A summary of current research identifying communication skills in various organizational contexts. *Communication Education* 29:283–290.

12. Szilard, L. 1961. *The voice of the dolphins.* New York: Simon & Schuster, pp. 25–26.

13. Greenspan, A. 1995. Talk show. *Business Week,* July 3:6.

14. Pearce, W. B., Harris, L. M., & Cronen, V. E. 1982. Communication theory in a new key. In *Rigor & imagination,* edited by C. Wilder & J. H. Weakland (pp. 149–194). New York: Praeger, p. 157.

15. Lawson, J. 1980. *The principles of classical dance.* New York: Knopf, p. 1.

16. Pearce, W. B., & Cronen, V. E. 1980. *Communication, action, & meaning.* New York: Praeger.

17. Pearce and Cronen (ibid) call these constitutive rules. They also have an elaborate system that explains how meanings are abstracted at various levels.

18. Gilchrist, J. A. 1982. The compliance interview: Negotiating across organizational boundaries. In *Communication yearbook 6,* edited by M. Burgoon (pp. 653–673). Beverly Hills, CA: Sage.

19. Watzlawick, P., Beavin, J., & Jackson, D. 1967. *Pragmatics of human communication.* New York: Norton.

20. Bateson, M. C. 1989. An interview with Mary Catherine Bateson. In *Bill Moyers: A world of ideas,* edited by B. S. Flowers (pp. 345–357). New York: Doubleday, p. 347.

2

What Is Communication, Anyway?

It requires a very unusual mind to make an analysis of the obvious.

Alfred North Whitehead

Describing communication as a dance can be illuminating and appealing to our more holistic, right brain. Yet, the more linear orientation of our left brain demands answers to more precise questions such as, "What actually happens in the mind of the sender? Of the receiver? Why do problems occur? Can communication breakdowns be described more specifically than to say that two people are not coordinating their actions?" This chapter addresses these issues by discussing seven propositions about communication and the related implications.

Propositions

Proposition 1: The Communication Process Can Best Be Described in Terms of Probabilities

Language is inherently ambiguous. We experience the ambiguity in the words we use, the sentences we utter, and in countless communication breakdowns. One researcher says that for the 500 most frequently used words in the English language, there are over 14,000 definitions.[1] Take, for instance, the word "run." A sprinter can "run" in a race. Yet, politicians "run" races but not exclusively with their legs. Although a horse "runs" with legs, it uses four of them, whereas sprinters use two. A woman can get a "run" in her hose, which is troublesome, but having a "run" of cards is good. However, having a "run" on a bank is bad. "Running" aground is not good at all for a sailor, but a "run" with the wind can be exhilarating. To score a "run" in baseball is different than a "run" in cricket. Hence we "run" into the ambiguity of language at every turn, even with simple, everyday words.

Given the inherent ambiguity of any message, we can assign probabilities to the various interpretations. The statement, "I am going down to the bank," when stripped of all contextual clues, could be seen as having a 50% chance of being interpreted as a financial institution and 50% chance as a riverbank. The communication process *increases* or *decreases* the probability of certain interpretations. Adding the phrase "to deposit a check" clarifies the operative probability. But it is not always that simple.

Communicators who fail to understand the probabilistic nature of interpretations may encounter serious difficulties. An incident at a hospital provides an intriguing insight into the difficulty. A young Green Bay, Wisconsin woman was taken to a hospital's emergency room for a minor injury at 7:00 p.m. on a Friday night. After the usual name and address part of the intake process, the conversation continued (see Figure 2.1).

The nurse walked away in disgust. The patient limped away in pain. Note how the probable interpretations started out one way, flip-flopped, and then reversed again. In the end, neither person recognized the true source of the conflict.

**Chapter 2:
By the Numbers**

76%
of corporate executives believe that oral and written communication skills should be emphasized heavily in MBA classes

14,000
The number of definitions for the 500 most commonly used words in the English language

51%
of employees are satisfied with organizational communication

3,155,760,000
Robert Hooke's estimate of the number of separate ideas the mind can entertain

1070,000,000,000
The number of possible neuron pathways for the brain

Conversation		Stage
Nurse:	How much did you drink?	
Patient:	I haven't been drinking at all tonight.	**1**
Nurse:	No, no I mean liquids.	
Patient:	Oh well, I'm not really sure. Normal, I guess.	**2**
Nurse:	Ok.	
Patient:	Why did you need to know about how much I drink?	
Nurse:	(caustically) I don't care how much you party! That's your business. But I see the results of you kids who drink and drive. It's not fair to those who don't.	**3**
Patient:	I didn't mean alcohol. I meant fluids, I meant . . .	

Figure 2.1   Conversation Analysis

In the beginning, (stage one), both people had different meanings for the question: "How much did you drink?" The nurse was referring to liquids (100% probability), the patient to alcohol (100% probability). Theoretically, both are plausible interpretations. For the nurse, the term "obviously" meant liquids. After all, the amount of liquid in the human body is a crucial medical factor. But another context is at work here, as well. For many people, on a Friday night, the term "drink" typically means alcohol. Nevertheless, eventually each person recognized the "mistake" in the other's interpretation.

The relevant information was abstracted in stage two with the patient adjusting to the interpretation of the nurse. Then, in stage three each assumes the other's interpretation, still at a 100% probability, as the operating rule for the conversation. On the surface, this switch appears to be the source of the conflict. Yet, on a deeper level, each communicator considered only *one* possible interpretation (a 100% probability) in each stage of the conversation (see Table 2.1). Neither the nurse nor the patient recognizes that "drink" has a probability of meaning *either* fluids *or* alcoholic consumption. Hence, the communication totally breaks down in stage three, resulting in frustration for both nurse and patient.

Incidents like this happen all the time because most people do not have a probabilistic view of communication. Yet, astute managers learn to adopt a probabilistic viewpoint and recognize a broader set of implications.

Implication A: Typically the message sender sees only one possible interpretation. Yet, for a receiver there are three different options. First, the receiver may see the same possibility—in which case, the two individuals understand one another. Second, the receiver may see a different possibility—which may go unnoticed or even be found amusing. Consider

Table 2.1   Using Probabilities to Diagnose a Communication Breakdown

Meaning for "drink"	Theoretical probability	Stage 1		Stage 2		Stage 3	
		Nurse	Patient	Nurse	Patient	Nurse	Patient
Alcohol	50%	0%	100%	0%	0%	100%	0%
Fluids	50%	100%	0%	100%	100%	0%	100%

the newspaper headline, "HERSHEY BARS PROTEST." Are candy bars on strike? Third, the receiver may be unable to determine the correct possibility. At this point, a clarifying question may be asked. Or the receiver may choose not to inquire about the precise meaning because the risk of asking exceeds potential gains. Fears of losing prestige, being ridiculed, being ignored, or being thought incompetent often stifle further communication. In most large group situations, for example, the pressures not to ask for clarification can be immense.

Implication B: The sender of a message may purposely use language that has multiple interpretations. Some speakers use a kind of verbal Rorschach. The famous Rorschach psychological test presents subjects with an ambiguous graphic: an inkblot. Then subjects are asked, "What do you see in this picture?" Theoretically, the interpretation of the inkblot reveals the subject's intellectual and emotional orientation. In the same way, statements can be designed that elicit different interpretations depending on the receiver's orientation.

Politicians provide a plethora of examples: "Our party believes in fiscal discipline." What does this statement precisely mean? It could mean almost anything. But it sounds good! Corporate executives are not above using such tactics. Consider this statement, "People are the key to our success." What does this mean? Will the company pay better wages than competitors? Are poor performers going to be fired? It remains unclear. But that does not imply that such statements are useless. On the contrary, such language can be extraordinarily powerful. Even though every person who hears such a statement may have a different meaning for the message, the ultimate effect may be favorable. The receivers read their own meanings into the statements, which might be quite positive. Yet, none of the *private* interpretations can be confirmed. Thus the speaker can forestall conflict, create the appearance of unity, or even allow people to save face. In essence, the ambiguity preserves the speaker's options. And if need be, the speaker can *publicly* deny any specific interpretations that become problematic.

Is strategic ambiguity ethical? The question is, in a sense, moot. Ambiguity, regardless of whether we acknowledge it, permeates our language. Both ethical and unethical people use such tactics. Ambiguity can stir creative ideas, allow people to save face, or resolve a conflict. For example, scholars discovered that employees deemed effective do not have to actually agree with

Table 2.2   Assessing the Value of Ambiguity

Potential Benefits	Potential Weaknesses
• Induces creativity • Allows people to save face • Resolves conflict through different interpretations of one message • Allows people to strategically delay making decisions • May enhance one's credibility in a conflict • Allows diverse groups to work together	• May not be useful with those desiring specific direction • May be used to deny personal responsibility • May result in unwanted misunderstanding • May delay conflict resolution • May create ethical concerns • May gloss over meaningful differences • Allows for plausible deniability

their managers on the regulative rules guiding conversation. Yet, they must be perceived by their managers as agreeing with these rules.[2] So ambiguity may serve to create the perception of unity, if not the reality. On the other hand, the unscrupulous do use such tactics for deception, power plays, and fraud (see Table 2.2). Thus thoughtful managers look at their own motives but are also aware of how others might misuse or even abuse ambiguity.

Implication C: The receiver may purposely misunderstand. In some circumstances, receivers exploit the probabilistic nature of communication in order to meet their goals. In short, they have a need to misunderstand. My favorite example involves the artist who sculpted figurines adorning the top of a prominent building in London. When city officials saw that the building was rimmed with statues of nude males, they ordered the artist to "cut off the offending parts." The artist complied, but in his own special way. He lopped off the heads of all the statues.

Employees often have a similar need to misunderstand communication they may find "offensive." For example, on a Wednesday afternoon, a manager sent his employee the memo, "I need the report first thing Monday morning." Monday rolled around and, lo and behold, no report. The angry boss confronted the employee, whereupon the employee remarked: "I thought you meant the following Monday." Sure enough, that is one possible interpretation. In fact, the memo could have been referring to any future Monday. No doubt, the employee understood precisely what Monday the boss was referring to. But the extra week of preparation met his needs at the time. The probabilistic nature of communication allowed him to legitimately argue that there was a "communication breakdown."

Proposition 2: Context Shapes the Probabilities by Creating Default Assumptions That Solidify Interpretations

If ambiguity permeates all messages, then how can two people ever understand one another? Some scholars might argue that there can never be 100%

understanding. However, people do seem to be able to understand each other well enough to get tasks done, communicate intentions, and effectively function in an array of situations. How? In part, the answer lies in the role that context plays in the communication process. The context either freezes or predisposes certain probable interpretations.

For instance, the term "bug" has a multitude of possible interpretations. It could stand for an insect, an eavesdropping device, a nasty illness, or a computer coding error. Consider the statement, "I've got a bug." Usually, we do not clarify how we are using the term. A sniffling, sneezing colleague need not explain what type of "bug" she refers to. Likewise, two software engineers talking about their latest program are most likely referring to a coding error. With astonishing ease and simplicity we understand the various uses of the term, without elaborate explanation. The context of the discussion increases the probability of some interpretation, while decreasing others (see Figure 2.2).

When communicators do not share assumptions about the context, they frequently misunderstand one another. My favorite example of this occurs in a Peter Sellers movie. Sellers, as Inspector Clouseau, is standing at a street corner with a dog at his side when a stranger approaches him. The stranger asks: "Does your dog bite?" The always forthright Clouseau responds, "No." Then the dog at Sellers' side promptly chomps on the leg of the bystander. The astonished man replies with justifiable anger, "I thought you said your dog does not bite." Sellers calmly replies, "It's not my dog." The humor of this episode lies in the incongruity between Sellers' context of interpretation and the other man's. The bystander assumed from the physical context that Sellers owned the dog standing by him. Or at the very least, Sellers would know which dog was the point of reference. Wrong on both counts. Inspector Clouseau should have known that the probabilities were shaped by the context to exclude references to all other dogs in the world and focus on the dog in sight. But such are the bumbling charms of this character. Yet, all incidents of this type are not so easily chalked up to a comic's antics; some are quite serious. For example, a deadline to submit a bid may be missed because the bidder assumes a different time zone than what was intended.

Intercultural scholars have noted that some cultures are more reliant on contextual clues than others. High-context cultures communicate in ways that depend greatly on the shared experiences and relationships of the communicators. The message itself relays little of this contextual information. High-context cultures, such as those found in Japan, Mexico, and Middle Eastern countries, tend to have collectivist values. In contrast, low-context cultures communicate in much more explicit ways, and are more likely to formalize agreements. They are comparatively less dependent on contextual clues. Low-context cultures, such as those found in Germany, Sweden, and the United States, tend to stress individualistic values.[3] Clearly, organizations operating in both cultures have a difficult challenge building an appropriate context. Even communicators in low-context cultures confront contextual challenges.

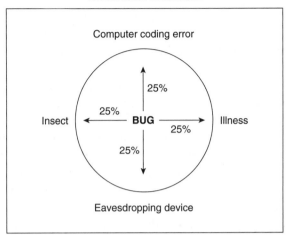

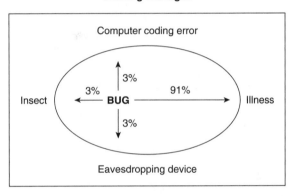

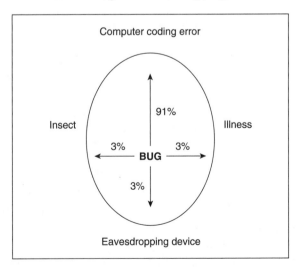

Figure 2.2   Probabilities Altered by Context

Proposition 3: Context Building Is a Dynamic Process

A unique context emerges as people interact, regardless of the culture. Even thoughtful analysts miss this point. Consider a typical model of communication in Figure 2.3. Note that the context is pictured as an element *outside* of the communicators. The implication: Communicators share and operate in the same context. It is as if the context is like air: Everyone breathes it, walks through it, and experiences it in a similar fashion. Therefore, many people assume that context exists *independent* of anyone's presence; it's something "out there." This image misleads. Situations may be commonly shared. Contexts are not. There is not one context; there are many. A context is not walked into; rather, we carry it around. Context is not some kind of ever-present ether; rather, it emerges from complex interactions between people and the setting. Our culture clearly shapes our perceptions, but, fundamentally, each individual has a personal and uniquely configured context. In short, we construct context through our relationships with each other, situations, and locales.

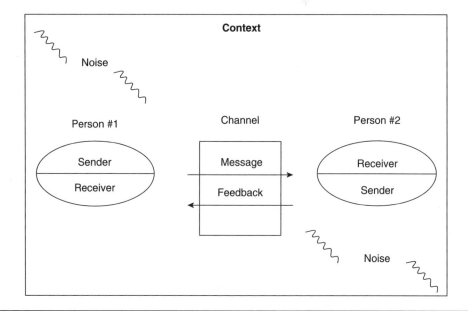

Figure 2.3   Typical (and Inappropriate) Communication Model

Greeting behavior demonstrates how contexts develop through a dynamic process. Think about the limitless number of possible responses to questions such as, "How you are doing?" In fact, the greeter faces an intriguing dilemma when someone actually proceeds to answer the inquiry in burdensome detail. Past experiences in the "greeting contexts" make it virtually certain that the responses will be quite limited. In fact, almost any response to a greeting will be interpreted as a simple acknowledgment because of the contextual rigidity. Some of my students tested out this notion by responding to greetings with wildly inappropriate responses, like the following:

Greeting (test subject):   "How's it going?"

Response (student):   "Not so good. My dog just died and a truck ran over my foot."

Reply (test subject):   "Hey, good to talk to you."

Such inattentive replies were all too typical. Why? People repetitively experience certain roles, under similar circumstances, and in comparable settings. Consequently, a series of probable interpretations are highlighted and others deemed less likely. Therefore, many people play their part in this obligatory ritual without really listening.

The dynamic nature of context building allows for a highly flexible but efficient method to reduce the interpretation probabilities. All comments do not have to be clarified in precise detail for two people to effectively interact. As a result of certain interpretations being *pushed* into the foreground and others being *pulled* into the background, people can reasonably assume that meanings will be shared, except perhaps when talking to Inspector Clouseau.

Proposition 4: The Context Can Become so Powerful That it Acts Like a Black Hole

Astronomers, as well as science fiction buffs, have a fascination with black holes. These are places in space in which the heavens collapse into a concentration of super gravity that warps space-time to such a degree that light cannot escape from it. Celestial objects that get too close to a black hole can get sucked in and never return. Nothing, not even light, escapes from a black hole. In a similar but perhaps less dramatic way, a context can exert such a strong force that the probable interpretations can become severely warped. Indeed, the meanings that are inferred can have little or no relation to the actual realities of the situation or the intentions of the sender.

The proverbial tale of the boy who cried "wolf" once too often is a case in point. The first time he cried wolf, everyone came running, only to find that it was a ruse. The second time, the same story. Then an actual wolf appeared and gobbled the boy up. Figuring it was just another ruse, no one came running to help him. The boy created a real contextual black hole. The context created by the previous incidents implied that the probable interpretation of "wolf, wolf" was that it was a "joke." The shift of probable interpretations from the first incident to the final episode shows the powerful role that context plays in the communication process. The irony, as well as the moral, is that in the end the boy was actually being truthful, but, because the context was so strong, he had no means to communicate his message. In essence, a black hole can destroy the capability for communication.

Unfortunately, the simple lesson of this child's tale goes unheeded in too many organizations. The situations vary in the particulars but not in kind. Past communication builds a very powerful set of contextual cues. For example, the manager who continually criticizes and berates employees and then suddenly praises them may be seen as trying to placate or appease employees. His motives are suspect even when offering honest praise.

Contextual black holes can also be a positive force. "Success breeds success" in part because useful meanings are accentuated by the context, whereas potentially negative ones are ignored. In many ways the reputation of Microsoft acts as a positive black hole. Even if a new Microsoft product may be inferior to others, buyers view it positively. One purchasing agent for a major company, keenly aware of the halo effect, said, "No one ever got fired buying a Microsoft product." The corporate philosophy, past successes, and image all serve to skew meanings in a positive way, regardless of more objective interpretations.[4] In sum, the black hole may act positively, as in the case of Microsoft, or it may function negatively, as it did for the boy who cried wolf once too much.

Proposition 5: Context Construction Is Uniquely Sensitive to Time Sequencing

The message in Figure 2.4 appeared outside a church on its marquee. If these two statements are read as question and answer, sequentially, then this church had a rather unusual approach to piety. Indeed, the humor comes from the fact that the first line was not intended to form the context for the second line. If the statements on the marquee were reversed, the faux pas no longer exists because the context did not necessarily suggest a sequential reading of the sign (Figure 2.5). This amusing incident illustrates a more profound principle. Unlike basic mathematics, communication lacks a commutative property: $A + B \neq B + A$. The manager, who, while reading the *Wall Street Journal,* finds out about his organization's plans to restructure, has a completely different perspective on the company than the manager who hears about the plans first-hand. Employees who depend on the grapevine first and the formal network second for accurate information come to different understandings than those who reverse the process.

Message order matters. Each message forms the context for the next message, as one musical phrase does for the next. But it is not quite that simple. Some messages are seen as being connected to one another, whereas others are not. This, too, influences the interpretations. Why some messages

Figure 2.4   Church Marquee A

Figure 2.5   Church Marquee B

are seen in the same context, as the first church sign, and others are seen in different contexts, like the second sign, remains somewhat of a mystery. Why do people connect some events or messages and not others? Future communication researchers will have to answer that question. This issue greatly influences our communicative experiences.

Take the case of 9-year-old Wendy Potasnik of Carmel, Indiana. She filed a lawsuit against Borden Inc. because she did not get her free prize in her box of Cracker Jacks. She wrote a complaint to the company but failed to receive a reply within 12 days. A Cracker Jack spokesperson stated that a letter of apology and a coupon for another box was sent within 13 days, but by then, the suit had been filed. Expectations formed at one point in time became part of the context, which then influenced all subsequent interpretations.

Clearly, silence is not always golden. Some communication scholars extend the argument further and claim that, "You cannot not communicate." In practical terms, that quip is nonsense. There are countless people with whom we do not communicate, with whom we do not intend to communicate, and who do not perceive an intent to communicate.[5] Rhetorically, however, this often-quoted maxim highlights that every person can be seen as a walking grab bag of potential messages, waiting to be interpreted. The type of clothing worn, the briefcase carried, the haircut, the accent, the rate of speech are just a few of the potentially interpretable messages.

Managers may find it disconcerting that, to a large extent, message senders are at the mercy of the interpretations of receivers, regardless of the sender's actual intent. The supervisor who does not respond to a written request from a subordinate, whether by design or carelessness, "communicates" a very important message. The valued employees who do not receive adequate feedback about their performance "read" that they are unappreciated and start searching elsewhere for more desirable working conditions. The marketing representative who fails to return a phone call from a client "sends" a potentially negative message. Discussions about this feature of the communication process are always difficult, messy, and confusing because even the language we use obscures the issues. The term "receiver" only derives meaning in relationship to the term "sender." Using the term "receiver" implies that there was a kind of action on the part of some "sender." But the aforementioned examples demonstrate that communication occurs all the time, without any "sender's" action. Why? Because expectations formed at one point in time influence interpretations at a later point, even without an explicit message.

Proposition 6: There Are Multiple Messages in Every Communication Event

For any primary message there are countless other messages that can alter the context and change the interpretations. For example, Mr. Arrow might confirm the spelling of his name like this: "Mr. Arrow; 'A' as in alpha, 'R' as in rover, 'R' as in rover, 'O' as in orange, and 'W' as in wagon." A functional equivalent that could be given by the stereotypical flirtatious man to a waitress could be: "'A' as in adorable, 'R' as in rich, 'R' as in really rich, 'O' as in obliging and 'W' as in willing?" To which the clever waitress might reply: "'N' - 'O'; 'N' as in never and 'O' as in offensive." The secondary messages are quite obvious. These statements provide the same information on the surface—a redundant expression of the spelling—but carry vastly different secondary messages.

In a similar sense, it was no accident that the Arrow manager preferred to be addressed as Mr. Taylor and the Circuit manager by his first name, Mark. When formal titles are used as a form of address, a more rigid and authoritative relational base is developed. The use of a first name implies a relationship of equality, openness, and flexibility. However, forms of address are not the only ways to express secondary messages. The tale of the recently inaugurated University Chancellor illustrates the point. He sent the memo in Figure 2.6 to all university employees. A number of employees, particularly long-term ones, were offended by the last point on

---

Upper Midwest University
_____

Walhain, Wisconsin 54321
Office of the Chancellor

7 November 2000

MEMORANDUM

TO: ALL UNIVERSITY EMPLOYEES

FROM: O.W. Caulder, Chancellor

SUBJECT: WINTER STORM PROCEDURES

1. Campus closings are rare.

2. The campus will be open unless you hear otherwise on
   your favorite local radio station.

3. Calls to the Information Center from students about
   specific classes will be referred to appropriate
   academic units.

4. If you commute by car, be sure it is properly equipped and
   maintained for foul weather driving.

Thank you for your cooperation.

OWC: pc

And be
sure to brush
your teeth
every night.

Figure 2.6   Example of Unintended Message

the memo—which implied that they needed to be reminded about how to take care of their basic responsibilities. It was as if a parent was talking to a child. Indeed, one graffiti artist added, "And be sure to brush your teeth."

Most professional speakers are quite skillful at exploiting the impact of secondary messages. Take the case of a management consultant addressing an audience of potential clients. While trying to illustrate the usefulness of a particular appraisal system, she reveals: "When I was working for IBM, Microsoft, and 3M, we used a similar system and recorded an immediate 20% improvement in production." Ostensibly, her statement provides evidence for her claim that the appraisal system works. Yet, there are other messages implicit in that comment, as well:

1. I have used this system.

2. I have been a manager, just like you.

3. IBM, Microsoft, and 3M have greatly benefited from this appraisal system.

Management consultants who use experiential examples to prove their points are more likely to be successful than those who rely exclusively on theoretical or statistical proof. The potent secondary messages provide a context—an aura of credibility—that makes the consultant more believable to listeners.

In many cases, people react as much to the secondary messages as they do to the primary message. Ultimately, these secondary messages, intended or unintended by the speaker, act as elements in forming the context of interpretation. Often secondary messages are not processed consciously. No wonder we are sometimes baffled about the source of misperception. Thus, the effective communicator pays attention to both the primary and secondary messages.

Proposition 7: Communication Content and Context Interact to Produce Meaning

Content consists of the actual words or behaviors of senders. The naïve communicator thinks of this as the "meat" of communication. But, as previously discussed, this is only part of the picture, as the context basically functions as the background for the content, much like the canvas for a painting.

Content alone cannot produce any meaning except in a very rudimentary sense. "Ceci est un message de la part de cette société" is certainly a message. It has content but does it have meaning? That depends, of course, on whether you can read French. Only then can you provide enough context to make an interpretation. Yet, when translated into English, does meaning magically appear? Only in a narrow sense. The sentence translates as follows: "This is a message from the organization." That reveals a little more about the message, but the "meaning" still appears ambiguous.

However, this sentence, in a certain context, can have a very precise meaning. For example, one manager was given a lateral move in an organization. The manager was faced with the task of determining if this was a message from top management. In some companies, a "lateral move" means the kiss of death; an indicator of poor performance. In other companies, like Japanese organizations, a lateral move indicates nothing at all about performance.

Pulitzer-prize-winning author, Douglas Hofstadter, provides a deeply penetrating explanation of this issue.[6] He postulated that there are three layers of any message. Layer one, the frame message, says: "I am a message; decode me if you can!" In the previous example, the manager had to decide if a "lateral move" was an actual message. In some cases, a manager may be unaware that there is a message in the move. On the other hand, if the manager determines that there is, indeed, a message in the move, then a layer two issue arises.

Layer two, the outer message, tells us how to decode the message. What decoding mechanism should the manager use? The corporate culture and the unwritten organizational rules determine how the message should be decoded. Yet, a manager may be able to recognize the message in the lateral move but not know how to interpret it. The situation would be similar to someone recognizing that French is being spoken but being unable to interpret the actual utterance.

The inner message, layer three, is the meaning as intended by the sender. In this case, top management may be saying, "Your performance has been lackluster. You better shape up!" In essence, the top two layers provide part of the context so the actual meaning can be extracted.

Therefore, context provides two important pieces of information to properly interpret the message. *First,* it designates what counts as a message and what does not. Is being left off a circulation list an oversight or a message? What about not being invited to certain social events? People are continuously faced with some kind of ambiguity. *Second,* the context tells what decoding mechanism should be utilized. If, for example, an organization has gone through some radical changes to become "leaner and meaner," how should being left off a circulation list be decoded? Should the old interpretation rules be used or the new ones? Clearly the decoding mechanism significantly alters the interpretation. A message must have a context for interpretation to take place. Part of that context emerges from the message itself but the most significant part arises from the unwritten organizational rules.

This complex process of meaning construction raises some disconcerting questions. Can managers ever be completely sure their words or actions will be interpreted as intended? In a word, no. Yet, does this process make it impossible to predict how employees will probably interpret a message? No. A manager cannot look for total certainty of interpretation but rather must learn to live with the probable and plausible. How can managers achieve reasonable certainty that their actions and words will be interpreted as intended? They do so by fully understanding how people interpret messages. Although the interpretations people make are relative, the process is not. We all use a similar process to construct meaning. Inferring how the context and content will interact in the receiver's mind lies at the heart of effective communication. As a dancer grows in familiarity with her partner's capabilities and the music, she learns to better predict her partner's movements.

Implications of the Propositions

The implications of these propositions are woven into the fabric of the following chapters. However, several deserve to be highlighted at this point.

Explore the Employees' Context

The more managers know about the context in which employees interpret actions and messages, the greater the likelihood that they can accurately predict the probable interpretations. For example, MBWA (Management by Wandering Around) helps managers learn about employee attitudes, environment, needs, and desires. This, then, helps managers develop an intuitive understanding of their employees' context of interpretation.[7] This kind of knowledge can help the manager implicitly, if not explicitly, structure communication so it will be interpreted as intended. One executive summarized it best:

> Perceptions form around tiny bits of data and become stronger as supporting evidence accumulates; they are never completely accurate, nor are they completely wrong. Staying in touch with others' perceptions is difficult, however, partly because these may not be wholly conscious and partly because only the tip of what may be a large threatening iceberg will be known to any one employee. So managers must piece together the overall picture for themselves by listening for the tone, or context, or shading that doesn't quite match their own perceptions. Moreover, managers (particularly those at high levels) must consider carefully how their decisions will be perceived. If a decision is right in some business sense but wrong (for whatever reason) from the employees' perspective, its implementation will be erratic at best.[8]

Carefully Manage Employee Expectations

Because employee interpretations are highly dependent on message sequences, the well-worn counsel to "under-promise, over-deliver" makes perfect sense. Expectations act as silent benchmarks that measure performance and gauge trustworthiness. Consider the executive who must announce a wage freeze. If the messages preceding the announcement created an expectation of a wage increase, then employees will be greatly disappointed and perhaps question the executive's integrity (over-promised, under-delivered). If messages preceding the announcement focused on potential job losses or wage decreases, the news would be greeted more favorably (under-promised, over-delivered). Note that employees have vastly different interpretations of the same announcement depending on their expectations, not the manager's expectations. Expectation management attempts to tap into the mental calculus employees use to make sense of organizational events. If executives and managers do not shape employee expectations, others will and often in ways that run counter to organizational objectives.

Think About the Possible Interpretations (and Misinterpretations) of Messages, Events, and Symbols

Typically managers only think about how to best structure their messages to get their points across. They rarely think: "How might my message be misunderstood?" Because communication is probabilistic in nature, it seems reasonable to try to lessen the possibility of likely misinterpretations. Osmo Wiio, a former Finnish parliament member turned organizational communication scholar, put it this way, à la Murphy's Laws:

- If communication can fail, it will!
- If you are satisfied that your communication is bound to succeed, it is bound to fail.
- If a message can be understood in different ways, it will be understood in just that way which does the most harm.[9]

With tongue only partly in cheek, he makes the fundamental point that managers cannot be 100% certain that their messages will be understood as intended.

Clarify Potentially Ambiguous Comments With the "Blackout" Tactic

Occasionally a speaker will make a statement and follow it up with a series of, "I am not saying X; I am not saying Y." This may seem a bit odd, for certainly most speakers know what they are saying. Yet, on closer examination, this tactic can be exceedingly useful for the audience because it clarifies the precise meaning of the speaker. In essence, the speaker has blocked out certain probable interpretations of his remarks. When the original remark is made, it is as if the stage manager turns on numerous spotlights to illuminate the stage. As the speaker says, "I do not mean," he extinguishes each light one by one until only one remains illuminated. So the speaker clarifies his precise meaning, while signaling his sensitivity to other potential interpretations. This strategy could be modified to black out only a few possibilities and still leave a number of possible meanings highlighted, like illuminating only a sector of the stage.

Pay Attention to Secondary Messages

Sometimes employees unwittingly undermine their credibility by sending inappropriate secondary messages. Consider this scenario. One manager spent close to one hour interviewing a potential employee. The interviewer was suitably impressed by the candidate's experience, skills, and education. That changed in an instant. At the end of interview, the manager asked the interviewee if she had any questions. Her response: "Tell me more about the vacation schedule." Fair or not, the manager concluded that the candidate did not have the right work ethic. Was this a legitimate question? Sure, but not for the first question. It signaled an inability to focus on important issues.

Be Aware of the "Law of Large Numbers"

Statistician Persi Diaconis noted, "If you look at a big enough population long enough, then 'almost any damn thing will happen.'"[10] Likewise, any message sent to enough people could be interpreted in almost any conceivable way. In fact, we should expect wacky interpretations from at least a few people. Several years ago, Pepsi ran a commercial campaign in which consumers collected points that could be used to purchase "Pepsi Stuff." As a humorous clincher, the ad suggested that anyone collecting seven million points could redeem them for one Harrier jet. How could anyone think this was a serious offer? Well someone did. A Seattle man even convinced several investors to help him collect the required number of points. Of course, when he went to redeem his prize, Pepsi shot down his dreams quicker than a sidewinder missile. The whole mess ended up in the court. Fortunately sanity prevailed and Judge Kimba M. Wood ruled, "No objective person could reasonably have concluded that the commercial actually offered consumers a Harrier jet."[11] Pepsi had fallen victim to the "law of large numbers" by communicating to millions of reasonable people but also some unreasonable ones.

Carefully Frame Messages

Gail Fairhurst and Robert Sarr describe framing in the following way:

The essential tool of the manager of meaning is the ability to frame. To determine the meaning of a subject is to make sense of it, to judge its character and significance. To hold the frame of a subject is to choose one particular meaning (or set of meanings) over another. When we share our frames with others (the process of framing), we manage meaning because we assert that our interpretations should be taken as real over other possible interpretations.[12]

The frame acts as a lens through which the other issues are viewed, highlighting certain images and refracting others. The frame alters the probable interpretations. Consider Tom Cashman, who adeptly managed a large and complex unionized plant that manufactures paper products. He also skillfully framed a critical message. After months of grueling decision making, the corporate headquarters decided to make a $25 million capital improvement at his plant. Unfortunately, this also meant shutting down a sister plant in Pennsylvania—good news for his plant, bad news for the other plant. Announcing this news required a deft touch. He had to simultaneously signal his excitement at winning a difficult corporate battle, his resolve to meet the new challenge, and his sadness for workers (also unionized) at the sister plant. What to do? He began his address to the hundreds of gathered by asking, "How many of you guys remember when you proposed to your wife?" Hands shot up all over the room. He continued,

Do you remember your emotions at the time? Perhaps you recalled all the crazy things you did during your courtship. Maybe you remember wondering whether she would accept the offer. And you might even feel a tinge of guilt because you wooed her away from your best friend.

That was the frame. Now the message: "That is how I feel today . . . ." He went on to explain why, over the last few years, he asked the plant to do some "crazy things" like taking on new projects—"They might not have made sense then, but we were positioning the plant for the future." He expressed concern over the sister plant by comparing the news to the guy who marries his best friend's girlfriend. The entire presentation was designed to set the tone for the coming challenges, and to help employees make sense out of a stressful situation filled with conflicting emotions. One wonders how the news would have been received without this frame. Would employees have been as motivated to meet the new challenges? Would they have understood the significance of the decision? Would they have felt honored? I don't think so.

Sculpt the Proper Context

Build enough frames and a context emerges. Skilled managers and companies carefully craft contexts by artfully accentuating certain interpretations while chiseling away others. Consider Johnson & Johnson, a company that routinely tops the "Best Corporate Reputations" list. No single incident accounts for their stellar image. J & J is passionate about putting customers first. The first several lines of their credo say it all: "We believe our first responsibility is to the doctors, nurses, and patients, to mothers and fathers and all others who use our products and services. In meeting their needs, everything we do must be of high quality. . . ."[13] You can see the credo everywhere: Web pages, sides of buildings, posters, and so on. The company uses it as the basis for training programs and performance appraisals.[14] The result: Customers learn to expect this level of commitment and employees feel obliged to meet those expectations. In other words, J & J carefully crafts the context so that employees pay attention to the right things: customer needs. The context shapes interpretations such that employees become accustomed to viewing events from the customers' perspective. No wonder J & J deftly handled the 1982 Tylenol tampering scare.

Conclusion

A probabilistic view of communication does not provide the certainty that most Arrow managers desire. The propositions highlighted in this chapter point to a far more fluid and dynamic situation than may seem comfortable. Even Circuit managers may find it disconcerting to find that meanings are not simply the product of interpersonal relationships, but instead are influenced by a broader context that includes the organizational rules, corporate environment, and culture. Effective managers, after all, are more comfortable with a realistic view of communication than a convenient one.

Notes

1. Haney, W. V. 1979. *Communication and interpersonal relations: Text and cases.* Homewood, IL: Irwin.

2. Eisenberg, E. M., Monge, P. R., & Farace, R. V. 1984. *Coorientation on communication rules as a predictor of interpersonal evaluations in managerial dyads.* Paper presented at the annual convention of the International Communication Association, San Francisco, CA, May.

3. Hofstede, G. 2001. *Culture's consequences: Comparing values, behaviors, institutions and organizations across nations.* Thousand Oaks, CA: Sage.

4. See, for example, Fombrun, C., & Shanley, M. 1990. What's in a name? Reputation building and corporate strategy. *Acadamy of Management Journal* 33 (2):233–258.

5. Motley, M. 1990. On whether one can(not) not communicate: An examination via traditional communication postulates. *Western Journal of Speech Communication* 54 (1):1–22.

6. Hofstadter, D. R. 1979. *Gödel, Escher, Bach: An eternal golden braid.* New York: Vintage Books.

7. Peters, T. J., & Waterman, R. H., Jr. 1982. *In search of excellence.* New York: Harper & Row.

8. Peace, W. H. 1986. I thought I knew what good management was. *Harvard Business Review* 64 (2):59–65, p. 65.

9. Wiio, O. 1978. *Wiio's laws - and some others.* Espoo, Finland: Welingoos.

10. Persi Diaconis as quoted in, Paulos, J. A. 1998. *Once upon a number: The hidden mathematical logic of stories.* New York: Basic Books, p. 162.

11. 1999. Attempt to sue Pepsi over jet is a flameout. *Houston Chronicle,* 6 August.

12. Fairhurst, G., & Sarr, R. 1996. *The art of framing: Managing the language of leadership.* San Francisco: Jossey-Bass, p. 3.

13. http://www.jnj.com/our_company/our_credo/index.htm). Date visited: November 10, 2003.

14. Alsop, R. 1999. Johnson & Johnson turns up tops. *Wall Street Journal,* 23 September:B1, B6.

3 Communicating the Corporate Culture

Culture includes the entire symbolic environment. Culture defines reality: what is, what should be, what can be. It provides focus and meaning. It selects out of the myriad of events and interactions in the world those we pay attention to. Culture tells us what is important; what causes what, how events beyond our lives relate to us. Culture gives us values and standards of value. What we may distinguish analytically (and at our peril) as fact, value, and goal is existentially integrated in culture–in identifications, expectations, and demands of individual persons.

Jeane Kirkpatrick

The technical cause of the tragedy was easy enough to figure out. It was a piece of foam that hit the vehicle at the wrong time and place. But the Accident Investigation Board believes that the "organizational culture and structure had as much to do with this accident" as the foam.[1] The safety

---

Chapter 3: By the Numbers

4X

Companies that live by their stated values experience 4 times the growth in revenues compared to those that do not

1 of 4

Corporate culture is 1 of 4 business fundamentals that high-performing companies must master

39%

of employees are cynical about organizational life

#2

ranked characteristic of top employers in the biotechnology and pharmaceutical industry is "having work and personal values that are aligned"

50%

of mergers and acquisitions actually end up adding value as intended

---

culture "over time, slowly and unintentionally" became "reactive, complacent, and dominated by unjustified optimism."[2] The investigators noted that the following traits were at the core of the organizational culture:

> . . . reliance on past successes as a substitute for sound engineering practices (such as testing to understand why systems were not performing in accordance with requirements); organizational barriers that prevented effective communication of critical safety information and stifled professional differences of opinion; lack of integrated management across program elements and decision-making processes that operated outside the organization's rules.[3]

How could an organizational culture devolve into this state? How might organizational culture structure our view of reality in destructive ways? How can leaders and managers cultivate a more desirable culture? And how can we use organizational culture to prevent future disasters like the one that destroyed the Space Shuttle Columbia and claimed the lives of seven astronauts? These are the types of issues discussed in this chapter.

What Is Culture?

The word "culture" has agricultural overtones, as in the word "cultivation." Historically, "culture" meant to prepare the ground or to till the soil in order to foster a particular kind of growth. To the early Christians, culture involved a kind of worship.[4] "Culture" still encompasses both definitions. Organizational cultures foster certain types of growth, provide fertile ground for certain types of enterprises, and weed out other types of behaviors. Although an organization's culture does not cause growth, it does cultivate the conditions of growth. Cultivation of the "organizational soil" allows for the reproduction of compatible and beneficial behaviors, practices, and policies. And in many companies, a kind of religious zeal permeates the organizational culture. Wal-Mart associates, for instance, often start the day with a ritualistic cheer or chant. ("Give me a W, give me an A . . . . What's that spell? Wal-Mart. Who's Wal-Mart is it? My Wal-Mart. Who's number one? The Customer! Always!")

Culture can be thought of as both a process and a condition. An organization's culture is simultaneously somewhat stable but constantly evolving as new challenges are encountered. Judgment lies at the core of the concept. Implicit or explicit decisions are made to encourage some values and discourage others. Jacob Bronowski, a 20th-century Renaissance man, said: "For the values rest at bottom on acts of judgment. And every act of judgment is a division of the field of experience into what matters and what does not."[5] These choices or "ways of being" become so thoroughly ingrained that other "ways-of-doing-things" are precluded.

Organizations, like countries, have styles of action and typical patterns of thought that slowly evolve. If there is "an American way" then we can also say there is the "Microsoft way." *Corporate culture, then, is the underlying belief and value structure of an organization collectively shared by the employees and symbolically expressed in a variety of overt and subtle ways.* Out of a host of individual practices emerge a company style, which ultimately reflects "the way we do things around here."[6] Faced with the frenetic pace of corporate life, few managers take the time to contemplate what the organization has become and is becoming. Although they may not be able to clearly articulate the values, they certainly function by them.

Culture for an organization is like music for dancers. It does not strictly determine movement but it does constrain options. Likewise, culture does not create communication patterns but it does foster certain types of interactions. Psychologists tell us that from the time we are infants, music regulates our social behavior and promotes bonding.[7] In a similar way, organizational culture creates bonding between employees and the organization. The communication practices of leaders contribute to the harmonies and rhythms of an organization. A strict adherence to a rhythmic structure might appeal more to an Arrow manager, whereas a Circuit manager might focus more on form than substance. Such are the tendencies of the Circuit manager's culture. Furthermore, music can express discord, confusion, turmoil, or even randomness, just as many employees stumble to the beat of an erratic culture. The Dance manager seeks to harmoniously and creatively blend form and substance, rhythm, and melody.

Does Culture Matter?

Corporate culture influences the organization in a variety of ways. This section highlights four of the more notable consequences.

Culture Impacts the Bottom Line

James Kotter has devoted much of his scholarly life to investigating the habits of visionary and value-oriented cultures. In a study of 207 companies over an 11-year period, he found that the companies that lived by their stated values experienced four times the growth in revenues than their counterparts.[8] Two other well-regarded researchers, Collins and Porras, concurred that the fit between the stated and actual values was critical:

> In short, we did not find any specific ideological content essential to being a visionary company. Our research indicates that the authenticity of the ideology and the extent to which a company attains consistent alignment counts more than the content of ideology.[9]

Another groundbreaking study of 160 companies over a ten-year period revealed that culture was one of four business fundamentals that high-performing companies must master. As the researchers note:

> Our study made it clear that building the right culture is imperative . . . one that champions high-level performance and ethical behavior. In winning companies, everyone works at the highest levels. These organizations design and support a culture that encourages outstanding individual and team contributions, one that holds employees—not just managers—responsible for success.[10]

These findings should not be surprising. The right culture coupled with the correct strategy and structure provides employees with focus, purpose, and motivation. In a sense, a strong culture allows employees to read the minds of executives, efficiently coordinating actions. The result: less waste, more innovation, higher productivity, and ultimately higher profits.

Culture Influences How an Organization Analyzes and Solves Problems

Few business activities have more significance on the profit and loss statement than how decisions are made and carried out. Paul Bate, a noted scholar from University of Bath, England, wrote in a thought-provoking article:

> . . . people in organizations evolve in their daily interactions with one another a system of shared perspectives or "collectively held and sanctioned definitions of the situation" which make up the culture of these organizations. The culture, once established, prescribes for its creators and inheritors certain ways of believing, thinking, and acting which in some circumstances can prevent meaningful interaction and induce a condition of "learned helplessness"—that is a psychological state in which people are unable to conceptualize their problems in such a way as to be able to resolve them. In short, attempts at problem solving may become culture-bound.[11]

His research confirms that culture can, and in fact does, restrain organizational thought. Indeed, poor decisions can result from such cultural restraints. Meaningful alternatives are not explored because "that's not how things are done around here." For instance, one small but growing company had several problems with how various departments interrelated. The normal procedure was to forward all such problems to the president and let him resolve the issue. After all, such procedures worked well in the past and the president, a corporate hero, was legendary for his ability to solve problems equitably. Yet, as the firm grew, it became increasingly difficult for the president to know the necessary facts to make appropriate decisions. A simple and obvious solution was to have a middle manager's meeting to solve many of the problems and coordinate activities. Strangely, no one in the company had thought of this idea. Why? Because of the "way things are done around here." To put it another way, the value of respect for the chain-of-command precluded even thinking about such a solution. The culture had put perceptual blinders on the entire management team. The consultant who suggested the change was not constrained by these blinders and was widely praised for this "revolutionary idea." Once the meetings began to take place, many of the problems were quickly and easily resolved.

Culture Influences How the Company Will Respond to Change

Culture can actively encourage quick and decisive change when conditions demand it. Consider Amazon.com, run by the disarmingly understated Jeff Bezos. His goal is "universal selection, the earth's biggest river, earth's biggest selection." Some of Amazon.com's innovations, like one-click ordering, are legendary. Others are complete failures. No matter. Few traditional companies would take such risky, costly, and bold steps. Yet, this is exactly what the culture demanded of its employees.

On the other hand, the organizational culture can act as an impediment to change when it is needed. Universities are almost legendary for such resistance. If the need arises to develop a program that crosses departmental boundaries, the budgetary and bureaucratic obstacles are almost overwhelming. Why? In a word, tradition. The entire system conspires to maintain the traditional departmental structure and it underscores a belief that knowledge should be compartmentalized. Hence, universities develop barriers to ensure that no one fundamentally challenges this belief. In some ways, such barriers to change may be beneficial, but the benefits should be weighed against the costs. All organizations should closely examine the environment to determine how much change they need. Then the question becomes: Does the culture foster the necessary degree of change? The answer has critical consequences for the organization's long-term survival.

Culture Impacts Employee Motivation and Customer Satisfaction

There can be no greater motivation for employees than when they believe in what they are doing, what the company does, and what the company

stands for. Excellent companies are motivating because of their corporate
cultures. When a company espouses one philosophy but practices another,
employees become disheartened and disillusioned. An organization with
a corporate philosophy that says "all employees should be treated with
respect" but does not respond to employee inquiries and unfairly rewards
employees, is doomed to an unhealthy culture. Likewise, the organization
that says it believes in offering a "fair pricing system" to its customers and
then regularly deceives clients as to the actual price of goods and services,
fosters disrespect among employees. When practice and belief are incongruent, the culture demotivates employees. Hypocrisy has its price. George
Gilder in his book, *Wealth and Poverty,* summarized it best:

> Matters of management, motivation, and spirit—and their effects on will-
> ingness to innovate and seek new knowledge—dwarf all measurable inputs
> in accounting for productive efficiency, both for individuals and groups
> and for management and labor. A key difference is always the willingness
> to transform vague information or hypotheses into working knowledge;
> willingness, in Tolstoy's terms, transferred from the martial to the produc-
> tive arts, "to fight and face danger," to exert efforts and take risks.[12]

In essence the organizational culture provides a unique point of identity
and commonality for all employees. It distinguishes employees from those in
other companies; it's like an exclusive club with all the requisite symbols of
distinction and powers of inspiration.

Successful companies link employee motivation to customer service. For
example, Disney World has a legendary culture of customer service. Rick
Johnson, who conducts seminars about the Disney culture, explains:

> You can't force people to smile. Each guest at Disney World sees an
> average of 73 employees per visit, and we would have to supervise
> them continually. Of course, we can't do that, so instead we try to get
> employees to buy into the corporate culture.[13]

Then employees are expected to behave according to these general principles as unique situations occur. Employees usually prefer to work with a
manager who has a set of values rather than a set of rules, who challenges
others to share values instead of enforcing regulations, and believes in people
over procedures.

How Can We Discover the Culture?

Anyone trying to detect cultural values should remember the old adage,
"Fish were the last creatures to discover water." Detecting culture requires a
degree of detachment and insight—qualities difficult to master when we are
immersed in an organizational culture. Think, for instance, about how much

you learn about your own national cultural when you travel abroad. Another difficulty faces the cultural detective; namely, distinguishing between the stated and actual cultural values. The *stated* culture is what the organization aspires to be, whereas the *actual* culture represents the way the organization truly behaves. The cultural detective needs to understand both to have a firm grasp of potential organizational difficulties. Table 3.1 reviews a variety of ways to detect an organization's culture. Some of the more revealing techniques are highlighted in this section.

Table 3.1   Discovering an Organization's Cultural Values

Signs	Potential Questions
Physical Design	
• Buildings	Where are they located? Why?
• Parking lots	Where do customers park? Executives?
• Office design	What activities are encouraged? Discouraged?
Symbols	
• Logos	What values are highlighted? Where are logos displayed?
• Dress codes	Whose needs are underscored?
• Philosophy statements	What concepts are emphasized?
• Taboos	What actions are prohibited? Why?
• Totems	What objects are revered? Why?
• Slogans	What actions or thoughts are highlighted?
• Heroes/Villains	Who are the "good guys" and "bad guys"? Why?
Conversations	
• Jokes/anecdotes	What jokes/anecdotes are considered funny? Why?
• Stories	What stories are repeated? What is the moral of the story?
• Naming conventions	How are employees routinely referred to? What nicknames are used? What do titles represent about the organization?
Policies and Activities	
• Financial rewards	What activities get rewarded? Ignored?
• Personnel policies	What kinds of people succeed? Fail? Why?
• Rituals	What routine activities take place in the organization? Why?
• Ceremonies	What events get commemorated? Why?

Examine the Corporate Slogans, Philosophies, and Value Statements

Click on the Web sites of almost any of the world's most admired companies and you will find a clear statement of their corporate values and slogans. Wal-Mart, for instance, routinely ranks in the top ten on this list.[14] The company Web site boldly asserts, "Our success will always be attributed to our culture." It elaborates by outlining three basic Wal-Mart beliefs: "1) respect for the individual, 2) service to our customers, and 3) strive for excellence."[15] Statements like these provide a brief and concise view of how the corporation views itself and its mission—a sort of corporate self-image. Publicizing the cultural values to both employees and customers creates internal and external pressures to act in concert with the values. Executing based on core values may explain why over 80% of U.S. households purchased something at Wal-Mart during the last year.[16]

One note of caution: Creating catchy value statements, of course, does not guarantee organizational success on the magnitude of Wal-Mart. Official organizational rhetoric often provides the cultural detective with a clear understanding of leaders' aspirations for the company (the stated culture), not necessarily the actual cultural values. The cultural detective looks for other, more subtle clues to discover the actual culture. We discuss two of the more important ones next.

Reflect on the Type of People in the Organization

Employees, particularly those at the highest levels, are at once creators, carriers, and consequences of culture. The people hired, their backgrounds, biases, prejudices, and styles shape corporate culture. In turn, these employees carry or embody culture. The daily rituals, the inside jokes, and the taken-for-granteds, are all reflections of the values.[17] Employees are also consequences of the culture, because even as they are shaping the culture, they are being shaped by it. The entire past, present, and future of the company are reflected in the employees, just as a broken corner of a hologram reflects the imagery of the entire picture.[18]

To be more specific, by questioning, probing, and observing the behavior of others, one can get a vision of the corporate values. Why are certain individuals hired, fired, or promoted? What makes a person successful in the organization? Unsuccessful? What does top management value in an employee? How are decisions made? Why?

The "why" questions are the most difficult and revealing, for the answers disclose the underlying thought patterns, beliefs, and values of the organization. More often than not, the "whys" are implicit and unconscious. For instance, why do most organizations go through the ritual of asking for more information than they can possibly use? The practice often reflects an underlying commitment to "making informed decisions." Or, why would a company take time to interview a number of people it has little likelihood of hiring? A silly practice? Perhaps. But it may reflect a corporate value of giving everyone "a fair chance."

Pay Attention to Corporate Symbols and Heroes

Corporate heroes frequently provide a rich source of information on organizational values. For example, during one seminar with bank employees, the discussion turned to some typical difficulties tellers had in dealing with "uncooperative" customers. In the middle of the discussion the bank president stood up and told a story. In a rather lengthy soliloquy, he told how he had handled a similar situation when he was a teller and went on to explain with great relish how he had become president from his modest beginnings. Whereas I was a bit surprised, the employees were not. In subsequent discussions it became apparent that such an event was not without precedent. Edward, as the president liked to be called, was one of the corporate heroes and those stories were common knowledge among employees.

What purpose did Edward's story serve? Fundamentally, the message reiterated the value that top management was "employee-centered" and that anyone can "make it." The president, who they on knew on a first-name basis, was a co-worker who understood their difficulties and troubles. Most of all, he cared. He communicated, consciously or unconsciously, the secret to this organization's success. For most employees at this seminar, the significance of this little event was short-lived. After all, it was common knowledge. Yet, the wise manager understands the deeper meaning of the commonplace and finds significance in everyday events.

Symbolic clues into corporate values abound. Some are more explicit, such as corporate heroes, slogans, and philosophies. Others are more implicit, such as parking lots, graphic designs, and company newsletters (see Table 3.1). But culture does not exist in the symbols themselves; they are really the manifestations of culture. Culture evolves as employees come to understand, react, and relate to the symbols. Note that this fluid process implies that organizations often have various subcultures that compete to create the dominant culture. Through this dynamic interplay, a culture emerges that may or may not be appropriate. We now turn to this difficult issue.

How Can We Evaluate the Culture?

This issue perplexes many analysts because of the inevitability and pervasiveness of culture. Yet, wise managers often find the roots of fundamental problems are buried deep within the culture. The following three tests can reveal fundamental troubles with the culture.

1. Does the Organization Seek to Close the Gap Between the Stated Culture and Actual Culture?

The stated culture always differs from the unstated one. No one, not even preachers, can entirely practice what they preach. The important question revolves around the nature of the gap between the two. Large gaps can promote cynicism, discouragement, and poor performance. Consider the following situation. A small university prided itself on its commitment to teaching. Prospective students were told of the stellar teaching qualities of the faculty. Even new faculty recruits were indoctrinated about the importance of quality teaching. Then one day, a new dean became enamored with seeking a special certification for one of the largest departments on campus. This particular certification required that the department's professors have terminal degrees. The only problem was that some of the best and most experienced teachers in the program had Masters degrees, not Ph.D.s.

What to do? Here was a real test of values. If teaching really mattered, then the leadership would either seek a way around the certification requirements or abandon the quest. But that did not happen. The dean decided to terminate the contracts of those with Masters degrees, one-by-one as their contracts expired. He also terminated any pretense that teaching really mattered. Image was all that counted. Even that was tarnished, as it became clear years later that the certification would never materialize. As many predicted, the initiative failed for lack of resources and commitment. Student complaints about the quality of teaching increased dramatically for a while, but abated when they realized they just had to "jump through the hoops" to get the degree. Cynicism, apathy, and pretense prevailed because the chasm between the stated and actual culture was too wide to bridge.

2. Is the Actual Culture Suited for the Organizational Challenges?

A strong culture can actually be a bad thing for an organization because it can create resistance to other ways of doing things. The culture needs to be consistent with organizational strategy and the demands of the marketplace.[19] Consider, for example, the scandal ostensibly precipitated by the notorious Jayson Blair at the *New York Times*. One of the world's greatest newspapers was forced to admit that it published dozens of Mr. Blair's stories that were either fabricated or plagiarized.[20] On the surface, it may appear that Mr. Blair was solely responsible for these misdeeds. But, Warren Bennis, an esteemed management theorist at the University of Southern California, argues that the problem really resides in the culture:

> For all of Raines's (NYT executive editor) liberal politics and Southern gentility, he was an ego-driven autocrat who ruled by fear, played favorites, had an idiosyncratic news judgment . . . and loathed hearing unwanted truths. Again and again, he gave Blair plum assignments despite warnings from other editors that the hyperactive, erratic rookie reporter was a disaster in the making.[21]

In essence the executive editor failed to produce a culture of candor, which is vital to maintaining and augmenting the credibility of the newspaper. In short, the newsroom culture was not in sync with the demands of the business for accurate and honest reporting. The subsequent firing of Mr. Blair and resignations of senior editors did much to readjust the culture.

Likewise, organizations with cultures that are not compatible with the competitive pressures cannot survive for very long. Some companies are wise enough to know it. In the late 90s, the full-service brokerage firm, Merrill Lynch, decided to break with tradition because they saw the proverbial "handwriting on the wall." Only it wasn't "the wall" they ran into, it was the net. The growing power of the Internet, discount brokerages, and day traders signaled a major market shift. The old Merrill Lynch culture prided itself on fostering close relationships with customers through well-trained, full-service brokers. This kind of enterprise could not survive in the e-commerce age. Consequently, they decided to reinvent the culture before it was too late and break from their tradition by offering discount brokerage via the Internet. Many Merrill Lynch veterans bristled at the cultural changes, but they were necessary to remain competitive. In short, when the competitive situation dramatically changes, so must the culture.

3. Does the Actual Culture Fit the Employees' Beliefs and Values?

Most company mergers and acquisitions fail to live up to their promise. In fact, researchers have consistently found a 50–60% failure rate.[22] This makes perfect sense because employees from one company do not often share the values of the other company. In one instance, a large regional financial firm acquired a local banking chain that prided itself on its unique culture. The local chain offered highly personalized customer service, even serving tea to customers as they entered the bank. When the regional firm took over, the tea parties stopped. So did the personalized service. They were replaced by standardized procedures and formalized relationships. The result: Employee turnover soared while customer satisfaction plummeted. No wonder mergers rarely live up to their promise. Few employees quickly or gleefully assimilate a new culture.

How Can Leaders Effectively Communicate the Culture?

The effective leader teaches employees what the corporation values, why it is valued, and how to transform values into action. Education of this sort requires special skills. Employees, like students, do not always see the value of what they are doing until after they have done it. They may tire, get discouraged, or even resist. Yet, the thoughtful manager overcomes these hindrances while engendering commitment to corporate values and inspiring employees to enact them. They view the values as DNA which should be replicated throughout the organization. Ultimately, the values must move from objective statements to subjective realities. In other words, employees must transform corporate rhetoric into personal commitments and experiences. How can managers facilitate this process? In a word, communication.

Most organizations construct their culture through an unplanned, haphazard, and trial-and-error process. Effective organizations with healthy cultures contemplate, plan, and manage their corporate values. Every manager creates a kind of subculture in the organization, as well. Effective managers consciously construct cultural cues for their employees. This section reviews ten useful strategies for communicating values.

Craft Actionable Cultural Statements

Organizational value, mission, and purpose statements are inherently ambiguous, and with good reason. This bit of equivocation can inspire a variety of creative but disciplined responses. If the cultural statements are too narrow, they straightjacket employees, inspiring only the automatons. If the statements are too ambiguous, they unleash employees, inspiring the disruptive elements. Consider the following statements:

- We are in the business of serving customers.
- Our employees are our number one resource.
- Our mission is to make the best damn product we can.

They may sound nice but a proper employee discussion would quickly expose their banality and insipidness. For example, how well should customers be served? Resources can be bought, sold, and bartered. What about employees? And what if customers do not want the "best damn product" the company makes because of the cost? In short, the statements do not motivate, inspire, or compel the right action. Overly ambiguous statements dominate the organizational landscape. Why? Probably because writing purpose, value, and mission statements have become fashionable. Companies can even purchase fill-in-the-blank, "tailored-made" mission statements, no doubt, guaranteed to inspire even the indolent. This boggles the mind; it has plagiaristic overtones and the same degree of authenticity.

Cultural statements should be carefully contemplated. Ideally, get as many people as possible involved in crafting and even wordsmithing the statements. This allows everyone to understand the nuances, test out examples, and discuss implications. A group of consultants specializing in these issues expressed it this way:

It pays to spend more time in the planning and gathering and discussing of the analysis, mission and vision, because the buy-in will be substantially stronger and the implementation phase will just be a continuation of the process, rather than a disjointed hand-off from planners to doers.[23]

Consider the experience of our consulting team with one dairy plant. We spent hours discussing the implications of one value statement, Purpose Directed Energy. We discussed what it meant and more importantly, what it did *not* mean. We also developed a secondary list of statements designed to clarify the value (see Figure 3.1). Milking the statement for all it was worth, we even created a PDE index for meetings (e.g., "On a 0–10 scale, how much of our energy in the meeting was 'Purpose Directed'"?) Ideally, the discussions should focus on how to link cultural statements directly to measures.

PURPOSE DIRECTED ENERGY

- What *we* do is *directed* at set targets.
- *Everyone* has a clear picture of the plant's objectives.
- *Our* time and efforts are *directed* at things that matter.
- *Everyone* understands *why* we do *what* we do.
- *All* employees meet defined *expectations*.

Figure 3.1   Actionable Value Statement

Appropriately Socialize Employees

From the moment potential employees enter the organization, they begin to develop a picture of the corporate values.[24] The manner in which they are treated, the way employees talk to one another, the office design, and even the hiring process are all indicators of the corporate culture. After being hired, the training procedures, daily rituals, and practices further reinforce "what this company is all about." So the socialization process slowly and steadily builds the pieces of the corporate value structure for the new employee.

Through this process managers can actively encourage the appropriate values. Who does the hiring and interviewing, for example, can send equally powerful messages. Admiral Hyman Rickover, the founder of the nuclear Navy, was notorious for his rigorous interviews of all cadets who wished to serve on the submarines. In fact, the title of President Jimmy Carter's book, *Why Not the Best?*, came from a comment by Rickover during one of those interviews.[25] Here was one of the most powerful men in the world interviewing a cadet, and asking him if he always did his best. Rickover thus set in motion the standard of excellence he expected from all those in his charge. In fact, his legendary commitment to quality was so great that his programs were usually considered "untouchable" during defense budget cutting days.[26]

Research indicates that the initial weeks of employment are a critical period for the manager to exert influence.[27] Supervisors, to some extent, lose their power to shape the values, beliefs, and behaviors of employees after the first month or so. This makes the initial training period extremely important, for managers are not only teaching specific skills but also the corporate philosophy. Detailed discussions of corporate history, corporate successes, and failures help instill corporate values into employees. Some companies, like IBM, go through extensive discussions of corporate values—not just the "whats" but also the "whys" of policy. One IBM employee remarked, "After you're done with their training, you know what they believe, why they believe it and you end up believing it."

Employees not only need to *think* about values but also *feel* them. It is silly to recite over and over again a fact such as, "The speed of light is 186,000 miles per second." Once is enough. Yet, repeating a slogan or value statement can act as an organizational mantra, reiterating words that weave a magic incantation.[28] We do, in fact, listen to the same music over and over again. It replenishes our strength, focuses our spirit, and energizes us, similar to the effect of "Why not the best?"

Develop Symbolic Reminders of the Core Values

Employees should live in a symbolic environment dominated by the organization's core stated values. The symbols reinforce the critical values, acting as continual reminders of what the organization stands for. The creative powers of many managers would be well spent in thinking of simple and novel methods to symbolize critical corporate values. Consider the ideas of various organizations highlighted here:

- *Appleton, a producer of specialty-coated papers.* The company does more than paper the walls with its core value of CFQ, which stands for Customer Focused Quality. Customers can park in specifically designated CFQ spots close to the office buildings and plants. The company has a special program that compensates employees for purchasing designer license plates that contain the CFQ acronym. On the streets in town you cannot help but notice CFQ license plates with gems like "IM4 CFQ" and "FORE CFQ." One almost senses a religious sect casting a magic spell. In fact, one citizen wrote to the local newspaper inquiring about the "CFQ cult." Appleton's prayers were certainly answered with publicity like that.
- *Imperial Inc., a national distributor of quality maintenance supplies,* uses an intriguing rhetorical device to reinforce the value of "customer service." As seen in Figure 3.2, the company organizational chart is "upside down" with the customer at the top as the "chairman of the board."
- *A church.* The minister believed that church members should volunteer for church responsibilities instead of the usual practice in which various members are "begged" to serve. Not only did he preach that "God calls people to serve" from the pulpit but he also signaled the value through a simple rhetorical device. Instead of a "nominating committee" that sought volunteers for various church functions, he reversed the spelling to coin the term "ETANIMON Committee" in which members applied to serve the church. Here, in this deceptively simple act, he reversed the nominating process in both spelling and deed.

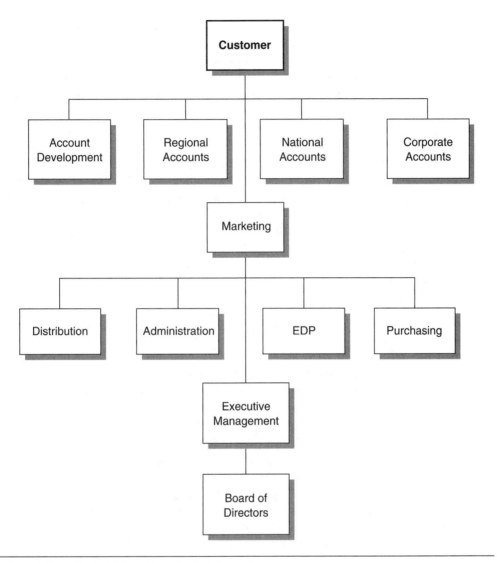

Figure 3.2   Imperial Inc. Organizational Chart

Slogans and other symbolic acts may appear to be simple-minded and trivial. Yet the far-sighted manager never underestimates the power and elegance of the simple. These symbolic acts provide meaning, purpose, and a unique point of identity and commonality for employees in these organizations.

Link Values With Specific Behaviors

Values are necessarily abstract concepts. Hence, there are countless specific behaviors that could spring from one value. Wise managers not only encourage certain behaviors but also link those behaviors to a specific value.

Thus, the value becomes the focal point, which in turn, encourages other novel behaviors that also express the value. One classic example occurred during the 1984 Olympic trials for the U. S. basketball team. Leon Wood, a stand-out offensive player at Cal State Fullerton, was a leader in scoring and assists but was not known for his defense. That was bound to change when Mr. Wood met Coach Bobby Knight, who was known for the prowess of his devastating defense at Indiana University. Not one to disappoint, Coach Knight gave Mr. Wood a lot of "personalized" instruction on how to play defense. At one point Leon reported that "Coach Knight came over to me and said, 'Leon, you took a charge, didn't you? That's your first one in camp, isn't it?' I said it was, and so he told me to go to the spot on the floor where I took the charge and sign the court."[29] The coach linked the person (Wood) to the value (defense) to a specific action (taking a charge). There must have been times when Leon was racing down the court that he looked over to that place on the floor and remembered the incident that was indelibly etched in his mind.

Moving from the hardwood to the office floor, we can find other compelling examples:

- *Imperial Inc.*—The national distributor of maintenance supplies has a "Two rings are plenty" policy. Whenever a phone rings at Imperial, someone always answers within two rings. The policy clearly links Imperial's corporate value of customer service to a tangible behavior.
- *Home Depot*—Enacts its value of "giving back to the community" by giving millions of dollars in grants to local charities and setting up teams of volunteers to complete community projects. For example, they have helped finance and organize projects to build affordable housing and playgrounds in numerous communities.[30]
- *Wal-Mart*—Associates are encouraged to abide by the "10-foot rule" to better serve customers. Sam Walton asked employees to pledge "to promise that whenever you come within 10 feet of a customer, you will look him in the eye, greet him and ask him if you can help him."[31]

Simple in design but powerful in effect, these acts symbolize and reinforce the core values of the organizations.

Filter Information Through the Values

Employees can pay attention to an infinite array of information, ranging from listening to the latest gossip to reading an ever-expanding stream of electronic communication. Effective organizations use the values to structure information to provide a focused reminder. *Focus* emerges by highlighting the most critical information while de-emphasizing less salient issues. Structuring information this way also provides a *reminder* to employees that the values permeate everything the organization does.

Consider how one task force restructured a plant's monthly production report. The original version of the thirty-plus page report (organized by departments) consisted of a mass of statistics wrapped in a morass of tangled and jumbled commentary. All too often, employees read only about their own unit. The committee cut through this thicket of information by reorganizing the report around the core values, disposing of pages of data, and slicing the report by twenty pages. For instance, for the core value of safety, all the safety data from various departments was grouped together in an easy-to-read chart designed to highlight the progress from month to month. Below the statistical data was a summary of the month's safety incidents and issues.

Focus groups revealed that employees liked the new format and were more inclined to read the entire report. Executives were particularly pleased by the emphasis on plant-wide issues. For example, when an employee sustained a peculiar injury in one department, employees in other departments would learn about the incident in the report. This kind of cross-departmental learning rarely happened with the old report format.

Tell the Right Stories and Create Opportunities to Originate Stories

As the insightful scholar, George Gerbner, said: "The control of any culture is dependent on those who control the stories that are told."[32] The wise manager seizes the power of the story and uses it as a tool to regularly communicate the core values. What happens if a manager *cannot* think of a good story that illustrates a critical organizational value? Nothing at all. Employees will not understand the values, much less try to abide by them.

Roger Schank leads a team of scholars trying to teach computers to "tell the right stories." This daunting task goes to the very core of human experience: "We are the stories we tell. We not only express our vision of the world, we also shape our memory by the stories we tell."[33] The storyteller's simple tale diverts our attention from their power and complexity. As Roger Schank put it: "If we all share the same stories, we feel part of a common group. Moreover, when we believe that our most intimate stories are shared by our listeners, communication feels most intense."[34]

A good story has a moral and that is what employees should remember and act on. In fact, in a wonderfully titled book, *Managing by Storying Around,* David Armstrong describes how his company uses stories:

We have found stories to be so effective; they've replaced our policy manual. . . . Storytelling is a much simpler and more effective way to manage. I don't have to make thousands of individual decisions—Is it okay to have a drink during (a company) dinner? How about charging an in-room movie to the hotel room (during a company trip)? . . . The story gives people our guidelines, and then it is up to them. Storytelling promotes self-management.[35]

The stories provide the mechanism to move the values from stale statements written on a piece of paper to a fresh testament written in the hearts and minds of employees. As the esteemed screenwriter, Robert McKee put it, stories "fulfill a profound human need to grasp patterns of living—not merely as an intellectual exercise, but within a very personal, emotional experience."[36]

Shrewd leaders are more than storytellers, they also create opportunities for others to develop meaningful stories. Ginger Graham, a group chairman for a medical technology firm, held a mock funeral to mark the demise of her old firm and the birth of a new one. The tale continued:

Someone dressed up as the Grim Reaper. Tombstone-shaped nameplates, with an executive's name on each, graced every place at the table. We each wrote our own epitaphs describing our roles in the demise of the company. Mine was slow decision-making . . . The funeral experience reinforced a sense of immediacy that made the epitaph exercises stick in our minds long afterward.[37]

Clearly, vivid memories can mark the point where values started to change and provide us a sense of future direction. One thoughtful writer may have best summed it up: ". . . we all bend our lives to fit the templates with which myths and archetypes provide us. We all tell ourselves stories and bring our futures into line with those stories, however much we cherish the sense of newness, of originality, about our lives."[38]

Use Rewards as Powerful Reminders

If you want to know what an organization really values, watch how it invests its resources. There are a variety of ways, large and small, to use rewards to reinforce values:

- Institute Employee Stock Ownership Plans.
- Link pay to performance on key value indicators.
- Provide special rewards (monetary and non-monetary) to individuals and teams who practice values-in-action.

Investing resources in the values usually pays off. As Carol Bernick, President of Alberto-Culver North America, wrote, "If you want something to grow, pour champagne on it."[39]

Manage Conflict Through the Values, Not the Hierarchy

Groucho Marx once quipped, "Those are my principles; if you don't like them I have others." Managers in a strong culture may chuckle at this wisecrack but they would never alter their values to deal with a difficult situation. Consider this incident that occurred at Appleton Inc. An hourly employee was arguing with a mid-level manager about how to pack a semi-trailer with a paper product. The hourly worker invoked CFQ (Customer Focused Quality): "This is the way the customer wants us to pack it. I thought we believed in focusing on the customer." Result: that was all the employee had to say; the trailer was loaded the way the customer wanted.

The story quickly spread throughout the plant. On the surface, the story circulated by the employee may appear to highlight the "victory" of the union worker over one of the "suits." After all, in many companies the hourly worker would quickly acquiesce to those in authority. But on a deeper level, it signals that Appleton tries to "walk the talk." Incidents like this more powerfully communicate the values than a thousand pep talks.

Unfortunately all organizational conflicts are not resolved as easily. Organizational conflicts often arise because of clashes between competing values. There are innumerable practical manifestations of one simple value. Practices that are congruent with one value may be incongruent with another one. Wise managers learn to reconcile the inevitable conflicts between values and seek a balance. Taken to the extreme, an employee might believe that "customer service" means providing an excessively costly service to clients. Of course, such practices need to be balanced with the "reasonable profit motive." The employee might retort: "I was only trying to serve the customer's needs. After all, that is what our company stands for. Is it wrong to serve the customer?" The effective manager then has a unique opportunity to guide the employee into an understanding of how the values balance one another. Indeed, values that seem to be at odds philosophically may, in practice, actually augment and strengthen one another. The wise manager toils and searches for this synergistic effect and encourages employees to do likewise. This discussion may sound something like the incantations of a Zen master, but successful managers artfully reconcile these tensions.

Routinely Evaluate Progress on the Core Values

Employee focus groups and surveys can provide insight into progress on core values. One medical clinic uses this process to reinvigorate a commitment, clarify the meaning of the core values, and develop specific action plans. Once a year they close the clinic for an afternoon to ponder the clinic value statements. All the employees and physicians rate the clinic on its seven core values using a "0" (low) to "10" (high) scale. After the ratings are compiled, everyone starts to discuss the reasons for their ratings. Sometimes the physicians' ratings differ greatly from the staff's. Sharing perceptions, for instance, on what "convenient patient care" actually means often proves revealing. In one instance, a physician who was notoriously late in completing follow-up reports, learned that his patients often complained about not getting back test results in a timely manner. One month later, after getting rid of the backlog, the problem was resolved. The collective scrutiny of the group was just the right prescription. The meeting ends with a decision about the projects most likely to improve the ratings for the following year. This organizational ritual not only provides a safe haven for conflict resolution but also symbolizes the importance of the value system. After all, the clinic never closes for any other reason. In short, a routine checkup on the culture provides an assessment of the organization as well as a source of renewal.

Assist in the Evolution of the Meaning of the Values

One of the signs of change can be the temporary clash between the stated values and the practiced ones. The conflict can be healthy. Not practicing what one preaches becomes unhealthy if there is not some movement toward greater congruity. Many corporations espouse the "wellness" value, which embraces advice such as "eat right," "exercise," et cetera. The et cetera is the tough part. How far should a company go? How fast? For example, in the late 1970s, Johnson & Johnson initiated the "Live for Life" program in which employees completed a comprehensive questionnaire about health risks. Based on the results, each employee was counseled by a nurse practitioner about appropriate lifestyle changes. Employees were encouraged to eat right, quit smoking, and exercise in the company-provided gym. But it was only in 1990 that the corporate headquarters became totally smoke-free. In other words, it took almost 15 years to fully integrate policies compatible with the wellness values. The wise manager recognizes the inevitability of the clash between word and deed while searching for specific ways to bridge the chasm.

Anticipating and shaping cultural changes can be beneficial in building employee commitment to the values. One wonders if a smoke-free environment could have been implemented in the late 1970s. Typically the corporate culture changes slowly, as it takes time for employees to fully embrace the values. But there are benefits in incrementally increasing employee commitment to organizational values. For example, programs like Johnson & Johnson's that have grown out of a commitment to the "wellness" value, have greatly reduced the health care costs of many organizations.[40] Indeed, a culture that does not change and continually renew its values can become stagnant and unhealthy.

Conclusion

As a youngster I remember watching an old black and white movie about a World War II naval battle. An American ship was dropping depth charges on a German submarine. Inside the sub, the results were devastating. Water was flooding one chamber after another, equipment was failing, and the crew faced what they thought was certain death. To make matters worse, the German crew had been instructed to maintain strict silence so that the American ships could not pinpoint their location. Morale was steadily eroding, which prohibited the necessary repairs from being made and the appropriate offensive tactics engaged. The crew was demoralized, exhausted, and terrified. Then, in a flash of brilliant insight and in direct violation of military procedure, the Captain ordered that the German national anthem be played over the speaker system. Because of the silence code, the Captain's officers were stunned. At first they refused. Then, with some gentle urging, one weary sailor placed the old scratch laden record on the record player. At first one by one, then two by two, and finally, the whole crew joined in the singing. And with each measure, the strength, the determination, and even the courage of the crew returned as if resurrecting a corpse. They still faced the grim task at hand but they were emboldened by their anthem, their music. And in the end they triumphed over their peril.

Likewise, many managers need to know when employee morale trumps procedure, how values can provide meaning and purpose, and why courage triumphs over all. They need to know when to play the music.[41]

Notes

1. Columbia Accident Investigation Board. 2003. *Columbia accident investigation report volume 1*. Washington, D.C.: National Aeronautics and Space Administration, p. 77.

2. Ibid., p. 180.

3. Ibid., p. 9.

4. Simpson, J. A., & Weiner, E. S. C. 1989. *Oxford English Dictionary* (2nd edition). Oxford: Clarendon Press.

5. Bronowski, J. 1978. *The common sense of science*. Cambridge, MA: Harvard University Press, p. 132.

6. Deal, T. E., & Kennedy, A. A. 2000. *Corporate cultures: The rites and rituals of corporate life*. Cambridge, MA: Perseus Publishing, p. 4.

7. Glausiusz, J. 2001. The genetic mystery of music. *Discover*, August: 70–75. See also, Trehub, S. E. 2003. The developmental origins of musicality. *Nature Neuroscience* 6 (7):669–673, and Kotulak, R. 2003. Rhythm, melody, life: Human hearts have always warmed to the rhythm of music. *Chicago Tribune*, 21 September: Section 2, p. 1, 3.

8. Kotter, J. P., & Heskett, J. L. 1992. *Corporate culture and performance*. New York: The Free Press.

9. Collins, J., & Porras, J. 1994. *Built to last: Successful habits of visionary companies*. New York: Harper Business, p. 87.

10. Nohria, N., Joyce, W., & Roberson, B. 2003. What really works. *Harvard Business Review* 81 (7):42–52, p. 4.

11. Bate, P. 1984. The impact of organizational culture on approaches to organizational problem-solving. *Organization Studies* 5 (1): 43–66, p. 44.

12. Gilder, G. 1981. *Wealth and poverty.* New York: Basic Books, p. 26.

13. McGill, D. C. 1989. A 'Mickey Mouse' class—For real. *New York Times,* 27 August:4f.

14. Hjelt, P. 2003. The world's most admired companies. *Fortune,* 3 March:82.

15. www.walmartstores.com. Date visited: October, 5, 2003.

16. Bianco, A., & Zellner, W. 2003. Is Wal-Mart too powerful? *Business Week,* 6 October:101–110, p. 102.

17. Pacanowsky, M. E., & O'Donnell-Trujillo, N. 1982. Communication and organizational cultures. *Western Journal of Speech Communication* 46:115–130.

18. Smith, K. K., & Simmons, V. M. 1983. A rumpelstiltskin organization: Metaphors on metaphors in field research. *Administrative Science Quarterly* 28:377–392.

19. 1999. The culture wars. *Inc. 20th Anniversary Issue,* 107–108, p. 108.

20. www.usatoday.com/life/books/news/2003–09–10-blair.book_x.htm. Date visited: September 18, 2003.

21. Bennis, W. 2003. News analysis: It's the culture. *Fast Company,* August:34–35, p. 34.

22. Cartwright, S., & Cooper, C. L. 1993. The role of culture compatibility in successful organizational marriage. *Academy of Management Executive* 7 (2):57–70, p. 57. Also see, 2000. Reed: Reflections on a culture clash. *Fortune,* 20 March:28.

23. Scott, C., Jaffe, D., & Tobe, G. 1993. *Organizational vision, values and mission.* Menlo Park, CA: Crisp Publications, p. 13.

24. Jablin, F. M. 1987. Organizational entry, assimilation, and exit. In *Handbook of organizational communication,* edited by F. M. Jablin, L. L. Putnam, K. H. Roberts, & L. W. Porter (pp. 679–725). Beverly Hills, CA: Sage.

25. Carter, J. 1976. *Why not the best?* New York: Bantam.

26. Polmar, N. & Allen, T. B. 1982. *Rickover: Controversy and genius.* New York: Simon & Schuster.

27. Clampitt, P. G., & Downs, C. 1993. Employee perceptions of the relationship between communication and productivity. *Journal of Business Communication* 30 (1):5–28. See also Jablin, F. M. 2001. Organizational entry, assimilation, and disengagement/exit. In *The new handbook of organizational communication,* edited by F. M. Jablin & L. L. Putman, (pp.732–818). Thousand Oaks, CA: Sage.

28. Broms, H., & Gahmberg, H. 1983. Communication to self in organizations and cultures. *Administrative Science Quarterly* 28:482–495.

29. 1984. Wood shows signs of defensive ability. *USA Today,* 1 August:2C.

30. Joyce, W., Nohria, N., & Roberson, B. 2003. *What really works.* New York: HarperCollins.

31. www.walmartstores.com. Date visited: November 1, 2003.

32. Gerbner, G. 1990. Personal communication.

33. Schank, R. 1990. *Tell me a story: A new look at real and artificial memory.* Menlo Park, CA: Crisp Publications, p. 170.

34. Ibid., p. 194.

35. Armstrong, D. 1992. *Managing by storying around: A new method of leadership.* New York: Doubleday Currency, p. 11.

36. McKee, R. 2003 Storytelling that moves people: A conversation with screenwriting coach. *Harvard Business Review* 81 (6):51–55, p. 52. See also, McKee, R. 1997. *Story: Substance, structure, style, and the principles of screenwriting.* New York: HarperCollins.

37. Graham, G. L. 2002. If you want honesty, break some rules. *Harvard Business Review* 80 (4):42–46, p.45.

38. Macfarlane, R. 2003. *Mountains of the mind.* New York: Pantheon Books, p. 271.

39. Bernick, C. L. 2001. When your culture needs a makeover. *Harvard Business Review* 79 (6):53–59, p. 57.

40. Simpson, S. 2003. Good for employees, good for business. *Occupational Health and Safety,* 30 September.

41. An interesting sidelight to this story is that the U.S. Army had for years lost international military contests that simulated small-scale skirmishes. In 1987 they won two of the most prestigious contests, and in part, they cited the use of rock and roll music in the training sessions. The songs played included the theme music for the movie *Top Gun* and "Born in the USA" by Bruce Springsteen. See, for example, Fialka, J. J. 1987. U.S. army units win battle contests for the first time. *Wall Street Journal,* 6 July:24.

4 Communication Ethics

It is strange that social scientists, who are by profession devoted to the application of reason to man's affairs, have been more impressed by the use and misuse of power than by the use and misuse of knowledge.

Harold Wilensky

Goodness is the only investment that never fails.

Henry David Thoreau

Ethics matter. It clearly matters to shareholders who have been deceived by dubious accounting tricks. Just ask former investors in Enron, Global Crossing, and WorldCom. In the wake of the scandals involving these companies, investors lost billions of dollars and the public's confidence in corporations was severely shaken.[1] Ethics also makes a difference to employees. They want to work for companies that share their values and

Chapter 4: By the Numbers

75%
of lies told in the workplace are
directed at supervisors

76 – 22 – 3
Percentage of lies that benefit a) the
liar, b) the person lied to, and
c) a third party, respectively

84%
of corporate recruiters believe
that personal integrity and ethics
are very important traits for
job applicants

60%
of corporate recruiters believe business
schools can provide students with
guidance on making ethical decisions

50%
of whistleblowers believe they were
fired for reporting misconduct

80%
of executives report having trusted
the wrong person at least once in
their career

80%
of information sent via the grapevine
is accurate

treat people honestly. Tobacco companies, for instance, have experienced difficulty in attracting top-tier talent.[2] Good people like to work for good organizations. Ethics impacts the bottom line, as well. To be sure, unscrupulous competitors have profited at the expense of organizations with high ethical standards. Bad things can happen to good organizations. Yet, in general, companies known for their integrity and commitment to acting socially responsible are more profitable than those that are not. Two scholars examined this issue by analyzing the results of over one hundred studies conducted during the last thirty years. They reported that most studies found a positive relationship between corporate financial performance and corporate social performance— only four reported a negative relationship.[3] Moreover, organizations that develop a reputation for integrity can better weather storms from the occasional scandal or crisis.

Behaving ethically is one of the continual human struggles. Organizations cannot ignore such a fundamental human dilemma. To do so disavows part of the human essence. Profits and morality are not polar opposites of one another. Ironically, one of the most famous champions of the profit motive came from a professor of *moral* philosophy—Adam Smith. But reconciling the tension between profits and morality presents managers and organizations with unique challenges. Thus, this chapter focuses on unraveling some of the complexities involved in distinguishing right from wrong in organizational communication.

Foundations

Three fundamental assumptions shape this discussion of ethics.

Every Communication Decision Has Some Ethical Dimension to It, Acknowledged or Not

There are countless complexities involved in the communication process, but communicators initially face a decision between three simple choices: to speak, listen, or remain silent. Each choice implies an ethical decision.

Choosing to disclose information, motives, or feelings to others inevitably involves an ethical element. Clearly, some messages should not be sent, like those sharing insider information (material, nonpublic information) with friends. To do so gives certain people an unfair advantage in the marketplace. But should one share a rumor about an organizational change with a colleague? Such actions are commonplace and appear to be less objectionable than insider trading. The timing and mode of communication add another layer of complexity to the ethical calculus. Is it ever wrong to "tell the truth"? Can one be too blunt? Should certain information only be communicated face-to-face? People inevitably make ethical judgments in choosing the timing, subject, and mode of their communications.

Clearly ethical concerns are inherent to the act of speech, but what about the act of listening? Alexander Solzhenitsyn, winner of the Nobel Prize in literature, experienced both the oppression of the Soviet Union and the immoderation of Western Society. His peculiar vantage point allowed him to experience the distinctive problems of each society. In an address at Harvard University, he cast his discerning eye on American society:

> Because instant and credible information has to be given, it becomes necessary to resort to guesswork, rumors, and suppositions to fill in the voids, and none of them will ever be rectified, they will stay on the readers' memory. How many hasty, immature, superficial, and misleading judgments are expressed every day, confusing readers, without any verification? The press can both stimulate public opinion and miseducate it. Thus we may see terrorists turned into heroes, or secret matters pertaining to one's nation's defense publicly revealed, or we may witness shameless intrusions on the privacy of well-known people under the slogan: "Everyone is entitled to know everything." But this is a false slogan, characteristic of a false era: people also have the right not to know, and it is a much more valuable one. The right not to have their divine souls stuffed with gossip, nonsense, vain talk. A person who works and leads a meaningful life does not need this excessive burdening flow of information.[4]

Unfortunately and perhaps inevitably, his deep insight and remarkable candor was never fully appreciated. He addresses not only the responsibilities of the speakers but also the listeners. Simply because someone will speak to us, does not oblige us to listen. Even choosing to listen means taking a moral stand.

Remaining silent may seem like the safest way to avoid ethical dilemmas. Yet, remaining silent in the face of unlawful behavior or a potentially harmful situation presents a serious ethical decision. Silence signals acquiescence or perhaps tacit agreement. In sum, there are ethical considerations whether communicators choose to speak, write, listen, or remain silent.

Communication Ethics Inevitably Involves Both Motives and Impacts

We easily condemn people who lie to pull off swindles. Their deceitful motives lead to immoral results. Yet, what happens when the good motives get mixed up with a questionable impact? Consider, for instance, a manager who wanted to boost charitable contributions in his unit. A noble motive, no doubt. He proceeded to attain salary information about each employee from the personnel department. On each employee's check he attached a note suggesting a fair percentage gift. The means used to attain this noble goal were, at the least, questionable. Indeed, most employees felt this action violated their privacy. The old adage, "the road to hell is paved with good intentions," still rings true. In short, noble motives are not enough; the ultimate impact of the actions must also be considered.

Suppose fellow employees discussed a project they were working on. This may seem perfectly ethical on the surface. After all, such discussions actually foster effective interdepartmental relationships, a worthy goal indeed. The problem may be that the discussion took place in a crowded bar and a competitor overheard the conversation. When the employees are confronted, they may well reply, "What did we say that was wrong? We weren't talking to a competitor." But this is, of course, the wrong question. The issue does not concern *"what"* was said or even *"who"* said it. The ethical issue revolves around *"where"* the conversation took place. Herein lies the complexity of ethical issues—evaluations must be made on more than one dimension. Ethical communicators are not concerned with just *"who"* or *"what"* or *"where"* or *"when,"* but with all four dimensions simultaneously, just as a physicist looks at the movement of a particle in four dimensions.

Fundamental Principles Should Guide Discussions of Ethics

When confronted with case studies of ethical dilemmas, people frequently probe for further information. There is nothing wrong with that. But sometimes they draw an erroneous inference from such an exercise; namely, that the uniqueness of the situation trumps deeper and more fundamental ethical principles. Consequently, discussions of fundamental ethical principles that apply across situations are trivialized.

Upon further examination, the "it depends" or "situational ethics" philosophy breaks down. Physicists have long known that the weight of an object depends on the gravitational field in which the object exists. A 180-pound person on earth weighs 30 pounds on the moon. Yet, physicists did not stop looking for fundamental principles of physics because weight varied with gravitational field. Indeed, they became intrigued by the problem. In the same way, it may be frustrating to come to grips with the fact that the same action can be deemed ethical in one circumstance and unethical in another.

The secrets of the universe lie behind physical complexities. Perhaps the secrets of the human condition lie behind the ethical complexities.

These foundational assumptions provide the backdrop for the following discussion of the ethical dilemmas managers face.

Ethical Dilemmas

Managers face many ethical dilemmas. Some of the more vexing ones are discussed in detail here.

Secrecy

Secrets are held for honorable and dishonorable reasons. In her thoughtful book, *Secrets,* Sissela Bok defines secrecy as "intentional concealment." Her definition does *not* imply moral judgment. Indeed, she comments that:

> Secrecy is as indispensable to human beings as fire, and as greatly feared. Both enhance and protect life, yet both can stifle, lay waste, spread out of all control. Both may be used to guard intimacy or to invade it, to nurture or to consume. And each can be turned against itself; barriers of secrecy are set up to guard against secret plots and surreptitious prying, just as fire is used to fight fire.[5]

Here then lies the challenge for the manager: to determine when secrets are justifiable and when they are not.

Think about the decision by some leaders in the American Catholic Church to use the veil of secrecy to protect priests who sexually abused children. It compounded the tragedy by adding even more victims to the already horrific list. Likewise, the engineer who remains silent about potentially catastrophic product failures has abrogated moral responsibility. Clearly secrets may have detrimental effects on our personal safety and our ability to make wise decisions. On the other hand, organizations have a legitimate need to protect certain information. If competitors, for example, gain access to proprietary research and development, they can produce that product for a much lower net cost because they do not have to absorb the R&D (research & development) expenses. Consequently, businesses would have little incentive to innovate, hindering not only the company but also slowing the general technological advancement of society.

Yet, there must be limits to even trade secrecy. Too much secrecy about trade practices creates just as many problems as too little secrecy. Having access to a wide range of new ideas provides the grist for the innovative mill. Dr. An Wang, founder of Wang Laboratories, believes that the great speed of computer technology development in the United States and Great Britain can be attributed to the openness of laboratories and the lack of secrecy required by the government.[6] In the haphazard ricochet of one person's ideas against another, and so on, new insights emerge. Innovation materializes as ideas whiz and rebound through a community—bouncing from conferences, to the university, to the business world, to government laboratories, to private research facilities, to publications, and back again. When the clamp of secrecy tightens too much, interactions diminish and innovation slows. And the net results are all too predictable: lack of innovation.

Thus, problems are evident at either end of the spectrum. Too much secrecy bogs down the creative process; too little secrecy removes incentives. There is a middle ground of sorts. Patent and copyrights allow for information to be used and generally circulated while providing a modicum of protection for companies, researchers, and authors. For example, Gillette used patents to "secure and sustain a market hold" on some product lines.[7] Others use a thicket of patents to "develop very favorable partnerships and licensing relationships."[8] Texas Instruments, for example, has earned billions of dollars from licensing revenues. In short, secrecy does not deserve blanket condemnation; rather, it should be regarded with a degree of healthy skepticism.

Dissent

Inevitably, employees will disagree with an organizational policy, procedure, practice, or decision. How the organization, managers, and employees deal with dissent presents an ethical challenge. Most employees are hesitant to discuss their concerns because they fear possible retaliation or that it will undermine critical relationships. Managers and organizations are often reluctant to encourage dissent because they fear it "poisons the atmosphere," disheartens other employees, and calls into question the competency of decision makers. Our research shows just the opposite; healthy constructive debate and dialogue actually build greater commitment to the organization.[9] The premier scholar in this area, Jeffery Kassing, reports that employees who dissent with their supervisors tend have more job satisfaction and identify more strongly with the organization.[10] Thus, ethical managers and organizations face two different questions: 1) Can we find healthy ways for employees to express their concerns to organizational leaders? and 2) How should we respond to these concerns? We deal with these matters later in the chapter.

Employees also face tough questions: 1) Should they voice their concerns? and 2) If they do voice their concerns, to whom should they talk? Employees grapple with the first question by reflecting on their own ethical or professional standards. The second question boils down to the choice between an internal or external audience (see Figure 4.1). Internally, employees may talk to co-workers or supervisors. Externally, they may talk to official governmental agencies or to their family and friends. In either case, these choices influence the likelihood of resolution.

Venting to family and friends may make the employee feel better, but it rarely settles the dispute. *Grousing* about concerns with fellow employees

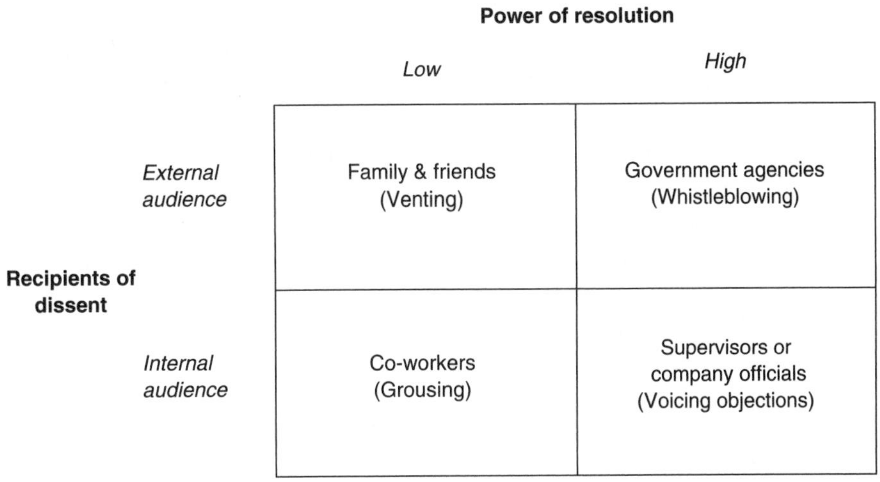

Power of resolution

	Low	High
External audience	Family & friends (Venting)	Government agencies (Whistleblowing)
Internal audience	Co-workers (Grousing)	Supervisors or company officials (Voicing objections)

Recipients of dissent

Figure 4.1 Voicing Dissent

may be a way to check perceptions of the situation and even start building a coalition to officially *voice objections* to an organizational policy. In fact, Sherron Watkins, who first voiced disapproval to her boss, Enron CEO Ken Lay, noted, "What I would do in hindsight is I would get more people to try and stand with me."[11]

Professor Kassing has identified five typical strategies employees use to voice disapproval through internal channels. They include: a) presenting a factual appeal, b) repeating the concern, c) presenting a solution, d) circumventing the normal chain of command, and e) threatening resignation.[12] Of course, we now know that none of these "upward dissent strategies" would have worked at Enron. So, Ms. Watkins took the most drastic step of all, whistleblowing, and she suffered the professional consequences, notwithstanding her notoriety as one of *Time Magazine's* "Persons of the Year."

Whistleblowers go to the media or a government agency with information about corporate abuses or negligence. Greed, jealousy, and revenge motivate some whistleblowers. That does not mean they are necessarily wrong but it does cast doubt. Some are simply misinformed. Some confuse public interest with private interest. Yet, the community has a right to know about corporate practices that are potentially hazardous and dishonest. No matter how virtuous the motives, whistleblowers often are committing career suicide. Typically they experience depression, severed friendships, shrinking professional networks, and trouble finding jobs elsewhere. After Sherron Watkins spoke to Ken Lay in good faith about Enron's accounting problems, the company thought about firing her but settled on relegating her to a meaningless job.[13] In fact, one study reported that half of the whistleblowers were fired after reporting their concerns.[14] Or as U.S. Senator Charles Grassley said, "Whistleblowers are like the skunk at a picnic."[15] He tried to correct these injustices by co-authoring key provisions of the Sarbanes-Oxley Act that protect whistleblowers from retaliation. Whether this helps the situation remains to be seen. After all, when Ms. Watkins was unpacking boxes from her Enron office, she came across a pad of paper Enron passed out to employees, imprinted with the Martin Luther King, Jr. quote: "Our lives begin to end the day we become silent about things that matter."

In fact, many employees choose to remain silent and "swallow the whistle." The result: potentially valuable information never surfaces, depriving many people of the choice to make reasonable decisions. The problems at Enron, WorldCom, and other companies festered because so many people swallowed the whistle.

Leaks

Some employees recognize the inherent problems with whistleblowing and whistle-swallowing. So, they anonymously blow the whistle by leaking information to influential sources such as the press. Politicians have used leaks for years to send up trial balloons, stall a plan, or even defame an opponent. Employees may also leak information to the press for honorable or dishonorable reasons. Leaks may cause organizational plans to be altered or forgone altogether. Leaks can be a form of political maneuvering in the organization or a way to sabotage the career of a colleague competing for a job. For example, a supervisor at Georgia-Pacific received an anonymous letter accusing one of his workers of being drunk in public. The supervisor fired the "drunk" worker and reported the incident to one hundred employees at a meeting. The state appeals court awarded the employee $350,000 for defamation of character.[16] Clearly, this worker never had a chance to respond to the charges. This hit-and-run tactic makes it difficult to access the veracity of any claim and the motives of the accuser. The accusations cannot be fully debated, casting doubt on the credibility of the claim.[17] So, leaking has a deservedly dubious reputation and should be undertaken only in the rarest of circumstances.

Rumors and Gossip

Is there anything inherently wrong with sharing news about the birth of the supervisor's baby? What about speculating about a supervisor's sexual affair? Or what about passing on an unconfirmed report of a corporate takeover? Rumors and gossip seem to be an inevitable part of everyday corporate life. Even though rumors and gossip often travel through the same networks, there is a distinction between the terms. Rumors tend to focus on events and information, whereas gossip focuses on people.

Managers appear to be on slippery ethical ground when they listen to gossip about fellow employees. Even though managers usually treat the information as "yet to be confirmed," the juicy tidbit may cloud judgments about the employee in question. The information has a way of creeping into performance evaluations and promotion decisions, even if unintended. Moreover, the information may be completely inaccurate. Why would someone want to make a decision on the basis of inaccurate information? Consider this case. A new manager heard about one of his employee's sons having a drug problem. He decided not to promote the employee, reasoning that if this mother "couldn't control her kids then how could she manage a department?"—a dubious assumption at best. (Would a father be equally accountable?) Of course, he never said that, per se, but the assessment of her "leadership skills" was lower than warranted. Such practices appear unethical on several accounts. First, the employee could never confirm or deny the information, even if it could be shown to be relevant. Thus, there was no mechanism for correcting the inevitable distortion. Second, the manager did not have access to the same type of information about all the other candidates. What if the manager found out that the son of another candidate was a drug dealer? No doubt, such information would have altered the rankings of the other employees. The supreme irony was that this employee's son was not on drugs; he was helping other kids get *off* drugs.

In fairness, others take a different position on this issue. Blythe Holbrooke, the author of *Gossip: How to Get It Before It Gets You,* says, "A commanding knowledge of gossip and gossipers gives you the edge in conversation and helps keep you clear of potentially damaging situations at work."[18] Other social critics have argued that gossip allows people to develop their moral sensibilities. Gossiping about the boss's affair also indicates a moral condemnation.[19] By gossiping, people develop and expose their moral judgments. If so, the moral training often occurs at the expense of running roughshod over other peoples' reputations.

Indeed, rumor mongering could be justified on similar grounds. Rumors can have a disastrous effect on organizations. Procter and Gamble spent years and thousands of dollars fighting a rumor that their corporate symbol represented the devil. Rumors that McDonalds added worms to its meat in order to increase protein content lowered sales in some states. Both rumors were unequivocally false. Passing along such hearsay seems ethically unjustifiable.

The seminal research in the area was done by Allport and Postman who studied rumors during wartime.[20] They found that rumors were passed from person-to-person; hence, distortion was inevitable. They identified three fundamental types of distortion. First, *leveling* may occur, which means that details of the original message are left out. Second, *sharpening* may happen, in which certain parts of the message are overly highlighted. Finally, *assimilation* may occur, in which case communicators twist the information to fit some preordained prejudice or predisposition. What part of the rumor has been leveled, sharpened, or assimilated? Managers have no way of knowing. Thus, no one can really be sure what type of distortion has taken place. But managers can be sure that distortion almost always occurs.

Rumors are more apt to occur in ambiguous situations in which people have a high interest in the topic. Announcing that "changes" are forthcoming in an organization without providing any specifics cultivates the perfect environment for rumors to flourish. Passing along unverified information in these circumstances often helps employees cope with anxiety, shaping their expectations for possible contingencies. Even though organizational leaders will never be able to entirely control rumors, they should provide timely information, even to the point of admitting when something remains unknown. Employees find rumors and gossip almost as irresistible as sailors found the mythological Sirens, whose beautiful voices lured them to their death. The allure seems inevitable. Perhaps. But remember that the sailors in Homer's *Odyssey* easily resisted the temptation. They had plugs in their ears.

Lying

Of all the ethical dilemmas discussed thus far, lying would appear to be the least morally perplexing. Most would agree that "one ought not to lie." A lie is a false statement intended to deceive. Yet, lies in business are more common than many would care to admit. A letter similar to the one in Figure 4.2 was sent to a small group of executives in a major organization by the corporate lawyer. Within days, hundreds of employees

---

ACME Oil Company

Legal Department

January 15

To: All Managers

From: Wm. G. Howard

Re: Pension Litigation

During the pendency of this litigation, we have had numerous inquiries about the status of the case. Recently, rumors have surfaced that the case has settled. These rumors were further fueled by a misleading broadcast on CNN reporting that a settlement had been achieved. In the past, when calls were received from former employees, we suggested that ACME respond by saying that no settlement negotiations are underway between the parties.

On November 28, the plaintiffs tabled their first settlement proposal....

If you have any questions on this matter, please call me directly.

Figure 4.2   Example of an "Objectionable" Corporate Memo

had "mysteriously" received copies. The bold-faced admission of past deception had a predictable effect on morale; anger, cynicism, and apathy resulted. Those who dealt with this lawyer, no doubt, questioned the veracity of all his past comments. He moved ever so close to the linguistic "black hole" discussed in Chapter 2. Like most lies, this one harmed both the deceiver and those deceived.

Good intentions are frequently used to justify duplicity. Some people argue that "white lies" designed to flatter or to avoid hurting someone's feelings are inconsequential and have little actual impact. However, the very people who vigorously defend a falsehood on such grounds are rarely comfortable with others telling them "white lies." Moreover, there can be some long-term unintended consequences. Consider the tale of the "broccoli soup." A couple, married for thirty-five years, sought the help of a marital counselor. In one of the final sessions with the counselor, the following conversation took place:

Husband: And another thing—why do we always have broccoli soup on Tuesday nights? I hate broccoli soup!

Wife: I hate it, too!

Husband: Then why do you make it?

Wife: I only make it because I thought you liked it. Don't you remember, the very first meal I ever cooked for you? It was broccoli soup. I asked if you liked it. You said you loved it.

Husband: I only said that to be nice to you.

For thirty-five years they both ate broccoli soup that they both hated. I wonder how many "broccoli soup" management practices are stirred up by little white lies.

Even if some lies are used for the best of intentions, scholars have discovered that most falsehoods are uttered for less altruistic reasons. In one study researchers found that 76% of lies benefited the liar, 22% benefited the person lied to, and 2.5% were told for a third party.[21] Equally alarming was the finding of another researcher who determined that 75% of lies told in the workplace are directed at superiors.[22] Lying inhibits the free-flow of potentially valuable information that could be used to change a policy, alter a procedure, or mitigate potentially serious situations. For example, when an employee lies about actions during a crisis, the true cause of the disaster may never be known. Thus, the potential for recurrence increases.

The bottom line: Lying breaks down trust between individuals, shaking the very foundation of our discourse. How does one communicate in a community of liars? Which remarks can be trusted? Which cannot? Sissela Bok insightfully summarized the issue:

The veneer of social trust is often thin. As lies spread—by imitation, or in retaliation, or to forestall suspected deception—trust is damaged. Yet trust is a social good to be protected just as much as the air we breathe or the water we drink. When it is damaged, the community as a whole suffers; and when it is destroyed, societies falter and collapse.[23]

In short, when words lose their power, only force remains.

Euphemisms

By definition, a euphemism is using a less offensive expression instead of one that may cause distress. Mourners, for example, often say "passed away" instead "died" when talking about the deceased. This usage is no doubt understandable. Yet, frequently a euphemism becomes the first cousin of a lie. Lenin reportedly once said, "If you want to destroy a society, corrupt the language." A purchasing agent has a far easier time accepting a "consideration fee" than a "bribe." Petty office theft gets passed off as merely "permanently borrowing" the item, instead of "stealing." People use these terms not only to obscure the truth from others but also from themselves. Indeed, researchers have determined that communicators most frequently "use euphemisms more for self-presentational purposes than out of concern for their addressees' sensibilities."[24]

Yet, euphemisms cannot be universally condemned. The user's motivations and the impact of such language need to be carefully evaluated. Few people would justify euphemistic expressions to rationalize unethical activity such as bribery or theft. The deeply contemplative Dag Hammarskjöld, the former Secretary General of the United Nations, poignantly wrote of what should be our attitude towards language:

> *Respect for the word* is the first commandment in the discipline by which a man can be educated to maturity—intellectual, emotional, and moral.
>
> Respect for the word—to employ it with scrupulous care and incorruptible heartfelt love of truth—is essential if there is to be any growth in a society or in the human race.
>
> To misuse the word is to show contempt for Man. It undermines the bridges and poisons the wells. It causes Man to regress down the long path of his evolution.[25]

Ambiguity

Because all language contains some degree of vagueness, there might be some question about why the subject should be discussed in this chapter. Yet, ambiguity, like secrecy, can be used for both ethical and unethical purposes.[26] For example, an employee who asked his superior about the possibility of promotion was told, "We have the very best in mind but we can't discuss it now." The supervisor implied that the subordinate would, in fact, be promoted. That was one possible interpretation and the most likely one. But what the manager actually meant was that he had "the best" in mind for the company, which meant that the employee would be fired. That, of course, was another possible interpretation. There can be no doubt that only the most cynical of employees would come away with the latter interpretation. Was such a statement an ethical way to stall further discussion? When later confronted with the true facts, the employee justifiably felt lied to. Technically this may not have been a lie because it was not a "false statement." Yet, the *intent* clearly was to deceive.

With a lie, the onus of responsibility for veracity clearly rests with the sender of the message. Even when someone chooses to remain silent, the onus of responsibility falls on the secret keeper. But with ambiguity, where does the responsibility rest? That remains unclear. There can be no question that, in this example, deception was the obvious intent and indeed the effect. In this sense, the manager's action was unethical. Moreover, there were legitimate alternatives open to the manager. If he wanted to stall on the issue, then he could have simply said, "We will have to discuss it later." Such an expression implies no commitment and doesn't lead the employee astray.

Communicators are to some extent held responsible for possible misinterpretations.[27] This means that managers must be aware of the probabilistic nature of communication and to consider not only their intentions but also how their messages might be misunderstood. Communicators have a responsibility to anticipate at least *some* of the possible reasonable misinterpretations. This does not mean that speakers are responsible for *all* possible misinterpretations, as any remark can be twisted into thousands of different meanings. (Note: Recall the discussion of the law of large numbers in Chapter 2.)

Purposeful vagueness or equivocation can be ethical, as well. Managers may equivocate when setting up certain tasks in order to encourage creativity. Employees are more likely to come up with new ideas when asked to come up with "a new marketing strategy" than when told in highly specific terms what the strategy should be like. Equivocation can be an effective and legitimate persuasive tool. Professor Lee Williams of Texas State University has done extensive research on the topic and found:

> If the speaker knows that certain issues are disagreeable and if he feels that the circumstances seriously limit the probability of successful persuasion, then equivocation appears to be the best alternative available. It provides the speaker with an effective means for avoiding premature exposure of his innermost feelings, it leaves the receiver with a neutral to moderately favorable disposition, it minimizes the chance of recalling the disagreeable issues, and it avoids negative connotations which might jeopardize future persuasive attempts.[28]

Hence, managers, when considering difficult issues, might legitimately use equivocation as a strategy.

Equivocation also serves a useful function of uniting people while allowing diversity. Dr. An Wang encouraged employee commitment with the philosophy of "providing specific solutions to clients' problems." He did not make a commitment to a specific product, per se. Thus, when he decided to move out of the calculator market—one in which the company had enjoyed great success—and into the computer market, he was being completely consistent.[29] If the change was perceived as a total shift of corporate position, then the strategic move would have been met with even more resistance than it was. Indeed, Wang's move proved prescient. Although values are necessarily ambiguous, the commitment to the values endures long after the passing fancy of the marketplace. Such commitments engender trust and stability amidst the turbulent seas of technological change. In short, ambiguity allows for freedom to maneuver when circumstances change.

Apology

Inevitably, managers and organizations are involved in situations that require an apology. This special communication challenge calls into question motives and reputations. Such concerns strike at the very heart of effectiveness—potentially damaging credibility, and undermining influence. There are two basic strategic responses to a perceived or actual offense. First, a manager may seek to *reform* perceptions of the offense by denying the allegations; clarifying the situation; or identifying with independent, credible sources. For example, one manager was accused of making racist comments at an off-site party. When questioned by the vice-president, the manager not only denied that the episode occurred, but also encouraged the VP to question colleagues, who were minorities, about his racial attitudes. Clearly, the manager was seeking some independent verification of his position. Second, a manager may seek to *transform* perceptions by placing an incident in a broader context of events or showing that the incident was an aberration.[30]

The fundamental issue in choosing between the "reforming" and "transforming" strategies involves responsibility. Is the organization or manager going to accept responsibility for the incident? The appropriate strategy depends on the incident. But regardless of where the responsibility for the episode lies, the manager or organization must take responsibility for *resolving* the situation. Consider the 1982 Tylenol tampering case that resulted in the deaths of seven people who took Extra-Strength Tylenol capsules laced with cyanide. An unknown terrorist had perpetrated the crime; Johnson & Johnson was not directly responsible for the mishap. However, they did have a duty to respond to the situation in a responsible and decisive way.[31]

When an organization accepts responsibility for a mishap, effective communication can limit the damage and actually build the corporate reputation. Consider AT&T's classic response to a major service disruption that affected long distance service across the United States. Clearly, this kind of difficulty threatened AT&T's reputation.[32] The letter in Figure 4.3 was the centerpiece of their strategy and provides an appropriate model for an apology:

AT & T

Robert E. Allen
Chairman of the Board

550 Madison Avenue
New York, NY 10022

Dear AT & T Customer:

AT & T had a major service disruption last Monday. We didn't live up to our own standards of quality and we didn't live up to yours.

It's as simple as that. And that's not acceptable to us. Or to you.

Once we discovered the problem, we responded within minutes with every resource at our disposal. By late evening, normal service was restored. Ironically, the problem resulted from a glitch in software designed to provide back-up in a new signaling system we were installing to bring even greater reliability to our network. It has now been fixed.

We understand how much people have come to depend upon AT & T service, so our AT & T Bell Laboratories scientists and our network engineers are doing everything possible to guard against a recurrence.

We know there's no way to make up for the inconvenience this problem may have caused you. But in an effort to underscore how much we value our relationship with you, we've filed with the FCC to offer a special day of calling discounts on Valentine's Day, Wednesday, February 14:

> Discounts all day for residence and business customers on most out-of-state calls made on the AT & T public network throughout the U.S. and on international calls to all 158 direct-dial countries.

We've also extended the provisions of our AT & T 800 Assurance Policy to cover this extraordinary situation.

For more than 100 years, we've built our reputation on superior quality, reliability, and technological innovation. Our goal is to ensure that you always regard us that way.

Sincerely,

R.E. Allen
Chairman

Figure 4.3   Example of a Corporate Apology

1. *It was timely.* The letter appeared in major U.S. newspapers in less than five days after the service disruption.

2. *It openly acknowledged the problem and expressed remorse.* The company did not equivocate about the nature of the incident but admitted it in the first sentence.

3. *It unambiguously accepted responsibility.* The letter cleverly acknowledged that AT&T caused the problem, while simultaneously suggesting that they had higher standards.

4. *It discussed action steps to prevent future occurrences.* AT&T's decisive action was vital in securing customer loyalty and signaling that the disruption was an aberration.

5. *It was brief.* The letter did not go into a lot of detail and did not make it appear that the company was trying to hide behind technicalities.

6. *It provided a type of restitution.* The Valentine's Day discounts could not compensate consumers for their problems but it did show that AT&T was remorseful. Moreover, consumers were aware that the restitution impacted the bottom line.

The company succeeded in limiting damage to the company's reputation because the letter was based on sound ethical principles. Some organizations and managers are reluctant to apologize out of fear for further legal entanglements. But two researchers have concluded that in the United States, "A company can apologize to someone who has been injured by a product or an employee without creating a legal liability."[33] Moreover, even when legal judgments are rendered, an apology can actually reduce the amount of the settlement.[34]

A Strategic Approach to Corporate Ethics

Cultivating an organization that ethically deals with the dilemmas previously discussed requires actions in three basic areas: 1) the corporate culture, 2) organizational policies, and 3) personal commitments. Ethical organizations are created and sustained by individuals of personal integrity, operating in a culture of principle, and governed by conscientious policies (see Figure 4.4).

Corporate Culture

As suggested in Chapter 3, organizational leaders can cultivate an ethical climate by their words and deeds. Indeed, the ethical organization must have a culture that symbolically signals its commitment.[35] There are a variety of ways to do this, including developing a set of fundamental operating principles that

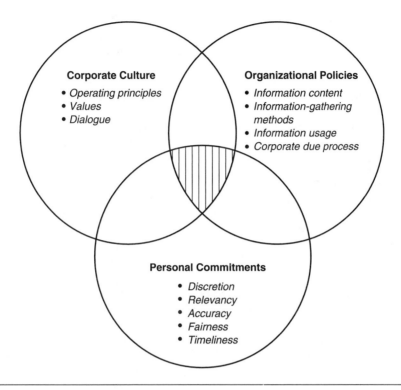

Figure 4.4   Creating an Ethical Organization

are widely circulated. For example, when Charles Brewer started MindSpring (now EarthLink) he used nine principles to guide the business. As shown in Table 4.1, over half of them relate to matters of ethics.[36] Ethical values emerge through the dynamic interplay of practice and philosophy. The very existence of an ongoing debate communicates the importance of ethical sensibilities. One thoughtful commentator put it this way:

> It is through discourse that individuals develop their own views of morality; through discourse that organizations develop and inculcate core values and ethical codes; and through discourse that incongruities within individual and organizational value-sets are managed and contradictions between the value-sets of different persons are negotiated.[37]

But discussions are not enough. Notions and principles that emerge from the dialogue must be translated into policy. We now turn to this issue.

Organizational Policy

Many ethical concerns about organizational policy relate to the management of information. In this section, we focus on critical policy issues. First, what information should the organization gather about employees,

Table 4.1   EarthLink's Core Values

These are EarthLink's "Core Values and Beliefs." If we don't seem to be living up to them, call us on it!

- We respect the individual, and believe that individuals who are treated with respect and given responsibility respond by giving their best.
- We require complete honesty and integrity in everything we do.
- We make commitments with care, and then live up to them. In all things, we do what we say we are going to do.
- Work is an important part of life, and it should be fun. Being a good businessperson does not mean being stuffy or boring.
- We are frugal. We guard and conserve the company's resources with at least the same vigilance that we would use to guard and conserve our own personal resources.
- We are believers in the Golden Rule. In all our dealings we will strive to be friendly and courteous, as well as fair and compassionate.

competitors, and others? Second, how should the organization gather the information? Third, how should the organization use the information?

Policy Issue 1: What information should the organization gather? Because the cost of gathering and retaining data has steadily decreased, many organizations routinely gather information for which they have little use. Companies often reason: "Who does it hurt? Besides, it might be useful someday." Yet, this cavalier attitude often runs roughshod over employee rights to privacy and may unfairly influence decision making.[38] There are important ethical considerations when one gathers information and organizations need to carefully consider the implications of their procedures.

We can capture the complexity of this issue by examining the tension between who possesses information and who potentially desires it. In particular, three fundamental parties are involved—employees or potential employees; the organization; and other external audiences such as community members, regulatory agencies, and the media. A proper information policy should consider the often conflicting needs and desires of each of these three groups. Some of the more common dilemmas are identified in Figure 4.5.

What information does an organization legitimately need about employees? Some points of controversy are identified in Sector 1. Does an organization really need information about a person's marital status, employment of spouse, medical records, and off-job behaviors? Organizations routinely collect such information. For example, in most cases, the health background of an employee has little relevancy to promotion decisions. Hence, a manager, when making such a decision, should not even have access to this information, so that there is no possibility of it influencing decision making. Of course, companies routinely screen for drug abuse as a hedge against potential lawsuits and problem employees. Other issues, like the use of DNA screening and personality tests, present potential concerns for employees. Employee privacy and personal dignity lie at the core of all these issues.

Information Possessed By	Information Desired By		
	Employee	Organization	External Groups
Employee		• Medical records • Purchasing patterns • Marital status • Off-job behaviors • Personality tests • Social security number • Drug abuse history Sector 1	• Corporate misconduct • Trade secrets • Corporate strategy • Policy disputes Sector 2
Organization	• Personnel files • Performance appraisals • Salary projections • Promotional prospects Sector 3		• Employee performance history • Product information • Employee names & contact numbers • Customer databases Sector 4
External Groups	• Affirmative action guidelines • Professional & ethical standards • Legal rights Sector 5	• Competitor strategy • Government policies • Forthcoming media stories Sector 6	

Figure 4.5   Concerns in Gathering Information

Organizations can eliminate many of these problems by asking a simple question: Is this information actually relevant to the decision at hand?

Sector 2 represents the quandary often faced by employees in resolving their respective responsibilities to external groups. Employees need to have a clear sense of what they *can* and *cannot* discuss with members of the community-at-large. Organizations need to respect employees' freedom of speech while simultaneously protecting vital information. Employees should be aware that trade secrets, marketing plans, and the like are out of bounds. Making the community privy to internal policy disputes is another questionable activity, although employees of public agencies are allowed a little more leeway in publicly criticizing policy.[39] Yet, employees are ethically obligated to reveal corporate misconduct and consumer safety concerns if the organization proves unresponsive. The code of corporate secrecy, while important, is subject to a higher code of societal responsibility. Or as the California Supreme Court succinctly ruled, "The privilege ends where the public peril begins."[40]

Sector 3 addresses the degree of access employees should have to files about themselves. A number of companies allow employees to see almost all job-related and non-job-related information in their files. If they feel an error has been made, they can insert explanatory material. This policy of open employee files may sound burdensome to the organization but few companies have found it so.[41] Clearly, organizations need secrecy but not metasecrecy (secrecy about the secrecy). Employees can be told what information will be screened from them and why. There are a few areas, such as promotional prospects or salary plans, to which the company might rightfully restrict employees' access to their records.

Sector 4 represents the information external audiences may desire about the organization. Publicly-held companies have a legal responsibility to provide certain information, such as their profit and loss and cash flow, to their stockholders. Product information presents another arena of concern. Certainly, clear warnings of potential hazards need to be provided by the company. Another concern regards how much information about employees can be released to outsiders without the employee's knowledge. Many companies will not release the company phone book to outsiders, even to charity organizations.[42] In the wake of September 11, some government agencies have requested information on customer databases. JetBlue Airways, for example, released five million passenger records to contractors working on security issues for the defense department. The company later e-mailed an apology to its customers.[43]

Sector 5 concerns information primarily under the control of the community-at-large that is desired by employees. Organizations have some responsibility to ensure that their employees are aware of laws and governmental policies that affect their well-being. Company newsletters often serve this function. Organizations also have a vested interest in fostering membership in professional organizations and societies that educate employees about ethical standards and obligations in their field of expertise.

Organizations, quite legitimately, seek information about the community-at-large. The environment has a tremendous impact on the business. Sector 6 presents some of the ethical decisions for the organization. How far should the organization go in trying to gather information about a competitor, consumers, the press, or government's future plans? These issues are particularly fuzzy because the restrictions are more often in terms of *how* the information is gathered rather than *what* information is gathered. Who, for example, could condone placing a spy in another organization to steal trade secrets?[44]

Policy Issue 2: How should the organization gather the information? Managers must not only be concerned with *what* information they gather but also with *how* it is gathered. It is legitimate, for example, to appraise employee work. But is it ethical to tape their telephone conversations? What about reading their e-mail? Many organizations do so. In fact, organizations based in the United States have a legal right to read employee e-mail.[45] For example, almost two dozen employees were fired from a *New York Times* business office for transmitting bawdy and lewd e-mail messages.[46] Would they have been fired for passing the same messages via the phone system or voice mail? These are the kinds of issues facing organizations today.

Organizations also need a clear set of guidelines concerning the methods used to gather information about competitors. There are entire books published about how to "legally spy" on competitors.[47] To what extent should a business go to secure information? Some firms have no problem with purchasing stolen documents. For example, Chien-Min Sung was accused of selling GE's secret formula for making industrial diamonds to a South Korean firm. The possible loss was conservatively estimated to exceed $5 million.[48] Tapping into another company's data bank is expressly forbidden. But what about using consultants to unwittingly provide information about competitors? Should trusted clients be pumped for information about the competition? The list of questions goes on and on. Fundamentally, the issue comes down to fairness. Most of the information needed about competitors can be legitimately gleaned from published sources that are widely available. That is fair. Other practices, decidedly, are not.

Policy Issue 3: How should the organization use the information? Information, unlike property, can be lost without the organization knowing it. Unlike the thief who steals jewelry, someone could read a personnel file and leave no clue that a "theft" has even taken place.[49] In this sense, information security presents a more difficult challenge than protecting property. Once released, the manager or organization loses controls of the information.

The problems occur when information collected for one purpose is used for another purpose. People selectively reveal information depending on the circumstances. A troubled employee, for example, might reveal information to a physician that he would not want shared with his supervisor. Fairly dealing with these kinds of issues means that organizations need to carefully consider three fundamental questions:

- *Who has access to information?* Clearly, the organization should respect the privacy of employees. Yet this need must be balanced with the needs of company and community-at-large. The consumer, for instance, rightfully needs to know the names of pilots fired for alcohol abuse.[50]
- *When can information be released?* The U.S. government operates under "The Freedom of Information Act," which sets a clear timeline for the release of classified documents. Companies might well consider a sort of "freedom of information act" concerning corporate decisions and future planning. In a crisis or time of uncertainty, employees feel more secure if there are guidelines about when information will be forthcoming.
- *When should information be destroyed?* Negative information in a personnel file often tags along with a person for years. Is there really any need in keeping an appraisal from ten years ago? This may unfairly influence decision making. For example, one executive was not given a promotion because his personnel file contained a note about "larcenous tendencies." It turns out that the characterization referred to a teenage prank.[51]

David W. Ewing, a former editor of *Harvard Business Review,* provides a proper perspective on all these policy issues. He coined the phrase "corporate due process," which means providing "effective mechanisms and procedures for ensuring equity and justice among employees."[52] The process grants "a neutral agency or person the power to investigate, adjudicate, and rectify" a dispute.[53] Some organizations use an investigator approach but most use one involving an appeals board. Regardless of the approach, the intent remains the same: to provide employees a vehicle for dealing with grievances outside the normal chain-of-command. Corporate due process provides a kind of organizational safety valve for employees. Why? Because some problems cannot be fairly resolved through the normal open-door policies. Grievance review boards typically disregard rank and status issues and focus on the merits of an employee's case. David Ewing suggests thirteen tests for an effective corporate due process system.[54] (see Table 4.2.). A small, but growing, group of organizations are using such systems with great success.

Table 4.2   Ewing's Tests of a Due Process System

- Does the procedure make a difference?
- Is access to the system a right, not a privilege?
- Is the procedure simple and easy to use?
- Is the board or investigator independent of the chain of command?
- Does the ombudsperson or board have the power to get the facts on both sides of the case?
- Is retaliation kept to a minimum?
- Is the response of the tribunal or investigator timely?
- Is confidentiality preserved?
- Is the system visible?
- Are cases approached rationally and objectively?
- Are the processes and decisions predictable?
- Are staff people ready to help and advise employees with complaints?
- Are the rules clear?

Personal Commitments

Corporate culture and organizational policy are powerful forces that can mold the ethical spirit of an organization but they are not a substitute for the character of individual employees.[55] In fact, one study revealed that 84% of corporate recruiters believed personal integrity and ethics are very important traits for job applicants.[56] Thorton Bradshaw, a former president of Atlantic Richfield was once asked about how to "infuse ethics into a huge organization." He responded:

> Well, I'm not sure it's a matter of infusing ethics into an organization, because I think most people that any good organization hires come with a set of ethics of their own, and live with because they're their own. What an organization should do—its objective should be not to twist or distort those ethics.[57]

Indeed research indicates that when employees behave unethically, they believe that others are often the cause. On the other hand, when they behave ethically, they cite personal values as the reason.[58] Personal ethics emerge from the rich interaction between a person's religious values, family background, and professional standards. But, an employee's supervisor also significantly impacts personal ethics. As Raymond C. Baumhart argued in *Harvard Business Review,* "If you want to act ethically, find an ethical boss."[59] Employees often feel compelled to adopt the values of their supervisors. This places an extraordinary burden on managers to foster ethical behavior.

How can managers successfully impart ethical standards? Typically employees are trained in what specific activities to avoid. Is this necessary? Perhaps. But ethics is more than a list of "thou shalt nots." Employees yearn for values they can believe in. As one ethicist said, "The value of an ideal is that it shifts attention away from what we know does not work and onto what we want to accomplish."[60] A commitment to these ideals, almost by necessity, means avoiding the questionable activities. Below are five suggested tests for communication that should engender a spirit of honorable communication.

Discretion

Sissela Bok, in her own moving and perceptive way, describes the quality of discretion:

> At its best, discretion is the intuitive ability to discern what is and is not intrusive and injurious, and to use this discernment in responding to the conflicts everyone experiences as insider and outsider. It is an acquired capacity to navigate in and between the worlds of personal and shared experiences, coping with the moral questions about what is fair or unfair, truthful or deceptive, helpful or harmful. Inconceivable without an awareness of the boundaries surrounding people, discretion requires a sense for when to hold back in order not to bruise, and for when to reach out.[61]

Respect for our fellow human beings, their privacy, and their dreams, requires a sense of discretion.

Relevancy

Communication should be structured around the norm of relevancy. Communicators should take care that their remarks are pertinent to the purpose at hand. It means that we only collect information relevant to a specific purpose; we dispose of the information when it is no longer pertinent. On the other hand, the norm of relevancy means that all pertinent facts are brought to bear on a decision. A manager who sugarcoats an appraisal review has not complied with the norm of relevancy. By not communicating important information, the employee does not know how to improve. Choosing what to express and what to repress involves making an ethical decision. The norm of relevancy aids the communicator in making that kind of critical choice.

Accuracy

A healthy respect for the truth provides the foundation of communication. The Biblical adage, "And the truth shall set you free," is more than a religious saying. Reliable information sets us free to make wise choices. Lies and half-truths rob people of fundamental choices. If an employee lies about the true cause of an accident, this behavior prevents the organization from protecting others from harm. So, all employees must be committed to the ethic of "accuracy," even when the implications prove personally painful. On the other hand, communicators must be reasonably certain that the information will be interpreted in the way intended. Philosopher William James may have expressed this concern best: "There is no worse lie than the truth misunderstood."

Fairness

Many questionable activities could easily be eliminated if we simply asked, "Would I want this done to me?" Lies and ambiguity meant to deceive can hardly be justified. Treating people in a judicious manner would eliminate much idle gossip, pain, and sorrow. Fair communication requires us to speak up to correct an inaccuracy, to defend someone's reputation, or to deal with impropriety. To be fair means to avoid the unjust but also to do the just. It compels us to speak and listen only under the proper circumstances.

Timeliness

Even accurate information can be useless if communicated in an untimely fashion. Why? Just as with a lie, choice can be restricted. Each day that an employer withholds news of impending layoffs may deprive some employee of another job opportunity that comes his or her way. Likewise, if someone communicates to the press about an indiscretion before the matter has been discussed internally, the test of proper timing has been violated. By timing communication properly, one communicates respect for the individual. Think, for instance, about the difference between remembering a spouse's birthday at the proper time rather than a week later. Proper timing allows us to build and honor relationships.

A pentathlon athlete must successfully compete in all five events. In the same way, an ethical communicator must run the good race on all five accounts. I can still vividly recall one cold Thanksgiving day from my teenage years. After a sumptuous meal with my family, we did what others were doing all across the land; we talked about various events and people. My grandmother began telling a wickedly funny story about an acquaintance of hers. We egged her on for more juicy tidbits. We all laughed. Then I said, "But Grandma, that's gossip." To which she responded: "No it's not. It's the truth." That caused us to roar all the more. Reflecting on that incident now, I see that "accuracy" is not the *only* ethical criterion that should be used to judge communications. Information may well be *accurate* and even *timely,* but may not be used with *discretion*. Each criterion must be balanced against the other. The dynamic tension in this pentad provides the challenge, compelling us to make the right tradeoffs. This requires judgment. It requires grappling with the complexity of communication. And it requires sensitivity as well as toughness. The only real losers in the pentathlon are those who fail to compete in all five events; so too with communicators.

Conclusion

Discussions of ethics seem to inevitably lead to great philosophical words such as "dignity," "freedom," "fairness," "right," and "wrong." For many, these words stay on the mind's bookshelf in the same dusty place where the Bible, the works of Aristotle and Plato reside in most libraries—untouched, unexamined, and unwelcome. But there are times when the force of circumstance or the compelling sense of place inspires one to dust off those forgotten tomes and contemplate those very words.

For me, it happened on a hot, muggy August afternoon in Washington D.C. One marvels at the Washington monument, the Lincoln Memorial, and the White House. But there is a different and inexplicable sense upon approaching the Vietnam War Memorial. The monument does not tower; it is carved out of the earth, like a healing wound. The hard black blocks of granite shimmer. The sun glares off the names of war heroes etched on the memorial. Strangely, unlike the war itself, the names on the face of the memorial are difficult to photograph. I thought perhaps this was a reminder that even though it was America's first "televised war," no photograph could ever tell of the true horror. There were people solemnly walking by. But there were a few who knelt down to pray. And then they reached out to the cold hard granite and touched the name—the life—of a loved one. They wept.

Down through the ages men and women like these have suffered and died for freedom. Freedom of choice, freedom of speech. These were not some philosophical abstractions to be debated; they were living principles that were bought and paid for in the blood of fighters and the tears of families. One feels a tremendous obligation to not make a mockery of such sacrifice, to not abuse the freedom but use it to pursue the very best in life. We often hear of the *freedom* of speech but on that hot humid day at this touching memorial, I thought about the *responsibilities* of speech. Ethical communicators ponder these obligations as well.

Notes

1. 2003. Scandal scorecard. *Wall Street Journal,* 3 October:B1, B4.

2. Smith, N. C. 2003. Corporate social responsibility: Whether or how? *California Management Review* 45 (4):52–76.

3. Margolis, J. D., & Walsh, J. P. 2001. *People and profits.* Mahway, NJ: Lawrence Erlbaum.

4. Solzhenitsyn, A. 1978. A world split apart. *Vital Speeches,* 1 September: 678–684, p. 680.

5. Bok, S. 1982. *Secrets: On the ethics of concealment and revelation.* New York: Pantheon Books, p. 18.

6. Wang, A. 1986. *Lessons.* Reading, MA: Addison-Wesley.

7. Rivette, K. G., & Kline, D. 2000. Discovering new value in intellectual property. *Harvard Business Review* 78 (1):54–66, p. 58.

8. Ibid., p. 58.

9. See discussion of the Pulse Process in Chapter 11.

10. Kassing, J. W. 2001. From the look of things: Assessing perceptions of organizational dissenters. *Management Communication Quarterly* 14:442–470.

11. Watkins, S. S. 2003. Ethical conflicts at Enron: Moral responsibility in corporate capitalism. *California Management Review* 45 (4):6–19, p. 18.

12. Kassing, J. W. 2002. Speaking up: Identifying employees' upward dissent strategies. *Management Communication Quarterly* 16 (2):187–209.

13. Lacayo, R., & Ripley, A. 2002–2003. Persons of the year. *Time,* 30 December: 30–33.

14. Dywer, P., & Carney, D. 2002. Year of the whistleblower. *Business Week,* 16 December: 107–110, p. 108.

15. Ibid., p. 108.

16. Hoerr, J. 1988. Privacy. *Business Week,* 28 March:61–68.

17. Near, J., & Miceli, M. 1995. Effective whistle-blowing. *Academy of Management Review* 20 (3):679–708.

18. Holbrooke, B. 1983. *Gossip: How to get it before it gets you and other suggestions for social survival.* New York: St. Martin's Press, p. 5.

19. Morrow, L. 1981. The morals of gossip. *Time,* 26 October:98.

20. Allport, G. W., & Postman, L. J. 1947. *The psychology of rumor.* New York: Holt, Rinehart & Winston.

21. Camden, C., Motley, M. T., & Wilson, A. 1983. *White lies in interpersonal communication: A taxonomy and (preliminary) investigation of social motivations.* Paper presented at the annual convention of the International Communication Association, Dallas, May.

22. Hample, D. 1980. Purposes and effects of lying. *Southern Speech Communication Journal* 46:33–47.

23. Bok, S. 1978. *Lying: Moral choice in public and private life*. New York: Pantheon Books, p. 26–27.

24. McGlone, M. S., & Batchelor, J. A. 2003. Looking out for number one: Euphemism and face. *Journal of Communication* 53 (2):251–264, p. 251.

25. Hammarskjöld, D. 1978. *Markings*. New York: Knopf, p. 112.

26. Bavelas, J. B., Black, A., Chovil, N., & Mullett, J. 1990. *Equivocal communication*. Newbury Park, CA: Sage Publications.

27. Austin, R. W. 1961. Code of conduct of executives. *Harvard Business Review* 39 (5):53–61.

28. Williams, M. L. 1976. *Equivocation: How does it affect receiver agreement and recall?* Paper presented at the annual convention of the Speech Communication Association, San Francisco, November.

29. Wang, op. cit.

30. Ware, B. L., & Linkugel, W. A. 1973. They spoke in defense of themselves: On the generic criticism of apologia. *Quarterly Journal of Speech* 59 (3):273–283.

31. Benson, J. A. 1988. Crisis revisited. An analysis of strategies used by Tylenol in the second tampering episode. *Central States Speech Journal* 39 (1):49–66. See also: http://iml.jou.ufl.edu/projects/Spring01/Hogue/tylenol.html.

32. For a more detailed account of a similar event, see Benoit, W., & Brinson, S. 1994. AT & T: Apologies are not enough. *Communication Quarterly* 42 (1):75–88.

33. Patel, A. & Reinsch, L. 2003. Companies *can* apologize: Corporate apologies and legal liability. *Business Communication Quarterly* 66 (1):9–25, p. 9.

34. Ibid.

35. Seeger, M. W., & Ulmer R. R. 2003. Explaining Enron: Communication and responsible leadership. *Management Communication Quarterly* 17 (1):58–84.

36. Grimes, B. 1999. Lessons from MindSpring. *Fortune,* 21 June:186(C)-186(G). Also see, www.earthlink.net/about/mission.html.

37. Conrad, C. 1993. *The ethical nexus*. Norwood, NJ: Ablex, p. 2.

38. Burgoon, J. K. 1982. Privacy and communication. In *Communication yearbook 6,* edited by M. Burgoon (pp. 206–249). Beverly Hills, CA: Sage.

39. Sanders, W. C. 1986. *Important and unimportant organizational communication: Public employee freedom of speech after Connick v. Myers*. Paper presented at the annual convention of the International Communication Association, Chicago, May.

40. See, for example, Wald, M. L. 1990. Whistle-blowers in atomic plants to be aided. *New York Times,* 11 March: Y13.

41. Ewing, D. W. 1983. *"Do it my way or you're fired!": Employee rights and the changing role of management prerogatives*. New York: John Wiley & Sons.

42. Westin, A. F. 1980. A profile of Bank of America's privacy experience. In *Individual rights in the corporation: A reader on employee rights,* edited by A. F. Westin & S. Salisbury (pp. 226–243). New York: Pantheon.

43. Carey, S., & Power, S. 2003. Responding to privacy concerns, JetBlue e-mails an explanation; CEO rues 'mistake'," says passenger records weren't passed on to U.S. agency. *Wall Street Journal,* 22 September:B3.

44. See, for example, Ingrassia, L. 1990. How secret GE recipe for making diamonds may have been stolen. *Wall Street Journal,* 28 February:A1, A11.

45. Bott, E. 2000. Are you safe? *PC Computing,* March:86–88, p. 88.

46. Carrns, A. 2000. Those bawdy e-mails were good for a laugh—until the ax fell. *Wall Street Journal,* 24 February:A1, A8.

47. See, for example, Fuld, L. M. 1985. *Competitor intelligence: How to get it—how to use it.* New York: John Wiley & Sons.

48. Ingrassia, op. cit.

49. The English language does not have an appropriate pejorative term to describe illicit copying of information. "Theft" implies the stealing of property but that is not quite the same as the unlawful perusal of a document.

50. Solomon, J. 1989. As firms personnel files grow, worker privacy falls. *Wall Street Journal,* 19 April:B1.

51. Ibid.

52. Ewing, D. W. 1989. *Justice on the job: Resolving grievances in the nonunion workplace.* Boston: Harvard Business School Press, p. 4.

53. Ibid., p. 35.

54. Ibid.

55. See, for example, Pastin, M. 1986. *The hard problems of management.* San Francisco: Jossey-Bass.

56. Alsop, R. 2003. Right and wrong: Can business schools teach students to be virtuous? In the wake of all the corporate scandals, they have no choice but to try. *Wall Street Journal,* 17 September:R9.

57. T. Bradshaw, as quoted in Freudberg, D. 1986. *The corporate conscience: Money, power, and responsible business.* New York: AMACOM, p. 230.

58. See, for example, Baumhart, R. C. 1961. How ethical are businessmen? *Harvard Business Review* 39 (4):6–21.

59. Ibid., p. 3.

60. Pastin, op. cit., p. 219.

61. Bok, *Secrets,* p. 41.

SECTION 2

Communication Challenges

5 Selecting and Using Communication Technologies

Organizations have swallowed technology, but now they have heartburn.

Harold J. Leavitt

Media choice is not the simple, intuitively obvious process it may appear to be at first glance. Appropriate media choice can make the difference between effective and ineffective communication. And media choice mistakes can seriously impede successful communication—in some cases with disastrous consequences.

Trevino, Daft, & Lengel

Who has most influenced the course of history? Unanswerable? Perhaps. Of course, the names of Jesus, Muhammad, Newton, and Einstein readily come to mind. Even if it were possible to construct such a list, what criteria should be used? And who would be qualified to construct

Chapter 5:
By the Numbers

75%
of people would have more difficulty living without e-mail for 5 days than living without a phone

$24
The savings for a company to process a customer's order over its Web site vs. over the phone

60,000
The estimated number of computer viruses currently in circulation

50%
of all e-mail is junk e-mail

45%
of American enterprises have implemented some manner of wireless networking

45%
of all capital expenditures in the U.S. are spent on information technologies

40%
of computer conferencing users do not know the gender of the other participant(s)

such a list? Michael H. Hart, a physicist and astronomer, took a stab at these intriguing questions.[1] He reveals his answer in a fascinating book titled, *The 100: A Ranking of the Most Influential Persons in History*. Disclosing who was ranked first would be like revealing the ending of a mystery book, so I will resist that temptation. Nevertheless, the person ranked seventh on the list would raise some eyebrows. Few Westerners have even heard the name before. Ranked ahead of Aristotle, Marx, Einstein, Moses, Luther, Hitler, and da Vinci is the inventor of paper, Ts' ai Lun. He was an official in the Chinese imperial court around 105 A.D. He developed the basic process for creating paper, which is still used today.

Before paper, communication was constrained by space and time. Generally, communication could only occur when two individuals occupied the same physical space and interacted in synchronous time periods. Paper changed all that, and along with Gutenberg's press (ranked eighth most influential), profoundly altered the course of history.

Few scholars have thought deeply about the impact of paper on society. In fact, many encyclopedias, ironically a paper product, fail to mention Ts' ai Lun's name. Paper was the first in a long line of communication channels that could readily be used by the masses. Yet, just as many Westerners overlook Ts' ai Lun's influence, most managers often fail to consider how communication technologies influence their communication.

Messages must pass through some kind of channel. Consequently the channel or technology necessarily alters the messages, just as the composition of an electrical wire affects the flow of electricity. In fact, Internet service slows because traditional copper wire cannot transmit the bandwidth of fiber optic cable. Likewise, some channels accentuate certain attributes of the message, while de-emphasizing others. For example, written messages typically imbue a sense of finality and formality that may not be intended by the sender.

Communication technologies can also radically alter the organization's social and physical structure. Certain channels restrict access to key individuals, whereas others encourage interactions. For instance, scholars have determined that the widespread use of e-mail has increased lateral communication (co-worker to co-worker communication).[2] Indeed one study reported that

60% of the messages sent via e-mail would never have been sent through another channel.[3] Technology also alters the physical structure of organization. One thoughtful commentator noted, "Without the telephone, buildings would have had wider stairways and fewer floors in order to accommodate the large number of runners needed to convey messages between departments."[4]

In addition, the communication channels affect organizational efficiency and effectiveness. Telephone tag wastes employee time; electronic mail has the potential to eliminate this futile game. Other new technologies will no doubt radically change the office environment in ways yet to be discovered. Learning to effectively manage communication technologies presents a major challenge. In what way does the technology impact a message? How should a manager decide what channel to use in communicating with employees? These are the types of questions considered in this chapter.

A Model for Selecting Appropriate Technology

Consider all the ways a typical employee can communicate today: memo, phone call, e-mail, bulletin board, Web pages, voice mail, fax, pager, and PowerPoint, to name the most familiar. (I am broadly defining "communication technology" and use it interchangeably with the term "channel." A technology is using a technical means to achieve a practical purpose.) With this bewildering array of options, many are tempted to just spin the wheel and select a channel. In fact, *personal convenience guides most channel selections*. As a technology's ease of use increases, so does the likelihood of use. Few employees consider how the channel filters the message. Yet, scholars have discovered that *effective* executives are sensitive to the impact of the medium and select the appropriate channel for their messages.[5] How do they do it?

Figure 5.1 presents a modified variation of the traditional sender (S), message (M), channel/technology (C), receiver (R) communication model. Executives can use this model to intuitively guide their technology choices. Selecting the appropriate channel resembles hitting a row of cherries on a Las Vegas slot machine. The goal should be to align four elements:

- The objectives of the sender.
- The attributes of the message.
- The attributes of the channel.
- The characteristics of the receivers.

Unlike a one-armed bandit, the alignment of these four communication variables should be a product of skill and insight rather than chance. The odds of "winning" can be markedly increased by carefully considering five fundamental questions.

Sender Objectives	**M**essage Choices	**C**hannel/Technology Options	**R**eceiver Characteristics
• Educate	• Terminology	• Fax	• Channel access
• Get attention	• Theme	• E-mail	• Personality profile
• Motivate	• Metaphor	• Phone	• Beliefs
• Flatter	• Non-verbals	• Face-to-face	• Values
• Persuade	• Stories	• Computer conference	• Age
• Compliment	• Facts and figures	• Bulletin boards	• Gender
• Confuse	• Arguments	• Group meetings	• Education level
• Equivocate	• Evidence	• Formal presentations	• Socioeconomic
• Ridicule	• Tone	• Web page	background
• Deceive	• Emotionality	• Hotlines	• Occupation
• Inform	• Length	• Audio and videotapes	• Religious orientation
• Express	• Complexity	• Voice mail	• Interest level
empathy	• Professionalism	• Videoconference	• Location
• Deny	• Formality	• Teleconference	• Race
• Impress	• Timing	• Pager	
• Ingratiate	• Sequencing	• PowerPoint	
• Honor			
• Entertain			
• Shift focus			

Figure 5.1   SMCR Model

1. Are the Sender's Objectives Compatible With the Attributes of the Intended Message? (S-M Test)

All messages have attributes that characterize their content. Messages can vary along numerous dimensions, including level of complexity, length, personal warmth, formality, and degree of ambiguity. Senders of messages also have a wide variety of intentions in communicating messages, including motivating, informing, persuading, and soliciting ideas or opinions.

Ideally, the needs of the sender should harmonize with the characteristics of the message. That does not always happen. A manager seeking to motivate employees should not communicate an overly complex message. But some do. Or consider the case of a manager who desired to "establish goodwill" with the executive team and proceeded to relay a sexist joke. Not very smart or effective. Communication efforts often fail because of incongruencies between the senders' objectives and their choices about message content and style.

2. Are the Messages Sent Compatible With the Channels Utilized? (M-C Test)

Every channel or technology has limitations. Consider PowerPoint, which has become the technology of choice for many business presentations.

Edward Tufte, who the *New York Times* dubbed as the "Leonardo da Vinci of data," argues that PowerPoint templates have "reduced the analytical quality of presentations" and "usually weaken verbal and spatial reasoning, and almost always corrupt statistical analysis."[6] He concludes his indictment by noting:

> PowerPoint templates may improve 10% to 20% of all presentations by organizing inept, extremely disorganized speakers, at a cost of detectable intellectual damage to 80%. For statistical data, the damage levels approach dementia.[7]

So, PowerPoint may not be as powerful as the name might suggest.[8] Simply put, critical message characteristics are not well suited to the technology, therefore hindering communicative effectiveness.

Likewise, managers must realize that every channel or technology has limitations that filter out parts of the message. Channels that are non-dynamic, such as memos or bulletin boards, are not effective in communicating extremely complex messages. On the other hand, bulletin boards can be useful and efficient when communicating a fairly simple message, such as the company softball schedule. Hence, to effectively communicate, managers must be alert to the dynamic interplay of the message and channel attributes.

3. Are the Sender's Objectives Compatible With the Type of Channels Utilized? (S-C Test)

Suggestion boxes have been used for years in countless organizations. Yet, most businesses have found them of limited utility. Why? First, many new ideas or suggestions are not readily captured on paper. Second, the suggestion box does not provide the personal recognition than many innovators desire. Indeed, employees are often told that suggestions should be made anonymously, which even further removes the incentive. One employee artfully described his feelings in a picture that nicely captures the essence of the problems with suggestion boxes (see Figure 5.2). This employee's motivations are not really compatible with the channel. Ideas are personal, warm, and alive. Impersonal media strip away these very elements from the message.

Because communication channels have certain attributes, senders must be sure that their intentions are congruent with the dynamics of the channel. One young entrepreneur who owned a successful limousine business took this principle to heart in an unusual way. He used the telephone almost exclusively as his communication tool. Why? Many of his clients with whom he had met face-to-face, and even some employees, did not take him seriously because of his obvious youth. With the telephone, the problems disappeared.[9] The lack of visual cues worked to his advantage; the channel was congruent with his purpose.

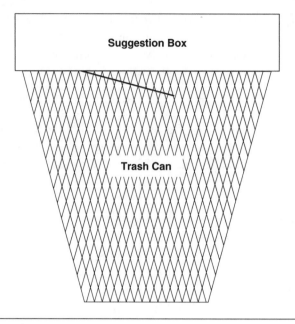

Figure 5.2   The "Suggestion Box"

Likewise, if the sender seeks to imbue a sense of formality, then more formal channels, such as written memos, should be used. If the sender seeks to relay a confidential message, then a face-to-face meeting beats the fax machine. If an executive wants to stimulate creativity but fears that status differences inhibit a free exchange of ideas, then computer conferencing would be best. If the CEO wants to instill an emotional commitment to corporate values, then a visual channel, such as a formal presentation or videoconference, would be the channel of choice. In sum, formal intentions require formal mediums; dynamic intentions require dynamic mediums; and so on.

4. Are the Messages Compatible With the Receivers' Characteristics? (M-R Test)

Effective communicators learn to craft their message in ways that are compatible with their receivers' characteristics.

For example, the choice of metaphors in a message should be adjusted to the occupational background of employees. A paper company executive was more successful in getting employee participation in a survey assessing organizational communication effectiveness when he changed his message from "it's like going to the dentist for a checkup" to "it's just like doing a routine inspection on your machine." Both metaphors "work," but employees can more readily identify with the machine assessment because it's an activity they do regularly to catch any mechanical glitches before they cause harm. Besides, how many people really like going to the dentist?

5. Are the Channels Utilized Compatible With the Receivers' Characteristics? (C-R Test)

The channels used must be uniquely suited to the receiver. For instance, sometimes managers assume that written communication is compatible with their receivers' abilities and preferences. It may not be. In one case, a man who was recently promoted to a job as shipping foreman had to shelve special orders until he could discretely ask for help reading the instructions.[10] The social stigma attached to his illiteracy often made it difficult to ask for help.

Historically, technologies (C) that meet users' unique needs (R) often prove successful. The fax machine, for example, rapidly gained prominence in Japan. Why? The written form of Japanese contains over 1,000 ideographic characters, which made the traditional Japanese typewriter extraordinarily cumbersome to use.[11] The fax machine had the ability to rapidly transmit handwritten messages that could not be easily transmitted through other devices at the time. Likewise, the extraordinarily rapid rise of WiFi (wireless fidelity) demonstrates the importance of understanding the C-R test.[12] WiFi allows users to tap into the Internet, networks, and other electronic devices, sans wires. This meets the needs of mobile employees who want convenient access to data housed on their PCs during meetings or want to receive messages while travelling.[13] In fact, the technology will eventually be available in most airplanes.[14] Some companies, such as UPS, believe that WiFi will potentially lead to a 35% boost in productivity.[15] In short, once receivers and organizations are convinced of their communication needs, they will often rapidly embrace a new communication technology that successfully addresses the need.

The five questions reviewed in this section provide a glimpse of the complexities involved in selecting a channel. Fundamentally, communicators need to find a fit between their objectives, messages, channel choices, and receivers' attributes (see Table 5.1). Suppose that for each of these four variables there were five possible alternatives, much like a column of a slot machine. Senders could have one of five possible purposes for communicating a message. Likewise one could choose among five possible channels: e-mail, computer conference, group meeting, telephone, or face-to-face. There are many more, but if we limited each variable to only five, then there would be 625 different combinations! This illustrates the wide range of choice facing communicators. The odds of correctly aligning each variable are exceedingly small. Yet, by pondering these questions, a prudent manager, unlike the gambler, can effectively manage this complexity.

Table 5.1   Sample Situations of Media Choice

Situation 1

A midsize construction firm wants to announce a new employee benefit program.

Poor Choice: Memo   **Better Choice:** Small group meetings

Rationale: The memo does not offer the feedback potential necessary to explain what may be seen as arcane information. Moreover, some employees might have a literacy problem. A group meeting will provide an oral explanation and will allow participants to easily ask questions about any of the complex material.

Situation 2

A manager wishes to confirm a meeting time with ten employees.

Poor Choice: Phone   **Better Choice**: E-mail or voice mail

Rationale: For a simple message like this, there is no need to use a rich and synchronous (sender and receiver simultaneously communicating) media when a lean and asynchronous one will do the job.

Situation 3

A midsize insurance company wants to garner support for a program that encourages employees from different departments to work on the same project teams.

Poor Choice: E-mail, voice mail   **Better Choice:** Face-to-face, telephone

Rationale: Persuasive situations demand that the sender be able to quickly adapt the message to the receiver in order to counter objections. This is not a feature of either e-mail or voice mail. Face-to-face communication offers the sender the greatest flexibility. The phone is the next best alternative.

Situation 4

A group of geographically dispersed engineers wants to exchange design ideas with one another.

Poor Choice: Teleconference   **Better Choice:** Fax, computer conference

Rationale: A teleconference may overly accentuate the status and personality differences between the engineers. Fax or computer conferencing would allow the quality of the ideas to be the central focus of interaction. Moreover, quick feedback is still possible in these media.

Situation 5

A company needs to describe a straightforward, but somewhat detailed, updated version of a sales promotion campaign to 1,000 geographically dispersed employees.

Poor Choice: Newsletter   **Better Choice:** Video conference

Rationale: As long as employees are already persuaded of the campaign's merit, the sender can use a less rich media. Also, the cost associated with the video conference indicates the importance of the campaign.

Lessons Learned

This section highlights some important lessons about channel and technology choice gleaned from the SMCR model and related research.

Use Rich Channels for Building Relationships, Managing Conflict, or Handling Ambiguous or Complex Tasks

Rich channels provide rapid feedback, establish a personal focus, and communicate multiple information cues. For example, communicating face-to-face provides us with instant access to a wide variety of personal cues such as vocal tone, body movements, and even smell. Almost unrestricted access to these signals can allow us to sense subtle distinctions necessary to understand complex issues. Moreover, the communicators, not a camera-person, determine what cues to attend to. Lean media lack one or more of these features. One can think of rich and lean channels on a continuum, with rich media—such as face-to-face discussions—on one end, and lean media—such as impersonal flyers or computer "pop-up ads"—on the other end. In between fall the telephone, e-mail, video conferences, and others.

The scholars who developed these notions in the Media Richness Model made this argument:

> . . . Face-to-face (communication) conveys emotion and strength of feeling through facial expressions, gestures, and eye contact. It is as important for a manager to know that participants are satisfied, angry, cooperative, or resistant, as it is to have accurate production data. . . . Memos and other written directives convey a predefined, literal description that can hide important issues and convey a false sense that everyone understands and agrees.[16]

No wonder teaching, training, managing conflict, and analyzing difficult problems are best handled in a face-to-face channel. No other channel permits communicators to send and receive messages of such an interpersonal nature, on the one hand, and cognitive complexity, on the other. Lean media such as e-mails and Web pages are effective tools for sharing *information* but they are poorly suited for sharing *knowledge*. Knowledge is more complex and subtle than information, therefore requiring a richer channel. Effective managers know that face-to-face communication nicely fits the bill, thereby, creating an S-C compatibility.

Even a teleconference does not effectively simulate the richness of a face-to-face meeting. One company holds a teleconference every Friday morning with up to 100 employees in five different locations to keep everyone informed of upcoming events. Although this provides a useful tool for information sharing, it limits knowledge sharing. Why? Employees tend to avoid secondary conversations because a single phone line transmits the communication[17] (see Figure 5.3). They rarely ask questions that they might ask in a face-to-face meeting.[18] Moreover, the lack of visual communication filters out many subtle cues necessary for conflict management and knowledge sharing. In short, a teleconference offers an efficient alternative to many face-to-face group conferences, but it cannot completely simulate one.

Face-to-Face Meeting

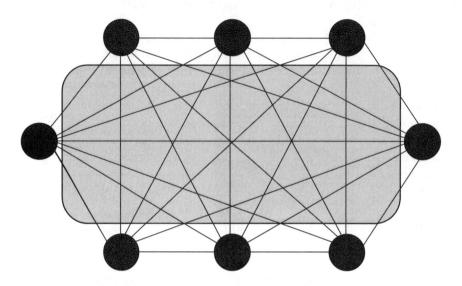

In the typical face-to-face meeting, participants can break into smaller groups for discussion without interrupting the primary conversation because all the communication lines are available.

Teleconference Meeting

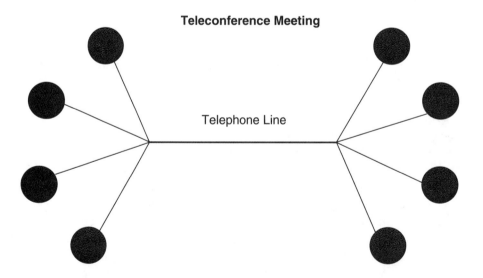

In a teleconference meeting, any person can talk to any other person—but the conversation occurs on a common communication line, unlike a typical face-to-face meeting.

Figure 5.3   Comparison of Teleconference and Face-to-Face Meetings

Select "Who" Channels to Highlight the Relationship, "What" Channels to Highlight the Task

Another model for gauging the S-C compatibility involves choosing a channel based on what the sender wants to highlight. *What* channels focus attention on the message, whereas *who* channels focus attention on the communicators. *What* channels, such as e-mail, Web pages, and computer conferencing (the formal counterpart of a chat room), tend to emphasize information and idea sharing. *Who* says it fades into the background. These channels muffle many cues such as frowns, verbal hesitations, and seating arrangements that signal status and role differences. For example, one study of computer conference participants indicated that 40% of the users did not know the gender of the senders and 32% had no idea of the sender's position in the hierarchy.[19] Some employees who feel physically unattractive report being more confident and participative in a computer conference than they do in a face-to-face interaction. The playing field differs in a chat room or computer conference; employees engage in a battle of wits and not of power. Due to the channel characteristics, the group processes less person-centered information. This may sound desirable but the lack of social cues may actually lead to a false sense of consensus and inhibit implementation of decisions.[20] Moreover, one study concluded that,

> "Given the money that organizations spend on (computer conferencing)—under the assumption that such systems produce higher quality decisions—it is ironic that the decision makers using them may not be as identified with their organization, team . . ."[21]

Who channels underscore the relational elements inherent in any communicative event, often accentuating status and hierarchical differences. Group meetings, formal presentations, and many teleconferences highlight person-centered messages. Consider one expert's counsel about conducting videoconferences:

> Video teleconferencing is a . . . medium where, in a sense, you become the visual aid. And just as you are not born with the ability to communicate brilliantly, so you are not born knowing how best to utilize video communicating. You must learn to make the medium work for you rather than the other way around.[22]

The expert's liberal use of the "you" pronoun signals the importance of personal presence. Television often tests one's ability at verbal ping-pong and imagery rather than the mental rigor of deep thought. On the plus side, *who* channels clarify relational ambiguities. On the negative side, *who* channels might actually inhibit certain employees from voicing concerns or even sharing better ideas.

What to do? Both kinds of channels have strengths and weaknesses. Wise managers recognize this and choose the appropriate channels for the situation. They often use different combinations of channels to maximize their effectiveness. They consider what some scholars have called the implicit "social presence" of the media. They recognize that some media, such as the telephone (*who* channel), are high in social presence and increase the likelihood of forming personal relationships. Likewise they know that other media, such as a generic memo (*what* channel), are low in social presence and diminish the possibility of creating an interpersonal dialogue.[23] In other words, effective managers routinely think about the implications of the S-C test.

Conduct Channel-Specific Training

Effective communicators learn generic speaking, writing, and listening skills. Those who lack necessary skills, such as writing with clarity and brevity, plague many organizations. For example, Figures 5.4 and 5.5 show

---

TO: All employees of Pas de Deux, International
FROM: Human Resources

Representatives from Pirouette Financial Group will be available on Tuesday, April 24 to acquaint you with ways that can help you build a secure, comfortable retirement. They will be discussing investment alternatives and will be happy to sit down with you for a few minutes to answer any questions you may have about your retirement and financial planning program.

There is no cost for this service and no appointment is necessary. Feel free to stop in any time between 10:30 a.m. and 1:30 p.m. in the alcove area for this review.

Total Word Count = 102

Figure 5.4   Traditional, Bureaucratic Memo

TO: All employees
FROM: Human Resources

Find out how Pirouette Financial Group can help you build a secure, comfortable retirement.

    Date: **Tuesday, April 24**

    Place: **Alcove**

    Time: **10:30 a.m. to 1:30 p.m.**

Representatives will discuss your personal financial concerns about your retirement planning.

No appointment necessary.

Total Word Count = 46

Figure 5.5   Short, "High-Impact" Memo

two different versions of the same memo. Figure 5.5, however, was drafted with almost half the verbiage. One study revealed that the high-impact style (e.g., Figure 5.5) took about 20% less time to read, was more effectively understood, and did not need to be reread as often as the bureaucratic style.[24]

George F. Kennan, a recipient of the Presidential Medal of Freedom and former U.S. Ambassador to the Soviet Union, warned about the danger of a society dominated by television by noting that "a mental world dominated by fragmentary images . . . can hardly be a thoughtful one."[25] The eloquent author, Annie Dillard, elaborated on the special quality of the written word:

> When you write, you lay out a line of words. The line of words is a miner's pick, a woodcarver's gouge, a surgeon's probe. You wield it, and it digs a path you follow. Soon you find yourself deep in new territory. . . . The writing has changed, in your hands, and in a twinkling, from an expression of your notions to an epistemological tool.[26]

Writing facilitates clear thinking. Sometimes ideas that make perfect sense in conversation turn to mush when you try to write them down. Why? Writing forces us to think in a more linear style. For instance, one computer science professor requires that all his students submit their class questions to him on e-mail. He claims that 90% of the time, the very act of writing down the question solves the problem. The rigors of writing often demand a greater precision of thought than speech.

Yet, effective communicators go beyond the basic speaking and writing skills; they learn how to maximize the utility of each channel. Different channels require different skill sets. For instance, composing successful e-mails requires somewhat different talents than composing effective memos (see Table 5.2). An effective e-mail need not contain finely honed prose. While brevity and clarity are highly prized business writing skills, they are even more critical in e-mails, because people can read and scan a printed page more efficiently than a computer screen. Likewise, holding a successful meeting requires more than merely knowing how to carry on a good conversation. Effective meeting management occurs when facilitators know what to focus on, what to ignore, how to build consensus, how to encourage discussion and how to stick to an agenda.[27] Facilitators must also must guard against "groupthink," in which employees fear sharing opinions contrary to the group norms.[28] Using a videoconference adds another layer of complexity on top of these skills. For instance, facilitators need to make employees comfortable with the limitations of the technology and the inevitable glitches.[29]

To sum up, managers cannot assume employees will be equally skillful in using every channel. As a result, they need to ensure that employees have basic communication skills as well as channel-specific proficiencies.

Table 5.2   Tips on Writing Successful E-mails

Tip	Rationale
Determine if an e-mail is the appropriate choice for the message.	E-mail is a lean channel and should be used for unambiguous tasks and information sharing.
Use action verbs in the subject line when making requests (e.g., "Provide input on slides.").	Users are more likely to open e-mail requesting specific action.
Double-check the subject line to ensure that it attracts the reader's attention.	The subject line is the gateway to further communication. If readers are not motivated by the subject line, they are less likely to open the message.
Preview the number of points or steps in the text (e.g., "Use the following 6-step process to update your computer.").	People scan e-mails and may not scroll through the entire message without a preview statement.
Selectively use the "urgent" designation.	Highlighting every message as urgent destroys your credibility. Wolf! Wolf!
Use the spell and grammar checker.	E-mail writers do not need to compose literary masterpieces but they should conform to basic writing conventions.
Write in short paragraphs.	Most readers glance over e-mails, scanning for the key points.
Think about how others might react to your e-mail if it was printed on the front page of the local newspaper (e.g., avoid off-color jokes and sarcasm.).	E-mail may appear private and confidential but it is not. In legal cases, attorneys routinely request copies of all employee e-mails. Also, employees can easily forward offending documents to others.

* This chart is based on O'Kane, P., Hargie, O., & Tourish, D. 2004. Communication without frontiers: The impact of technology upon organizations. In *Key issues in organizational communication*, edited by D. Tourish, & O. Hargie (pp. 74–95). London: Routledge; Munter, M., Rogers, P. S., & Rymer, J. 2003. Business e-mail: Guidelines for users. *Business Communication Quarterly* 66 (1):26-40.

Use the Speed of New Technologies to Build Understanding of Critical Issues

Managers committed to effective communication often feel tugged in two different directions. Information technology yanks the manager toward increasing the speed of communication, but a desire to fully explain events pulls the manager toward a slower, more deliberate form of communication. The effective manager recognizes the peril of either extreme. Arthur Shulman, an international consultant and researcher, points out that:

With the new information technologies we are presumably able to speed up the transmission and increase the storage of ideas much more than we could if we were relying on simple human 'connections' and the fallible human mind. . . . there is little evidence that information technology can act as a substitute for human communication, let alone do it better . . . the major consequence of the introduction of new information technologies within organizations has not been better communication, only faster misunderstandings.[30]

Although increasing the speed of information sharing may inhibit understanding if used as a "data dump," the other extreme may prove equally problematic. Many formal communication systems make extensive use of channels designed more for thoroughness than for speed. Some companies, for example, make extensive use of quarterly employee meetings designed to provide thorough briefings on the "big picture" items. Unfortunately, in our era, the "big picture" often changes more quickly than every quarter. Other organizations rely on regular newsletters to keep employees informed. But, again, the news may change more quickly than the beleaguered editorial staff can handle. In short, the responsiveness of the communication system often does not match the pace of organizational events.

Given the problems at either extreme, what should a manager do? Some executives reason, "Why not wait until all our 'ducks are in a row' before informing employees?" However, because executives cannot control the flow of information due to active grapevines, the corporate Intranet and Internet, the *ducks* start quacking long before executives can line them up. An employee may hear something from a vendor or a competitor and pass it along. As a result, employees' misconceptions, apprehensions, and resistance points often surface prior to any formal announcement. Consequently, building support and consensus proves more difficult. Increasing the speed of information sharing helps mitigate these problems. Consequently, the bias must be toward using *speed* to shape employee understanding of key issues.

On the downside, speeding up information sharing sacrifices the completeness of the story. Thus, executives will have to acknowledge gaps in understanding and future uncertainties. They often resist sharing partial information because it undermines their credibility. Yet, we do not expect the meteorologist to predict what will happen next month except in the most general of terms. We do, however, watch the daily forecast. It provides timely, but necessarily partial, information. Meteorologists allow the big picture to emerge over time by constantly focusing on well-understood metrics such as temperature and humidity. Their credibility emerges from their speed more than from long-range accuracy. The environment imposes this constraint on both meteorologists and organizational communicators.

The CEO of Novell, Eric Schmidt, put it this way: "The fastest learner always wins."[31] By routinely reporting on a limited number of key indicators, leaders can create a deep understanding of the performance drivers. They create a "no data dump zone" by providing an opportunity for everyone to analyze a few critical results and address the concerns. Some companies, such as the Progressive Corporation, have taken the idea to a new level by providing their investors with a monthly—as opposed to quarterly—report on key problems and metrics used in managing the company. Instead of increasing stock volatility (as many expected), it has dampened it. Instead of decreasing company credibility, the frequent and revealing report actually enhances it.[32] In days past, a more deliberate communication system may have met the C-R test. But no longer.

Recognize How Technologies Send Symbolic Messages and Impact Power Relationships

Several years ago a tale circulated about a "techie" who broke up with his girlfriend. He decided to e-mail her the news because he thought faxing was too impersonal. Ugh. Well, at least he had the right sentiments. The moral of the story: Our choice of channels also sends a message, by shaping the tone and character of our message. For example, memos and letters imbue a sense of formality and credibility, allowing recipients a document as a reference point. In general, written communication signifies authority, legitimacy, and responsibility. After all, judges issue a *written* not *oral* court decision. Face-to-face conversations often lack these qualities. Several researchers found that managers use face-to-face communication "to signal a desire for teamwork; build trust and goodwill; or to convey informality."[33]

These symbolic messages link to the underlying constraints of the particular medium. E-mail, for example, crudely communicates emotional messages. Consider the thoughts of two scholars:

> Attempts to introduce typographic cues become thin substitutes for nonverbal cues: There is no way to distinguish mild amusement from hilarity with a "smiley," :-). There are few reminders in e-mail of others or of the social context. When cues and controls are weak, people may pay less attention to the presence and opinions of others.[34]

Paying "attention to the presence" of others is often the point of communication; a point that our techie friend failed to understand. Miss Manners, no doubt, intuitively knew what the scholars discovered when she wrote this useful rule of thumb:

The more emotional the content, the more cumbersome should be the means of conveying it. Highly emotional communications are best made in person, where the effect can be assessed and the message tempered to the reaction.[35]

In short, the symbolic overtones of the communication technology influence social relationships.

Even the frequency of channel use sends powerful symbolic messages that greatly influence how messages are interpreted. Some organizations rarely use certain channels, such as all-division meetings. When the company does use this channel it signals that something "big" is going to happen. Bill Journey of PepsiCo Business Solutions aptly describes the consequences of such symbolic messages:

> "Employees know that the organization only gathers for 'weddings and 'funerals.' So once 'the big meeting' is announced, everyone starts speculating about who 'died.' In other words, the rumor mill starts cranking out stories about which division will be downsized."

In essence, the symbolic significance of the meeting may unintentionally override the actual messages shared in the meeting.

In a similar way technology choices may unintentionally alter power relationships. The former chairman of Citicorp, Walter Wriston once commented: ". . . The most basic fact about the world we live and work in is this: Information is a virus that carries freedom."[36] He might have added that communication technologies provide the delivery system. The CEO of Hewlett Packard, Carly Fiorina, argues that because of the Internet, information no longer constitutes power because everyone has it.[37] This fundamentally changes the job of leadership. Leaders can no longer control the flow of information through their organizations, so they must learn to shape the employees' interpretations of news, rumors, and opinions.

Executives and managers often find this state of affairs frightening. Why? First, their traditional levers of power no longer exist. Second, they don't know how to exert influence under the new rules of the game. In one organization, the computer conferencing system led to such internal revolts and lack of concern with traditional power/status issues that top management felt threatened and dismantled the entire system.[38] That's an extreme example, but instructive. Employees' (receivers') capabilities have changed. Consequently, executives (senders) must alter their messages in order to wield influence. When communication technologies began to emerge, some commentators forcefully argued that the technology would "democratize the workplace."[39] Maybe they took the argument too far. Power and status differences still prevail but they can be tempered by information technologies. As two scholars observed:

> In FTF (face-to-face) groups, higher-status people talk more than lower-status people, men talk more than women, and managers talk more

than subordinates. Those who participate have more opportunities to influence decisions. Because e-mail reduces status cues, status-induced imbalances also are weaker. E-mail can encourage more open and equal discussion, leading to decisions based on knowledge rather than on the influence of high-status members.[40]

No wonder many executives feel threatened by new technology.

Find the Right Niche for the Various Technologies

E-mail has become the communication channel of choice for many employees. In fact, one survey found that almost 75% of the employees would have greater difficulty living without e-mail for five days than they would without a phone.[41] Why? E-mail fills a niche because of its unique characteristics. It allows senders to reach many others simultaneously, creates a paper trail, increases speed of responses, and allows asynchronous communication.[42] It creates a human connection but only a minimal non-timing-consuming relationship.[43] Other channels, such as a phone call, take us beyond a mere connection. In other words, e-mail fulfills a particular role. As channels compete for employees' attention, they take on specific functions. Generally, old channels don't die; they find a new niche. AM radio did not die when FM came along, although many predicted it would. Talk radio thrives on AM stations.

In a similar way, different technologies in organizations evolve and secure a particular niche in the communication system. For instance, commentators have long complained about the quality of employee newsletters.[44] The dreaded "three B's"—birthdays, baby pictures, and bowling scores—dominate most newsletters. At one time, I thought this was an inappropriate use of this often costly communication tool.[45] Now, I believe that newsletters with this orientation may satisfy a particular employee need. After all, Abraham Maslow taught us about the fundamental need for recognition and esteem. The newsletter may provide a tangible and permanent communication designed to meet this need. This may not be the *best* channel, but it may be an *adequate* one, given other competing demands on the communication system.

Channels fill niches as they dynamically interact in the communicative marketplace of organizations. In the communication system of a paper mill, top management primarily used a bimonthly newsletter and quarterly meeting to keep employees informed. But, because of the rate of organizational change, employees often complained about not getting accurate and timely information. The newsletter and quarterly meeting did not, and indeed *could* not, meet the need. So they created a new communication channel, a biweekly supervisor meeting centered around sharing critical, timely company news. In the meeting, they presented and discussed "talking points," which explained several critical issues in detail. The supervisors, in turn, communicated this information to their employees in crew meetings. The new channel satisfied the particular communicative need. The lesson: Managers need to think about the right niche for each communication channel. Often existing channels fail to fully meet the needs of communicators. New channels may need to be created, and old ones may need to be renovated.

Detect and Respond to Patterns That Develop With Technology Usage

Who would embrace a new technology that promises to bring strange viruses into your home, annoy you with unsolicited advertisements, and expose your confidential information to potential criminals? Nevertheless, millions of Internet users take these risks every day. As we use technologies, unexpected problems, conventions, and norms emerge. For instance, many mobile phone users were originally sold on the idea because it provided them greater safety and security. Few people immediately went home and disconnected their landline phones. Yet, as their comfort grew, they realized that the technology could be used in unintended ways. So we see this step-by-step progression from "use only in emergencies" to "use to be more efficient as a business traveler" to "use all the time, any place, regardless of whether you have something important to say."

Insightful managers recognize both the positive and negative trends associated with new technologies and strategically respond to those insights. Spam (unsolicited and annoying e-mails), for instance, has emerged as a nasty nuisance in many organizations. Some experts estimate that spam constitutes close to 50% of all Internet traffic and wastes precious minutes of most employees' days.[46] Some legal experts believe that companies that fail to block pornographic spam could be in legal jeopardy because these offensive messages may spawn a hostile workplace.[47] Even though most companies report blocking an average of 54% of spam, other negative trends, such as security issues, continue to plague the Internet.[48] In addition, many employees and companies have been burned by the paper trail left by their e-mails. They often wrongly assume that deleting a message equates with destroying it.[49] Every technology/channel has a downside (even though vendors avoid talking about it), but the effective manager acknowledges these concerns and seeks to proactively respond.

On the flip-side, managers can exploit the more positive and unexpected trends that also emerge with new technology. For instance, the Internet was not originally conceived of as a commercial tool. But e-commerce thrives because consumers have grown more accustomed to using the Internet. They have learned to trust the technology and their own abilities to use it. The Internet takes the concept of self-service to a new level by empowering consumers while driving down transaction costs. One company estimated that taking a product order over the telephone costs about $20 to $30, but only $1 on the World Wide Web.[50] Wow! No wonder organizations readily embrace the Web. Indeed, many organizations with an eye toward reducing paper and administrative costs have turned to Web-based forms to help administer health care and benefit programs. For example, the Hewlett-Packard employee portal (a Web site only available to employees) has over fifteen hundred services available online and processes close to three hundred million transactions per month. This proves terrifically convenient for employees on the road or those who cannot wait for an HR rep to return a phone call.[51] In addition, many companies successfully use the Internet as an integral part of their crisis-management process.[52]

These technology success stories sound great, but think about the dynamics behind the scene. What factors fueled the success? Perceptive managers must ask this tough question before making investments in technology. They should consider the following subsidiary questions:

- *First, what unique costs and benefits does the technology offer?* In addition to the typical considerations of the amount of the investment and the resulting productivity improvements, there are more subtle impacts. For example, status often plays a role, which was quite evident when I worked with one Fortune 100 company caught up in Blackberry frenzy. These portable devices allow users to send and receive text messages from virtually anywhere. Every manager had to have one, and I soon realized why: All the senior leaders had one; it was really a status symbol signaling a manager's importance.
- *Second, what role does personal choice play in the technology?* Some channels tend to be used to *push* communication, whereas others allow users to *pull* the communication. *Push-oriented* channels like spam, pop-up ads, and required meetings, diminish the receiver's choice. They tend to have lower credibility and effectiveness compared to *pull-oriented* channels (such as a Web site or newsletter) that receivers choose to use.[53] So managers would do well to recognize that a choice usually trumps a decree.
- *Third, are the necessary precursors in place for the technology?* It takes time to build confidence in technology, adapt to the new possibilities, and exploit the advantages. Certain technologies and the related competencies need to be in place before taking the next step.[54] Consumers, for example, did not recognize the need for high-speed Internet service until they experienced the limitations of dial-up service and projected the possibilities of enhanced service. Without these experiences there will not be a *critical mass* of users to ignite further interest and sustain the technology.[55] Wise managers provide these critical learning experiences and build on them.

Pattern detection may be one of the most difficult skills managers must learn, but those who master it also learn how to skillfully use existing channels and new technologies.

Conclusion

Senders and receivers often evaluate the effectiveness of a channel choice in different ways. What channel should managers use to discuss an employee's performance problem? That depends on whose perspective you adopt and how you evaluate effectiveness. Usually employees (receivers) prefer face-to-face meetings, allowing them to ask timely questions, discuss details, and more accurately judge the severity of the issue. They want a dynamic and rich channel. Managers may not prefer face-to-face meetings, for the very same reasons. They don't want to answer questions, provide further details, or create a potentially emotional scene.

In fact, I have interviewed several managers about this issue. One manager, known by his employees as "Stealth," never left his office all day. He bombarded his employees with e-mails. I asked him, face-to-face, about his peculiar interface with his employees. He responded, candidly but anxiously: "They get too emotional and I can't handle it. I get my point across another way." His employees got *a* point as well—that "he doesn't care about us." They rarely got the point he intended. Stealth would have never communicated his concerns without e-mail. In fact, these less dynamic channels may be the *only* way some managers feel comfortable confronting conflict. Understandable? Perhaps. Justifiable? Probably not. As Swiss playwright Max Frisch sadly observed, some people have "the knack of so arranging the world that (they) need not experience it."[56]

What to do? There may be no perfect answer. Stealth will never be an effective manager (although he thinks he is) but at least his channel choice allows issues to surface that he would normally avoid. In a sense this conundrum brings us right back to the five congruency tests. Ideally, managers would use the guidelines outlined in Table 5.3. But, it may not always be possible to line up the channel with the needs of senders and receivers. As a sender, we should recognize when our personal needs may compromise the efficacy of our communication. And as receivers, we should be aware of how our colleagues' limitations alter their communications. A communicator, like a composer, seeks to choose the proper instrument to convey a particular theme or mood. To wisely select the proper instrument requires a complete knowledge of the possibilities and the complexities of the entire process. Then the message becomes something more than mere notes on a piece of Ts' ai Lun's paper.

Table 5.3   Effective Use of Channels/Technologies

Channel	Most effective use	Examples
Telephone	• Sending short, simple messages • Sending confidential messages • Providing feedback • Providing quick "turn-around" time	• Negotiating a meeting time and place • Discussing a work problem
Fax	• Sending informal messages • Seeing visual display of information • Providing "hard" copy	• Viewing a copy of brochure • Providing directions to a meeting
E-mail	• Sending impersonal, brief messages • Keeping employees updated on routine matters • Efficiently gathering routine information	• Conducting an in-house survey • Confirming a meeting time
Voice mail	• Sending short, simple messages • Sharing routine information • Informing others when feedback isn't needed	• Responding to an information request
One-on-one (face-to-face)	• Sharing potentially emotional, complex information • Communicating confidential material • Persuading and negotiating • Providing feedback • Communicating personal warmth • Reading nonverbals • Sharing knowledge	• Holding a performance appraisal • Promoting/firing an employee
Memo	• Sending short, simple message • Distributing to numerous receivers • Informing others when feedback isn't needed • Providing scannable information	• Communicating a routine update • Confirming a policy change
Letter	• Sending a message needing a personal touch • Conveying formality • Providing detailed information • Providing a written record	• Expressing thanks, condolences • Writing a complaint letter
Web page	• Communicating non-controversial, non-confidential, general information • Efficiently sharing routine information with large audiences	• Summarizing company's expertise, career opportunities • Responding to "frequently asked questions"
Video conference	• Connecting emotionally with large audiences • Sending non-complex, unambiguous messages	• Updating company performance • Outlining a major organizational initiative

Notes

1. Hart, M. H. 1978. *The 100: A ranking of the most influential persons in history*. New York: A & W Visual Library.

2. Conrad, C., & Poole, M. S. 1998. *Strategic organizational communication: Into the twenty-first century*. Fort Worth, TX: Harcourt Brace.

3. Rice, R. E., & Gattiker, U. E. 2001. New media and organizational structuring. In *The new handbook of organizational communication*, edited by F. M. Jablin & L. L. Putman, (pp. 544–581), p. 565. Thousand Oaks, CA: Sage.

4. Shulman, A. D. 2001. Putting group information technology in its place: Communication and good work group performance. In *Handbook of organizational studies*, edited by S. R. Clegg, C. Hardy, & W. R. Nord (pp. 357–374), p. 362. London: Sage.

5. Lengel, R. H., & Daft, R. L. 1988. The selection of communication media as an executive skill. *Academy of Management Executive* 2 (3):225–232.

6. Tufte, E. R. 2003. *The cognitive style of PowerPoint*, p. 3. Cheshire, CT: Graphics Press.

7. Ibid, p. 23.

8. For a further discussion on the limited power of PowerPoint, see Clampitt, P., & DeKoch, R. J. 2001. *Embracing uncertainty: The essence of leadership*. Armonk, NY: M.E. Sharpe.

9. Robichaux, M. 1989. Teens in business discover credibility is hard to earn. *Wall Street Journal*, 9 June, B1–B2.

10. Mikulecky, L. 1990. Basic skill impediments to communication between management and hourly employees. *Management Communication Quarterly* 3 (4):452–473.

11. Pierce, J. R., & Noll, M. 1990. *Signals: The science of telecommunications*. New York: Scientific American Library.

12. Nasaw, D. 2003. Wi-fi is becoming popular at the office. *Wall Street Journal*, 23 October:B4.

13. Levitt, J. 2003. Mobile desktops on the go. *Informationweek*. 29 September: 43–46. See also, Fitzgerald, M. 2003. Hand-held: The new mobility. *Informationweek*, 6 October:88–92.

14. Green, H. 2003. Wi-fi means business. *Business Week*, 28 April:86–92.

15. Ibid, p. 87.

16. Trevino, L. K., Daft, R. L., & Lengel, R. H. 1990. Understanding manager's media choices: A symbolic interactionist perspective. In *Organizations and communication technology*, edited by J. Fulk & C. Steinfield (pp. 71–94). Beverly Hills, CA: Sage, p. 88.

17. Williams, F. 1987. *Technology and communication behavior*. Belmont, CA: Wadsworth.

18. Note: Researchers have determined that dyadic exchanges constitute close to 50% of the conversation in six-person, face-to-face decision-making groups and many occur simultaneously. Many of these side conversations simply do not occur in a teleconference or videoconference. See Stasser, G., & Taylor, L. A. 1991. Speaking

turns in face-to-face discussions. *Journal of Personality and Social Psychology* 60:675–684.

19. Sproull, L., & Kiesler, S. 1986. Reducing social context cues: The case of electronic mail. *Management Science* 32:1492–1512.

20. Cornelius, C., & Boos, M. 2003. Enhancing mutual understanding in synchronous computer-mediated communication by training. *Communication Research* 30 (2):147–176.

21. Craig, S., & Fontenot, J. C. 1999. Multiple identifications during team meetings: A comparison of conventional and computer-supported interactions. *Communication Reports* 12 (2):91–97, p. 96.

22. Frank, M. O. 1989. *How to run a successful meeting in half the time.* New York: Simon & Schuster, p. 142.

23. Short, J., Williams, E., & Christie, B. 1976. *The social psychology of telecommunications.* London: John Wiley; O'Kane, P., Hargie, O., & Tourish, D. 2004. Communication without frontiers: The impact of technology upon organizations. In *Key issues in organizational communication*, edited by D. Tourish & O. Hargie (pp. 74–95). London: Routledge.

24. Surprisingly, the study also found that "bureaucratic" writing was seen as more "dynamic and forceful." A "bureaucratic" style included abstract language, passive verbs, no personal pronouns, and the purpose statement in the last paragraph. One explanation offered was that the bureaucratic style fits more closely with the organization's culture by allowing the writer coverage of his "vital assets." Perhaps, this is to be expected from a study conducted with U.S. Naval officers. Sometimes the culture demands a cluttered writing style. Suchan, J., & Colucci, R. 1989. Analysis of communication efficiency between high-impact and bureaucratic written communication. *Management Communication Quarterly* 2 (4):454–484.

25. Kennan, G. 1993. *Around the cragged hill.* New York: Norton, p. 177.

26. Dilliard, A. 1989. *The writing life.* New York: Harper & Row, p. 3.

27. For an excellent and short primer on how to hold effective meetings see, Tropman, J. 1996. *Effective meetings: Improving group decision making.* Thousand Oaks, CA: Sage.

28. Janis, I. 1982. *Groupthink: Psychological studies of policy decisions.* Boston: Houghton Mifflin.

29. Allen, M. 2003. Videoconferencing for practice-based small-group continuing medical education: Feasibility, acceptability effectiveness, and cost. Journal *of Continuing Education in the Health Professions* 23 (1):38–47.

30. Shulman, op. cit., p. 367.

31. Schmidt, E. 2000. Speech to the National Governor's Association, February 27.

32. Lublin, J. S. 2003. The naked truth: To counter investor skepticism, some CEOs are making public what was once considered private. *Wall Street Journal* 27 October:R12.

33. Trevino, Daft, & Lengel, op. cit., p. 86.

34. Garton, L., & Wellman, B. S. 1995. Social impacts of electronic mail in organizations: A review of the research literature. In *Communication yearbook 18*, edited by B. Burleson (pp. 434–453). Thousand Oaks, CA: Sage, p. 442.

35. Martin, J. 1997. *Miss Manners' basic training: Communication*. New York: Crown Publishers, Inc., p. 22.

36. Wriston, W. B. 1990. The state of American management. *Harvard Business Review* 68 (1):78–83, p. 83.

37. Fiorina, C. 2000. Speech to the National Governor's Association, February 27.

38. Zuboff, S. 1984. *In the age of the smart machine*. New York: Basic Books.

39. Brown, J., & Duguid, P. 2000. *The social life of information*. Boston: Harvard Business School Press.

40. Garton & Wellman, op. cit., p. 440–441.

41. Nowak, R. 2003. Behind the numbers: E-mail beats the phone in business communication. *Informationweek,* 19 May:66.

42. Ibid. See also, Munter, M., Rogers, P. S., & Rymer, J. 2003. Business e-mail: Guidelines for users. *Business Communication Quarterly* 66 (1):26–40.

43. Gopnik, A. 1999. The return of the word. *New Yorker,* 6 December: 49–50, p. 49.

44. D'Aprix, R. 1982. *Communicating for productivity*. New York: Harper & Row.

45. Clampitt, P. G., Crevcoure, J. M., & Hartel, R. L. 1986. Exploratory research on employee publications. *Journal of Business Communication* 23 (3):5–17.

46. Woellert, L. 2003. Out, out, damned spam. *Business Week,* 11 August: 54–56, p. 54.

47. 2003. Blocking porn at work. *Chicago Tribune,* 26 October:Section 5, p. 5.

48. Smith, L. 2003. Behind the numbers: Fighting spam cuts deeper into spending. *Informationweek,* 29 September:60.

49. O'Kane, Hargie, & Tourish, op.cit.

50. Peppers & Rogers Group. 2002. *An e-commerce blueprint: How to maximize ROI from your web strategy,* p. 11.

51. Tam, P. W. 2003. Communicate with employees. *Wall Street Journal,* 15 September:R4, R10, p. R10.

52. Perry, D. C., Taylor, M. & Doerfel, M. L. 2003. Internet-based communication in crisis management. *Management Communication Quarterly* 17 (2): 206–232.

53. Lawrence, S. 2003. The medium shapes the message. *Business 2.0,* July:32.

54. Farrell, D. 2003. The real new economy. *Harvard Business Review* 81(10): 104–112.

55. Rice & Gattiker, op. cit.

56. Frisch as quoted in O'Kane, Hargie, & Tourish, op. cit., p. 89.

6

Managing Data, Information, Knowledge, and Action

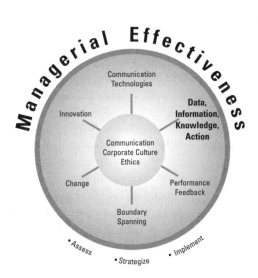

Information is not a neutral product of organizational activity, but is a result of an inherently political activity—a political activity often hidden from those engaging in it largely due to presumed neutrality.

Stanley Deetz and Dennis Mumby

Business isn't complicated. The complications arise when people are cut off from information they need.

Jack Welch

If information had nutritional labels, it would be intriguing to study a manager's dietary habits. The typical manager encounters a virtual smorgasbord of information. In fact, one commentator noted that, "A weekday edition of the *New York Times* contains more information than the average person was likely to come across in a lifetime in seventeenth-century England."[1] How do managers cope with this bountiful harvest? Some gorge themselves and face the inevitable consequences. Many subsist on informational McNuggets that are easily consumed but of little nutritional value. There are far too many managers who have grown fat on information but are starved for knowledge.

This chapter discusses how to effectively manage data, information, and knowledge in order to produce appropriate actions. Properly nourished organizations learn to shun bad habits and establish healthy ones. In the same way as wise nutritional habits cultivate healthy bodies, wise data-, information-, and knowledge-management practices cultivate healthy organizations.

The D-I-K-A Model

Chapter 6: By the Numbers

70%
of workplace learning is informal

100
The number of voice and e-mail messages the average manager receives each day

80%
of Cisco System's customer service issues are handled through its Web site

50%
of our brains are devoted to processing visual information

50%
of decisions made in organizations are not fully implemented or sustained

Intuitively, the relationship between data, information, knowledge, and action seems fairly clear. The detective solving a murder mystery provides a familiar template. The detective starts by examining the crime scene, interviewing potential witnesses, and researching various documents. These facts become the detective's database. Most of the data, such as the color of the victim's watch, prove irrelevant. But a few facts emerge that inform the detective of something useful, such as the time of death. The detective starts thinking, ruminating, and then pulls together all these tidbits to form a theory of the crime. Once confirmed, we know "whodunit." The final action sequence ends with a theatrical arrest.

This time-honored plot provides several useful insights:

• Note the skills needed by the detective: gathering data, assessing data relevance, transforming data into information, managing information, transforming information into knowledge, creating knowledge out of limited facts, managing knowledge, and transforming knowledge into action. Effective managers need all these skills.

• Note that the detective uses a winnowing process, starting with a lot of data and ending with a single action. Likewise, effective managers must use a similar process in deciding how to wisely respond to organizational events.

- Note the implicit definitions of the key concepts. Effective managers instinctively know the differences between data, information, and knowledge. More important, they know the limitations of data, information, and knowledge. The following section explores these ideas in more depth.

Figure 6.1 provides a model of the veteran detective or manager's view of the situation. Scholars debate the definitions of these terms, but for our purposes, the concepts can be described as follows:

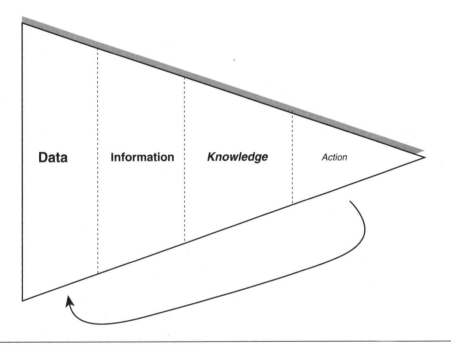

Figure 6.1   The D-I-K-A Model

Data = Representations of Reality

The detective who observes that the victim wore a Rolex watch chooses to depict or represent the situation in a particular way. This representation, like all others, may be flawed; the watch could be a fake. For a manager, data might be the results of a particular customer survey, which are also imperfect.

Information = Data That Provide Relevant Clues or News

The detective needs to know the time of death because that provides relevant clues about who could have possibly committed the murder. The manager scanning the customer survey usually ignores most of the data, focusing instead on key pieces of news. Perhaps the manager is monitoring a particular issue about customer service. The manager, like the detective, focuses on data relevant to the problem at hand. But distinguishing the *relevant* from the *irrelevant* often presents some unique challenges. What may appear relevant at one time *may* or *may not* be relevant at another time. The color of the victim's watch might, at some point, provide the crucial piece of evidence to solve the mystery. Likewise, the manager may look back on the survey results and spot an important trend.

Knowledge = The Framework or Schema for Organizing the Relationships Between Pieces of Information

Two well-respected scholars define knowledge in the following way:

Knowledge is a fluid mix of framed experience, values, contextual information, and expert insight that provides a framework for evaluating and incorporating new experiences and information. It originates and is applied in the minds of knowers. In organizations, it often becomes embedded not only in documents or repositories but also in organizational routines, processes, practices, and norms.[2]

Note how they define knowledge in a personal and subjective way. There is something elusive, subtle, and perhaps mysterious about knowledge. The key may be that the person or organization recognizes patterns that are often difficult to capture in words. The detective, for instance, takes all the relevant facts and pieces together a theory of what happened the night of the murder (they always happen at night). Likewise, a manager might connect the survey results to a particular management decision made months ago.

But how does the detective or manager learn to make the right connections? There are two possible answers. First, they may have *tacit knowledge,* which one scholar defines as "a set of particulars of which we are subsidiarily aware as we focus on something else."[3] In other words, tacit knowledge often lies beyond our immediate awareness, implicitly guiding our decisions. Passing along tacit knowledge often proves quite difficult. Second, they may have *explicit knowledge,* which can be readily discussed and passed on to other detectives and managers. Tacit and explicit knowledge are really the flip side of the same coin; good detectives and managers have a ready supply of both.

Action = The Deeds or Decisions Made Based on Knowledge

Easy enough—for the detective. Once she figures out who committed the murder, she arrests the culprit. Not so easy for the manager. Figuring out what went wrong may be only half the battle. Correcting the problem in the proper way through a new policy, procedure, or perhaps a personnel change, requires special insight.

These definitions are, necessarily, a bit fuzzy. That should not be a surprise. After all, philosophers have debated about the true nature of knowledge for eons.[4] Nevertheless, these distinctions can provide insight into the pragmatic problems facing managers. Table 6.1 summarizes the model, addressing the special combination of people, research, and intellectual skills managers need to acquire, along with requirements for producing, transmitting, and storing data, information, knowledge, and action.

Table 6.1   Summary of the D-I-K-A Model

	Data	*Information*	*Knowledge*	*Action*
What is an example?	• Victim's time of death • Stock price	• Timeline of victim's activities • Stock performance update	• Theory of the crime • Advice from stockbrokers (Hopefully they have a good theory!)	• Arrest of the criminal • Stock purchase
What form does it is typically take?	• Numbers • Impressions	• Facts • Tables • Charts	• Stories • Rules of thumb • Theories • Models	• Action plans • Procedures • Recipes
What are the criteria to measure effectiveness?	• Timely • Accurate	• Relevant • Timely • Accessible	• Applicable • Synthesized • Explanatory • Predictive	• Implemented
What skills do you need?	• Generate • Gather • Research • Store	• Filter • Organize • Analyze • Distribute • Interpret	• Think critically • Communicate • Analyze • Synthesize • Conceptualize	• Plan • Motivate • Lead • Communicate
What is required to produce it?	• Some • expertise	• Some expertise	• Much experience and expertise	• Some experience and expertise
How difficult is it to transmit?	• Easy	• Moderately easy	• Difficult	• Moderately difficult
What is the best way to store it?	• Computers • Web pages	• Computers • Databases • Books, journals, etc.	• Experts	• Historical record • Employee memory
What are typical organizational problems?	• Poor research skills • Information overload	*Lack of:* • Timeliness • Access • Distribution networks • Organization	• Few venues for sharing • Inadequate storage	• Resistance to change • Uneven follow-through • Ineffective communication

The D-I-K-A model assumes fluid feedback between the various phases. For instance, the detective may arrest a person, only to discover that after this action, a similar crime is committed. This situation creates new data and information that needs to be assimilated into the detective's mental model. Likewise, a manager might try to control customer complaints by a policy change, only to create even more customer dissatisfaction. In essence, the action sets in motion a whole new D-I-K-A cycle.

Variations of the Model

I would love to say that the D-I-K-A model actually describes what happens in most organizations. Unfortunately, it does not. Organizations do not typically process data and information as does the detective or scientist. Why? There are number of reasons, including office politics, time pressures, and cultural norms.

Constructing a map or drawing a schematic of how the organization *actually* manages the D-I-K-A relationships can prove revealing. Maps help managers identify gaps, shortfalls, and obstacles. For example, after discussing the D-I-K-A model with one executive, he realized his organization created a lot of data and information but did very little with it. His schematic was a big "D" and "I" followed by a little "k" and "a" (see Figure 6.2a). Another executive found a key insight by looking at the distance between D-I-K-A in his organization (see Figure 6.2b). He realized the problem was not one of

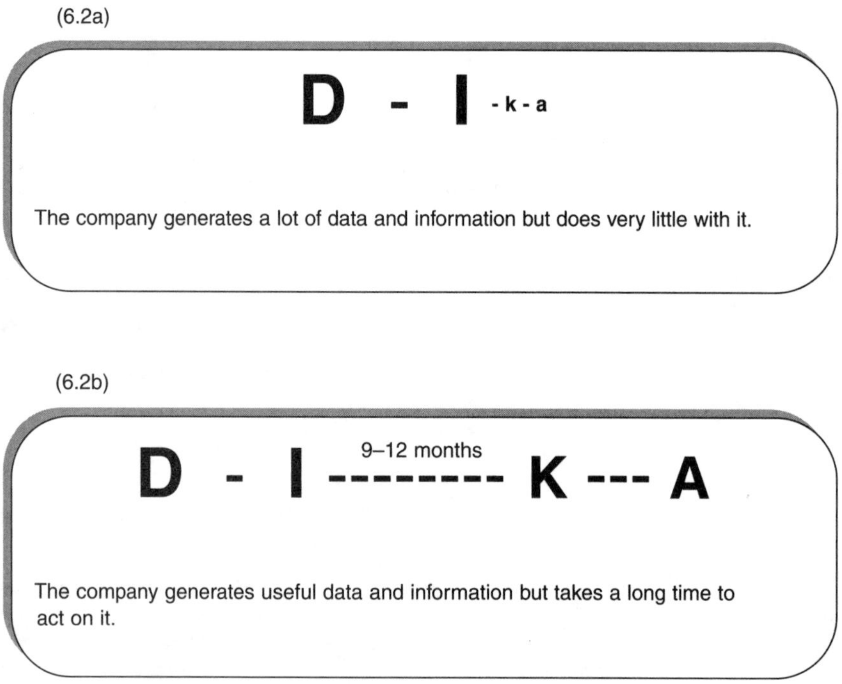

(6.2a)

D - I - k - a

The company generates a lot of data and information but does very little with it.

(6.2b)

D - I -------- 9–12 months **K** --- **A**

The company generates useful data and information but takes a long time to act on it.

Figure 6.2   Two Perspectives on D-I-K-A

generation, but of *speed;* how quickly data and information were transformed into knowledge and action. By the time the solution was agreed on and implemented, the problems had changed. One thoughtful scholar explains the challenge this way: "The manager really needs a research process that yields results faster than the time taken for the problem to change."[5]

In these cases, examining the size of the letters in the map or the distances between them allows us to understand underlying systemic problems in the organization. In fact, discerning analysts often think of data, information, knowledge, and action as blocks that can be arranged in any order. They may find evidence that the system can best be described by discarding one or two of the blocks. This creates some rather interesting relationships or dysfunctional loops. A few of the more typical ones are discussed next.

The D-I-K Loop

Academic institutions and government entities demonstrate a peculiar fondness for this pattern. Consider this typical example. The chancellor of a university commissions a study on faculty productivity. A committee dutifully develops a survey and generates data, which yield some interesting information. The committee reports that some departments produce a lot more research than do others. The interpretation of the information becomes pivotal. How does this finding fit into the existing conceptual frameworks and prejudices? Well, it probably will not. In fact, the low producers will not like the results, so they will want a new study conducted. The process starts over again, looping back to the data-gathering stage. Notice that action, per se, never occurs—only the appearance of it. To summarize: earnest activity but no action. And that's why some organizations appear to be very busy but not especially productive.

The K-A Loop

Will Rogers once said, "It ain't the things that people don't know that's the problem. It's the things they do know that just ain't so." He perfectly described the mindset of those stuck in the K-A loop. They are not open to new data, information, or interpretations. Consider, for instance, the stereotypical iconoclastic inventor who refuses to give up on an idea, even in the face of contradictory evidence. He is so committed to his model (knowledge) that he insists if he tinkers a little longer (action), it will work. On occasion his determination leads to some stunning achievement. More often, it doesn't. All the tinkering in the world cannot transform a fundamentally unsound idea into a smart one. To paraphrase George Bernard Shaw, "Knowledge becomes dangerous only when it imagines that it has reached its goal." Zealots caught in the K-A loop believe they possess "the truth" and nothing can dissuade them. They fail to recognize the fluid nature of knowledge and that abandoning previous conceptions in the face of contradictory evidence often proves illuminating. Or as two scholars put it, "Managing knowledge must also include attempts to manage forgetting."[6]

The I-A Loop

Managers caught up in the "program of the month" cycle unwittingly create an I-A loop. Here's how it works.

Step 1: They read about the latest management fad.

Step 2: They seize on a compelling fact about how the fad improves productivity, morale, commitment, and so forth.

Step 3: They implement the program.

Step 4: The results are less than spectacular.

Step 5: They return to step one.

The result: a workplace that spawns an endless supply of storylines for the Dilbert cartoon strip. Employees in these organizations become frustrated and cynically respond to the latest initiative. No one clearly thinks about how the new program fits with existing strategy and organizational culture. Information (the fad) leads to action, not knowledge of *how* the fad fits in with the big picture. Consequently, the managers look exactly like the dolts parodied in the Dilbert strip; they do inane things because they don't think about the meaning of the information.

Clearly, we could discuss more patterns that might emerge. But I'll leave those exciting discoveries to the inquisitive reader. The main lesson is that perceptive managers learn to first recognize the emergent organizational pattern and then determine the strengths and weaknesses of the pattern. Finally the manager needs to decide whether the pattern produces the desired outcomes. Some patterns clearly breed frustration, such as the I-A loop. Other patterns create seemingly odd manifestations elsewhere in the organization. Ideally, wise managers use the D-I-K-A loop or some related variant. Therefore, the remaining sections of the chapter discuss how to strategically manage the key relationships implied in the model.

Managing the Data-Information Relationship _____

Effectively managing this relationship requires generating timely and accurate data that can be transformed into relevant information. A wristwatch meets all three criteria.

Timely: When you want the information, you simply turn your wrist.

Accurate: Most watches provide enough precision to be useful.

Relevant: Knowing the time allows you to plan, organize, and accomplish tasks.

Wristwatches do not overwhelm us with irrelevant data; most are not synchronized with the atomic clock. They are inexpensive, easy to maintain, and styled according to our needs. In short, the wristwatch provides the ideal template for the characteristics of an effective data/information management system. Sounds great. But how do managers put together such a system? After all, before the wristwatch, were the sundial, town crier, and the clock tower. The lesson: Effective data/information systems evolve over time. The following strategies may not make managers digital watchmakers, but they may, at least, allow them to move the evolutionary clock forward.

Recognize the Inherent Flaws of All Data and Information

Thoughtful scientists, like Abraham Kaplan, appreciate the inherent limits of data. He observed that, "The fact is that no human perception is immaculate, certainly no perception of any significance for science. Even if perception itself were immaculate, the perceptual report exposes us to sin, as a necessary consequence of the way in which language works."[7] Managers who believe in "immaculate perception" create a false sense of security and certainty that precludes looking at a situation from various perspectives. A mousetrap works because the mouse believes that cheese is cheese. Of course, data, like cheese, is not just data. Companies gather data for certain reasons, from different perspectives, and report it in particular contexts. Consequently, this alters the nature of the data and the meaning we attach to it. For example, employees routinely express agreement with their supervisor in a meeting, only to share a different opinion around the water cooler. Supervisors who only rely on data generated in the meeting will unwittingly deceive themselves. Failing to recognize these potential problems with data gathering can lead to uninformed decisions, truncated discussions, and even seductive political traps. In short, data is not divinely conceived; it has all the stains and scars of distinctively human hands.

Information has related potential flaws. Reporters often pride themselves on their objectivity but their assertion lacks credibility upon closer examination. Reporters, like managers, have to determine what constitutes the news, the story. The choice itself reflects the values of the reporter. Why does the bloody crash of an automobile get reported on the evening news but not the successful blood drive at a local business? The choices are guided by the values of the reporter, which are usually not readily apparent. The values, in turn, influence what is seen, heard, and reported; what constitutes information. So, too, with managers. Assumptions underlie all observations. These assumptions or values determine "what counts" and "what does not count" as information. Choices are made about what is important and what is not. In short, all data and information are value laden. Skilled managers adjust their perceptions and judgments in light of these concerns.

Determine What Employees Really Need to Know

Gathering more data and information does not necessarily equate with better decision making. Some managers, especially Circuit ones, tend to wait until "all" the data has been gathered and processed before making a decision. Such a posture can lead to unnecessary delays, unwarranted uncertainty, and missed opportunities.[8] More data can never provide a 100% guarantee of what the future holds; the picture is never complete. Walter B. Wriston, former chief executive officer of Citicorp, said, "Our ability to discern what is important and what is not may be impaired if we are inundated by a sea of numbers. Too many numbers may make the decision-making process harder, not easier."[9] Laboratory studies echo the theme by revealing that decision makers seek more data and information than they can possibly use, even to the point of hindering performance. But the extra data serves to "increase the decision maker's confidence. The net result may be that decision makers arrive at poorer decisions but are more confident in their choices."[10]

Employees seem to have an insatiable desire for information.[11] In communication assessments, we asked employees to indicate how much information they *received* on a wide range of subjects versus the amount of information they *desired*. Remarkably, employees wanted more information in *every* topic area. Employees are naturally curious about their organization. Part of the problem is that employees naturally assume that those in management know about changes far in advance. This may not be the case. But effective managers learn to distinguish between desires and needs. Providing all the information employees desire may be costly and ultimately debilitating to the organization. Therefore, priority must be given to certain types of information. Our research has shown that employees most frequently complain about not being informed of changes, decisions, and future plans.[12] Expert data/information managers must become sensitive to the particular needs of their colleagues and not burden them with unnecessary data and information.

Analyze Both Quantitative and Qualitative Data

Data comes in a variety of forms. Corporate decisions are increasingly based on "hard data," or quantitative output. Yet, music cannot really be understood or appreciated through statistical analyses. Likewise, a problem cannot be fully understood or an opportunity realized with information gleaned from a spiritless set of statistics. Few people appreciate the rich wealth of information that lies silently at their fingertips, like some obscure composer's score waiting to be discovered. In sum, the wise manager listens to the right brain as well as the left.

Qualitative analysis includes studying metaphors, stories, and symbols like those reviewed in the chapter on culture (Chapter 3). Jonathan Miller, for example, notes that great strides were made in understanding how the human heart works when the dominant metaphor changed from a furnace to a pump.[13] This switch in perspective opened a new realm of explanations, theories, and treatments. Metaphors make reasonable what was heretofore unreasonable. They simplify the complex. They provide a structure for the experience of phenomena. And they highlight key attributes and obscure others. After all, the human heart looks no more like a pump than a furnace. Hence, unmasking the dominant metaphor reveals the way organizations implicitly structure data and information.

The organizational environment offers a cornucopia of captivating metaphors.[14] One telemarketing company had a room in which sales calls were regularly monitored by management. Employees referred to it as the "spy room." The image was completed with certain "spies" on the staff and a "need to know" communication policy. Amazingly, when the corporate executives were told about the metaphor they simply laughed and dismissed it as trivial. When coupled with quantitative data, which indicated that the staff felt mistrusted, we made a powerful case that revealed both the intensity and depth of employees' feelings. If taken seriously, this captivating metaphor could have been more useful to management than any detailed analysis of an employee survey.

Every organization has operative metaphors. Managers should be concerned about the unforeseen consequences of an undetected metaphor. Why? Because particular metaphors may narrow employees' vision, cutting off potentially rich sources of information and possibilities. In sum, we shape our metaphors and after that, they shape us.

Harness the Power of Product Embedded Information (PEI) and Just-in-Time Information (JITI)

A number of consumer products have started to harness of the power of what might be called "Product Embedded Information" (PEI) and "Just-in-Time Information (JITI). Consider these minor wonders:

- A washing machine that rings a bell upon completion of the cycle.
- A toothbrush that lets the user know when it's time for a replacement.
- A word processing package that provides a timely tip during a critical operation.
- A signal alerting a car driver to a potential hazard.
- A weather update directly delivered to your cell phone.

In each case, relevant information arrives at just the right time for the user. The product has the information embedded in it, so that the users don't have to locate the relevant fact in some long-ago-misplaced manual or flyer. Likewise, managers can harness the power of JITI and PEI by reviewing current data and information practices.

Cisco Systems, for instance, saves millions of dollars every year by handling a remarkable 80% of customer service issues through its Web site.[15] Customers receive information just in time and don't have to wait for a customer service representative to answer the phone. Personnel are freed to handle more complex matters, rather than routine requests. In fact, one study reported that 70% of the businesses surveyed are supporting initiatives to provide real-time business information to employees and other decision makers.[16] Table 6.2 provides some questions that managers can pose to help them implement JITI and PEI practices. But be cautious. Improving data and information efficiency often involves some unpleasant tradeoffs. The Internet, for example, provides JITI but it also creates extraordinary security issues for the organization.

Table 6.2   Efficient Information-Management Practices

Creating JITI Management Practices	*Creating PEI Management Practices*
• Can a portal be structured to provide employees with relevant information to meet their needs? • Can reports (e.g., benefits information, customer complaints, etc.) be generated when employees desire them? • Can tracking systems be developed to more accurately monitor the progress of a project or purchase order? • Can data be directly linked to report forms to allow instant updates? • Can products be electronically tagged to provide relevant information? • Can those who desire information serve their own needs (e.g., supermarket shopping)?	• Can machinery instructions be located on the equipment rather than in a manual? • Can forms include instructions on the document instead of on a separate enclosure? • Can special sensors provide alerts to potential dangers? • Can service reminders be embedded into the product? • Can products incorporate self-diagnostic tools to detect problems and warn users? • Can products be designed to recognize and adjust to different users?

Use Imagery to Personalize Information and Summarize Complex Data Sets

Over 50% of our brains are devoted to processing visual information.[17] No wonder images are powerful communication vehicles. Some data simply cannot become informative without the use of imagery. The Tropicana ad in Figure 6.3 is an excellent example of how imagery can personalize information. There are many ways to state the ad's essential message that "Tropicana orange juice is fresh." Tropicana, for instance, could explain the

Figure 6.3

juice extraction process. Although such an approach may prove enlightening, it fails to arouse the senses. Perhaps various consumers could testify as to the freshness of Tropicana. Yet, this approach still does not arouse the emotions. But everyone can relate to the straw and orange imagery. Clearly, no one can use a straw to extract juice from an orange. No one, except Tropicana. Through this vivid imagery, consumers can see, feel, and taste the freshness of Tropicana juice.[18]

Images can be created verbally, as well. For example, President Theodore Roosevelt once responded to his critics, "I have about as much desire to annex more islands as a boa-constrictor has to swallow a porcupine. . . ."[19] These remarks have power and verve, conveying something more than a simple denial. In short, the well-conceived image can often be more captivating than reams of statistical data or a finely honed argument.

Likewise, well-conceived illustrations or graphs can powerfully communicate to employees by economically summarizing a great deal of data and clarifying complex relationships. In his marvelous treatise, *The Visual Display of Quantitative Data,* Edward R. Tufte notes:

> Modern data graphics can do much more than simply substitute for small statistical tables. At their best, graphics are instruments for reasoning about quantitative information. Often the most effective way to describe, explore, and summarize a set of numbers—even a very large set—is to look at pictures of those numbers. Furthermore, of all methods for analyzing and communicating statistical information, well-designed data graphics are usually the simplest and at the same time the most powerful.[20]

For instance, three scientists developed one graphic, Figure 6.4, depicting the results of over 200 experiments assessing the thermal conductivity of copper.[21] Few people could imagine a better way to summarize the results of that much research, allowing viewers to transform a massive amount of data into meaningful information. Indeed, the National Science Foundation has recently recognized the power of imagery and started co-sponsoring an annual contest to recognize outstanding scientific images designed to help improve communication and visualization.[22]

Yet, as with any powerful tool, graphics, as well as imagery, can be misused. Some studies suggest that using graphics that are not accompanied by precise figures can actually undermine managerial confidence in decision making.[23] The sword cuts both ways. Information of import can be overlooked and the trivial can appear important. The wise manager understands this while recognizing that the form of the information may be as important as the substance. Or as Isadora Duncan, the famous ballerina, once said, "If I could tell you what it meant there would be no point in dancing it."[24]

If Possible, Reduce the Number of Links in the Communication Chain

The more links in the communication chain, the greater the likelihood that information passed along the chain will be distorted and context stripped away. The child at the end of the line in the game of "telephone" receives the least accurate, and usually, briefest message. Organizations are no different, except the results can be more tragic. Indeed, on a cold January morning in 1986, the civilized world was shocked by the fiery disaster that befell the Space Shuttle Challenger. The television pictures recorded in gruesome detail what the mind could not comprehend. In due course, the sorrow and grief

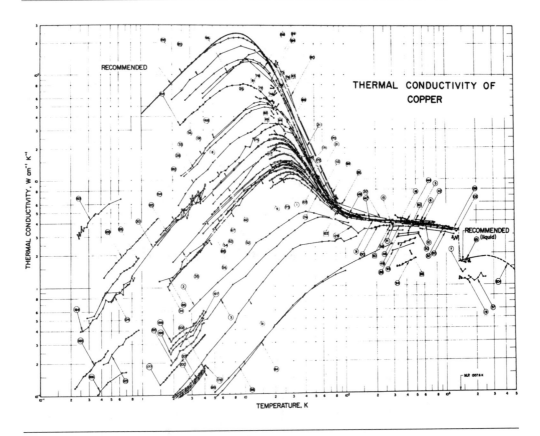

Figure 6.4   Properly Summarizing Complex Data

gave way to inquiry and investigation. One of the critical findings was that messages sent up the chain of command became severely distorted. In particular, engineers from both Rockwell and Thiokol were deeply alarmed about the impact of ice on the shuttle launch. Consider the following sequence of exchanges:

- Rockwell engineers reported to their superiors that they did not have a proper database on how the Shuttle would perform at temperatures below freezing. They concluded that the situation created an "unquantifiable hazard."
- Two Rockwell vice presidents reported to NASA that "Rockwell cannot be 100% sure that it is safe to fly."
- The Director of the National Space Transportation System reported to his team that "Rockwell did not ask or insist that we not launch." He "felt reasonably confident that the launch should proceed."
- NASA's associate administrator, who was in charge of the final decision, stated, "I never thought the ice presented a serious safety problem."[25]

This sad tale vividly illustrates the fundamental communication principle about what happens to a message as it is passed from person-to person. The distortion occurs quite naturally because people have different responsibilities, beliefs, and concerns. Details are omitted. Some are highlighted. Inferences become facts. Even a written memo can be interpreted differently at various levels of an organization. Priorities can shift; nuances are lost.[26] Indeed, NASA felt so much pressure for a launch that they actively discouraged any messages that might call for a delay. Two scholars aptly summed up the situation, "Messages in serial reproduction, like water in a great river, change through losses, gains, absorptions, and combinations along the route from the headwaters to their final destination."[27]

Managing the Information-Knowledge Relationship ____

Managing the I–K relationship requires the ability to judge, analyze, evaluate, and synthesize. Two scholars, with backgrounds in accounting, discovered that:

> . . . successful managers develop the ability to collect and use diverse, ambiguous, and sometimes contradictory information effectively and efficiently. They develop the capacity to evaluate the reliability of information by considering its source and their experience with that source. More frequently than not, that source is not the accounting systems in place in the firm. They develop the ability to know where to go to ask crucial questions about information that intrigues or troubles them.[28]

In other words, successful managers learn how to transform information into knowledge. How do they do it? To some extent this remains a mystery, but we know that these managers use strategies like the ones described in this section.

Recognize the Difference
Between Information and Knowledge

Scholars have estimated that 70% of the literature on "knowledge management" focuses on the use of information technologies, including issues such as "data warehousing" and "data mining."[29] Learning where and how to efficiently store data (warehousing) concerns many chief information officers. And "searching for unknown correlations in the data by looking for interesting patterns, anomalies, and clusters" (data mining) can provide managers with valuable insights.[30] But these important activities should *not* be confused with creating knowledge. Why? Knowledge goes beyond the facts; it connects and explains them. The "facts" often contradict one another. Knowledge seeks to reconcile seemingly disparate findings.

Consider the case of Rosalind Franklin who studied the DNA molecule at Kings College in London during the 1950s. She was the first person to take clear X-ray-diffraction photographs of the B form of DNA. Yet she was not the one who won the Nobel Prize. It was Crick and Watson. The photograph was the final piece of the DNA puzzle. And Crick and Watson put it all together to form a working model of the DNA molecule.[31] Franklin had information, exceedingly important information, but Crick and Watson went further. They transformed information into knowledge. The elegant simplicity of the DNA structure, with all its implications for explaining sexual reproduction and controlling disease, unfolded because Watson and Crick knew how to use information. Crick reflected on why others did not discover the DNA structure:

> They missed the alpha helix because of that reflection! You see. And the fact that they didn't put the peptide bond in right. The point is that evidence can be unreliable, and therefore you should use as little of it as you can. And when we confront problems today, we're in exactly the same situation. We have three or four bits of data, we don't know which one is reliable, so we say, now if we discard that one and assume it's wrong—even though we have no evidence that it's wrong—then we can look at the rest of the data and see if we can make sense of that. And that's what we do all the time. I mean, people don't realize that not only can data be wrong in science, it can be misleading. There isn't such a thing as a hard fact when you're trying to discover something. It's only afterwards that the facts become hard.[32]

In a similar vein, effective managers weigh the evidence, evaluate the information, and discern the salient features in the situation. All information is not equally relevant. Some crucial data may even be missing or unattainable. Assembling a lot of information is not enough (see Figure 6.5). Plans, theories, and models need to be set forth to organize the information. Hence, the data begins to "make sense," to have meaning. Tests can be conducted, projections made. The wise manager seeks a more encompassing perspective by linking fact to fact, like some kind of conceptual scaffolding. Those who produce information are important, but the prizes usually go to those who can produce knowledge.[33]

Evaluate the Credibility of the Evidence Before Theorizing

Like it or not, every message has a kind of credibility tag attached to it that determines, to a large extent, how that message will be treated. Because there are more messages than people, credibility provides an efficient screening mechanism. All messages emanating from a single source can be lumped together for assessment. In essence, credibility acts as a labeling system, tagging messages with, "PAY ATTENTION TO ME," "ignore me," or "I May Be True." Students, for example, will dutifully listen as the teacher

Employees connect the dots even with incomplete information

Figure 6.5   Reasoning With Incomplete Information

reflects on the importance of having a professional-looking portfolio. But when the HR director for Microsoft relates the same message, the students do more than nod their heads. Messages cannot be separated from people, for the source forms part of the context.

Who creates the data and sends the information also may provide an important insight into its reliability, validity, and utility. Indeed, consumers rarely doubt the veracity of something as "factual" as a photograph on a magazine cover. Think again. *Redbook,* for instance, has acknowledged they doctored up some cover photos of actress Julia Roberts.[34] Veracity can also be compromised for other reasons. Some messages never get transmitted because of who gathers the information. One of the top salespersons of a large pharmaceutical corporation quit her job in disgust over the practices of her immediate supervisor's boss. During the exit interview, when she was asked why she quit the job, she forthrightly told of her legitimate grievances about the situation. Yet, the information never reached the personnel office or the people who could do something about the problem. The reason: The immediate supervisor conducted the interview and he had to forward the report to this very person. On the exit interview form, under the question about why the employee was leaving, the supervisor wrote: "personal reasons."

The law of gravity does not always seem to apply to information flow in organizations. Information held at the top of the organizational hierarchy does not always filter down (e.g., financial results, pending mergers, etc.). And some information, such as major success stories held in the lower echelons, shows exceptional buoyancy in reaching the top, almost like defying the laws of gravity. Effective managers know that the hierarchy inherently filters information. Researchers have confirmed what Sir Winston Churchill noted long ago:

> The temptation to tell a Chief in a great position the things he most likes to hear is one of the commonest explanations of mistaken policy. Thus the outlook of the leader on whose decision fateful events depend is usually far more sanguine than the brutal facts admit.[35]

Sending the good news up is only natural for those who wish to get ahead in the organization. As several scholars noted, "This tendency is so strong that subordinates who do not trust their superior are willing to suppress unfavorable information even if they know that such information is useful for decision making."[36] Therefore, thoughtful managers evaluate the credibility and the sources of information before reaching any conclusions.

Organize the Same Information in Different Ways to Extract the Underlying Meaning

The organization of information significantly alters the meaning gleaned from it. Different relationships can be highlighted; different meanings discovered. For example, Figure 6.6a provides the raw data for five employee performance ratings. Figure 6.6b underscores the differences between them, by ranking them from highest to lowest. Yet, using the same data, when the employees are individually plotted, they all appear above-average as seen in Figure 6.6c. In Figure 6.6d, no real pattern seems to emerge from the same data. But displaying the average ratings by gender, as seen in Figure 6.6e, almost begs the viewer to draw a conclusion. The structure of the information acts like mirrors at carnivals; one stretches the reflection up and down, the other side-to-side. It's the same image but different parts are accentuated, causing the spectator to have dramatically different perceptions.

(a)

Employee Performance Raw Data

Name	Score*	Rank	Yrs. of Service	Gender	X Factor
Davis	9.1	1	2	M	?
Alexander	8.7	2	6	M	?
Newman	7.3	3	16	F	?
Clark	6.8	4	21	F	?
Eastman	6.5	5	1	F	?

1-10 scale; 1 = low, 10 = high

The only way to gain a true perspective on this information is to look at it from a variety of angles. Even then, there is always some unknown "X" factor that could provide further clarification.

(b)

Summary of Rankings: High to Low

Rank	Name
1	Davis
2	Alexander
3	Newman
4	Clark
5	Eastman

(1 = highest; 5 = lowest)

Probable Interpretation:
Davis is a much better employee than Eastman.

Better Interpretation:
All employees are above-average performers. Note in (a) that all the scores are above "5."

Figure 6.6a–e Employee Performance Ratings: Different Ways to Organize the Same Information

(Continued)

Figure 6.6a-e (Continued)

(c)

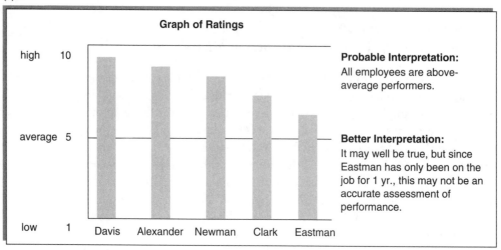

(d)

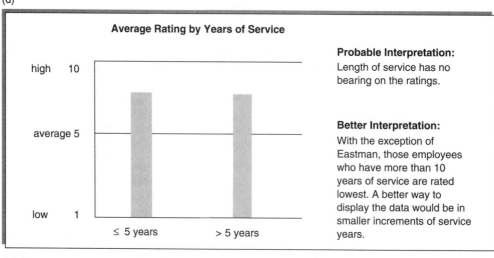

(e)

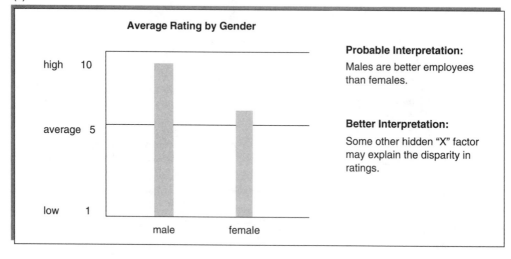

The leadership team at Harrah's Entertainment took this advice to heart. The company has tracked millions of customer preferences and transactions to create a vast data storehouse, which it mined for information and patterns. The analyses unearthed some nonintuitive informational nuggets such as the fact that the best customers were not necessarily the high rollers. Indeed by reorganizing and analyzing their data they found that company profits could be better explained by how much a customer spent *over time* rather than the amount spent on a *single visit* (e.g., high rollers). This bit of knowledge ran counter to conventional wisdom and partially explains why Harrah's has consistently beat the competition.[37]

Ask a Lot of Questions About What You Do Not Know

Why? This creates the proper climate for a dialogue in which knowledge can be shared and created through informal networks. Managers who know a lot of facts might be considered intelligent, but those who also know what they do *not* know are considered wise. We could call this kind of insight, "knowledgeable ignorance," representing the known unknowns.[38] The manager or the organization recognizes that something is missing. Knowing the right questions, even if the answers are elusive, usually proves illuminating.

- Saul Wurman who "reinvented the guidebook" and restructured the Pacific Bell SMART Yellow Pages said: "My expertise is my ignorance. I ask the obvious questions, the ones everyone else is embarrassed to ask because they are so obvious."[39]
- As a youngster, Albert Einstein asked, "What would it be like to ride on a beam of light?" Later in life he provided the answer: the theory of relativity.
- Jacob Bronowski said: " . . . the hardest part is not to answer, but to conceive the question. The genius of men like Newton and Einstein lies in that they ask transparent, innocent questions which turn out to have catastrophic answers."[40]

Asking penetrating questions provides the scientist, as well as the manager, the ultimate tool for creating knowledge.

Managers often unwittingly fall into an information trap. By devoting so much of their time to processing information already generated, they often fail to devote time to asking the insightful questions. An illusion can emerge that they already have all the necessary information. Walter Wriston, former Citicorp CEO, put it this way: "Since we are the prisoners of what we know, often we are unable to even imagine what we don't know."[41] Wise managers do not let existing information obscure their judgment of more fundamental issues. They acknowledge their ignorance and perhaps, as a result, a brilliant insight or theory will emerge.

Structure Informal Networks

Informal networks emerge from random associations, personal interests, and formal communicative structures. Scientific research has clearly established that we have limited knowledge about our personal informal networks. If, for example, you know 500 people and those individuals know 500 others, then you may have as many as 250,000 people one link removed from you.[42] Think about the daunting task of keeping track of those relationships, much less knowing about the special expertise of those individuals. These facts suggest that managers *cannot* and *should not* cultivate an informal system in which everyone connects to everyone else. As one group of scholars put it, "An indiscriminate increase in connectedness can be a drag on productivity, as people get bogged down maintaining all their relationships."[43] Instead skillful managers encourage informal relationships that have the greatest likelihood of strategic payoff and discourage those that don't.

Informal networks or communities work best when imbued with the following attributes:

- Understanding of who knows what.
- Norms of timely responsiveness.
- Willingness to mutually solve problems.
- Personal connections based on factors other than expertise (e.g., hobbies, community activities, etc.).
- Mutual trust and respect.[44]

Note the blend of cognitive, behavioral, and relational factors in the previous list. Skillful, knowledge workers and managers create useful networks by cultivating activities designed to address all these factors. One study, for example, examined the knowledge-management practices of over 300 organizations. The most innovative and financially successful firms structured informal networks by strategically bringing together employees for events such as "show-and-tell" sessions, informal brainstorming, and "After-Action Reviews" of projects.[45] These companies recognize that "knowledge does not simply flow through an organization but is bartered, blocked, exchanged, and modified."[46] By cultivating communities that add strategic value, they may, for instance, alter the network by changing who has responsibility for certain information and decisions, thereby shifting communicative incentives in the network.[47] In essence, they attempt to influence this seemingly random set of associations that lies beyond the awareness of even the most astute observers. No wonder the quest for effective knowledge-management practices has proven so elusive.[48]

Create and Continually Test Models and Theories

The quintessential detective, Sherlock Holmes said in his first adventure, *A Scandal in Bohemia*: "I have no data yet. It is a capital mistake to theorize before one has data.

Insensibly one begins to twist facts to suit theories, instead of theories to suit facts."[49] In contrast, the quintessential physicist, Albert Einstein, felt that if the evidence did not agree with the theory, then the evidence must be faulty. Such a perspective might explain why Einstein slept in peace and confidence the night his general theory of relativity was being experimentally tested.[50] Who should we believe, Holmes or Einstein?

Managers often face the unavoidable tension between the "facts" and the "theory." For example, the market surveys ("facts") showed there was no market for the Xerox machine. Yet, the marketing model ("theory") suggested that the device seemed like a sure winner. The model was clearly right; the "facts" incorrect. But the model or theory can also be flawed. A merger that makes sense on paper ("theory") frequently fails to work out in reality ("facts").

Ironically, the more money spent on a project, the more credible the idea becomes, regardless of the "evidence." The battle cry becomes, "It must be good, we paid a lot for it" or "We can't be wrong, after all we spent so much time on it." *The implicit but incorrect assumption is that money or time spent translates into theory confirmed.* The actual reason: No one wants to admit that a mistake has been made. Not only are money, time, and effort tied up in our theories, but also our passions, values, and reputations.

The thoughtful manager maintains a healthy skepticism about both facts and theory. Sometimes analysts do not have wrong answers but they have asked the wrong questions. Perhaps the Xerox researchers asked the wrong questions, the wrong people, or both. Good models are simple, elegant, and even beautiful. Scientists have long marveled at the simple elegance of the DNA molecule or even the theory of relativity. Einstein even dismissed certain ideas because they were not "beautiful enough." Likewise, business plans, strategies, and designs that are theoretically sound have an elegance and simplicity about them. Steven Jobs commented about the design plan for the original MacIntosh computer:

> If you read Apple's first brochure, the headline was "Simplicity is the Ultimate Sophistication." What we meant by that was that when you first attack a problem it seems really simple because you don't understand it. Then when you start to really understand it, you come up with these very complicated solutions because it's really hairy. Most people stop there. But a few people keep burning the midnight oil and finally understand the underlying principles of the problem and come up with an elegantly simple solution for it. But very few people go the distance to get there.[51]

Of course, since then Apple Computers has had its fair share of failures and successes. Thus, both Holmes and Einstein are correct; successful managers develop models and theories but they also actively and continually seek evidence that might contradict their conceptions.

Managing the Knowledge-Action Relationship

Knowing *what to do* and *doing it* are two very different things. In one study of over 350 organizational decisions, only 50% of the decisions made were ever fully implemented and sustained.[52] Why? One commentator explained, "Managers know what to do to improve performance, but actually ignore or act in contradiction to either their strongest instincts or the data available to them."[53] Consider the case of Southwest Airlines, as described by one scholar:

> Southwest Airlines is a firm that uses fairly simple business practices that are widely known, but it continues to have the best financial performance in the airline industry. Numerous books, case studies, and television shows have described Southwest's management approach, but the firm's competitors have either not tried to imitate what it does or, when they have, like the United Shuttle did, they have not been nearly as successful as Southwest.[54]

Clearly, bridging the chasm between knowledge and action (the "knowing–doing gap") requires special skills.[55] Effective managers learn to transform knowledge into action through a combination of experience and critical thinking. Experience comes through time, but critical thinking can be more finely honed by heeding the following notions.

Create Strategic Knowledge-Sharing Communities

For years scholars, commentators, and consultants have grappled with how to effectively share knowledge. Some advocated establishing vast organizational databases. It didn't work out. Others suggested that corporate intranets provided the answer. They failed, as well. As one thoughtful scholar and consultant, Thomas Davenport, concluded: "Knowledge is often sprawling and messy, and the ways in which knowledge workers use it are manifold and unpredictable. More to the point, early attempts to 'engineer' knowledge have often failed."[56] To sum up, knowing how to effectively share knowledge remains a fairly elusive goal.

Strategic knowledge-sharing communities seem to unravel at least part of the mystery because they can help workers communicate and act on tacit knowledge.[57] These communities are created in organizations as a strategic asset to facilitate knowledge sharing. They are strategic because they focus on broader goals than a task force. The agendas, procedures, and direction tend to be rather fluid and dynamic.[58] One such community allows supervisors to get together every two weeks for an hour to discuss major issues, share "war stories," and discuss problem-solving tactics. Other organizations, like Xerox, bring together groups of greater diversity, but the goal remains the same. Two primary forms of knowledge sharing emerge in these discussions:

> *Rules-of-thumb (Heuristics):* Experts in the community often know little tricks to solve typical problems that they can pass along in simply

stated rules. These often take the form of "If this problem occurs, then you should respond in the following way."

Case-based thinking: Cases tend to focus on more abstract and complex issues than can be captured in heuristics. Experts soon learn that stated problems may not equate with actual problems. Why? The person stating the problem may not have defined it properly or has difficulty articulating the precise concerns. Sharing cases or examples allows others in the community to quickly understand and solve the actual problems.

Two commentators who made an extensive study of such communities note that, "A strategic community forms and shares knowledge by 'pulling' individual members into an environment in which they learn from each other."[59] They also found that these communities often yield benefits such as:

- Higher quality knowledge creation.
- Fewer surprises and revisions in plans.
- Greater capacity to deal with uncertainty.
- Increased likelihood that decisions will be implemented.
- Further employee development.

Of course, reaping these benefits requires special skills and employee time. In particular, skilled facilitators are needed to assist members of the community in making sense of differing perspectives and minimizing political gamesmanship.[60] Organizations also need to provide employees the time to create a community, which only emerges when members have similar beliefs and a sense of belonging.[61] When denied this sense of community, employees feel a sense of exclusion, "lighting up" an area in the brain similar to that when experiencing physical pain.[62] For that reason alone, organizations should create knowledge-sharing communities.

But organizations profit in other ways because the communities assist in transforming knowledge into action. The CEO of British Petroleum, John Browne, observed, "In order to generate extraordinary value for shareholders, a company has to learn better than its competitors and apply that knowledge throughout its businesses faster and more widely than they do."[63] Bottom line: Strategic knowledge-sharing communities can create value for the organization and shareholders.

Restructure Organizational Reports to Focus Attention on Actionable Issues

Routinely circulated information has a way of shaping the beliefs, thoughts, and actions of organizational members by directing attention to certain issues and deflecting it from others. Reports can hinder performance in two ways. First, the report may contain too much information. In this case, employees either ignore it or pay attention to only those items that serve *their*—not necessarily the organization's—needs. Second, the report may contain too little actionable information. In this case employees learn to disregard it because they feel they cannot impact the results in any meaningful way. Between these two extremes lies the sweet spot where reports allow employees to learn how they directly impact critical organizational results.

Developing reports with this kind of dynamic requires considerable effort. But asking the following questions can put managers on the right track:[64]

- Are reports directly related to actionable tasks?
- Does information in the reports match the scope of responsibility and concerns of the employees?
- Do the reports present information in a simple, straightforward, and concise manner?
- Is the content in the reports presented in a familiar format?
- Are the reports timely?
- Do the reports allow readers to easily understand critical organizational relationships?
- Do the reports have a reputation for reliability?

Some organizations use these questions as criteria to grade the quality of their reports. They usually discover that the vast majority of their organizational reports fail to receive a passing grade. No wonder most companies experience difficulties moving from knowledge to action.

Speed Up the Transformation Process, Even at the Expense of Accuracy

How long does it take to move from data creation to action? This question dominates the thinking of an action-oriented manager obsessed with results. Why? Because they understand three important tendencies:

- *Data, information, and knowledge are perishable "goods."* Data and information tend to lose utility over time as they are processed, stored, and analyzed. Knowledge tends to last longer, but it, too, has a lifecycle limiting its utility over time.[65] Who would decide to take a rain hat to work based on yesterday's weather report? But that's exactly what many organizations do when they fail to insist on fresh intelligence.
- *Most people hedge their bets and preserve their flexibility when working with uncertain data and information.* Employees in organizations with fast-paced D-I-K-A cycles are more likely to experiment and look for errors rather than over-analyze the data and information. They feel less compelled to defend their analytical conclusions and are less embarrassed by "failures." They simply continue experimenting. A kid playing an action video game does not ponder missed opportunities for very long.
- *Most people eventually make the right decisions without totally accurate data and information.* Why? Because they factor the inaccuracy into their decision making and become highly sensitive to contradictory feedback.[66] A detective, for instance, might check out an anonymous tip, but shift focus to a more promising lead when new information becomes available.

In fact, one study confirmed that the price of creating accurate data, information, and knowledge may be too high. The study concluded that, "Any extra effort spent on improving the accuracy of top executives' knowledge *damaged* rather than *improved* performance."[67] That conclusion may sound far-fetched. But it perfectly aligns with the sensibilities of anyone who has been to meetings treated as "information dumps" or worked in an organization suffering from the proverbial "analysis paralysis." Clearly leaders need enough accurate data and information to sense underlying patterns, create reasonably sound models, and energize the organization toward appropriate responses. But beyond a certain point, data, information, and knowledge can actually become liabilities. So, wise managers recognize that speeding up the D-I-K-A cycle trumps all other concerns.

Conclusion

In the past, business schools taught that organizational excellence basically consisted of effectively managing people and tasks. Today a third dimension has emerged: managing data, information, and knowledge. This makes the traditional managerial functions of planning, organizing, leading, and controlling all the more complex and difficult. Yet, this may well be one of the greatest challenges facing the modern organization. Data and information may not be tagged with nutritional labels, but wise managers monitor their intake in order to create useful knowledge and actions.

Notes

1. Wurman, R. S. 1989. *Information anxiety.* New York: Doubleday, p. 32.

2. Davenport, T. H., & Prusak, L. 1998. *Working knowledge.* Boston: Harvard Business School Press, p. 5.

3. Tsoukas, H. 2003. Do we really need tacit knowledge? In *Handbook of organizational learning and knowledge management,* edited by M. Easterby-Smith & M. A. Lyles, (pp. 410–427), p. 425. Malden, MA: Blackwell Publishing.

4. Blackburn, S. 1999. *Think: A compelling introduction to philosophy.* New York: Oxford University Press.

5. Mackenzie, K. D. 1994. Some real world adventures of a bench scientist. In *Producing useful knowledge for organizations,* edited by R. H. Kilmann, K. W. Thomas, D. P. Slevin, R. Nath, & S. L. Jerrell (pp. 100–118), p. 113. San Francisco: Jossey-Bass Publishers. In particular, learning how to effectively manage the relationships between the variables proves useful.

6. Martin De Holan, P. & Phillips, N. 2003. Organizational forgetting. In *Handbook of organizational learning and knowledge management,* edited by M. Easterby-Smith & M. A. Lyles (pp. 393–409), p. 393. Malden, MA: Blackwell Publishing.

7. Kaplan, A. 1963. *The conduct of inquiry: Methodology for behavioral science*. New York: Chandler Publishing Co., pp. 131–132.

8. O'Reilly, C. A., Chatman, J. A., & Anderson, J. C. 1987. Message flow and decision making. *In Handbook of organizational communication*, edited by F. M. Jablin, L. L. Putnam, K. H. Roberts, & L. W. Porter (pp. 600–623). Beverly Hills, CA: Sage.

9. Wriston, W. R. 1986. The world according to Walter. *Harvard Business Review* 64 (1):65–80, p. 65.

10. O'Reilly, op. cit., p. 617.

11. Goldhaber, G., Yates, M., Porter, T., & Lesniak, R. 1978. The ICA communication audit: Recent findings, background, and development. *Human Communication Research* 5 (1):81–84.

12. See also Foehrenback, J., & Rosenberg, K. 1982. How are we doing? *Journal of Communication Management* 12 (1):3–9. These findings parallel a follow-up study by Foehrenbach, J., & Goldfarb, S. 1990. Employee communication in the '90s: Greater expectations. *Communication World*, May-June:4–10. Unfortunately, the complete results are not available.

13. Miller, J. 1978. *The body in question*. New York: Random House.

14. See, for example, Morgan, G. 1986. *Images of organization*. Beverly Hill, CA: Sage.

15. Reinhardt, A. 1999. The man who hones Cisco's cutting edge. *Business Week*, 13 September:140.

16. 2003. Behind the numbers: Real-time aspirations. *Informationweek*, 6 October:114.

17. Matter, C. 2003. Personal communication. October 5.

18. Grinder & Bandler have suggested that people process information in one of three primary modes: 1) Visual, 2) Auditory, and 3) Kinesthetic. This advertisement appeals to all three modes. Grinder, J., & Bandler, R. 1976. *The structure of magic II*. Palo Alto, CA: Science & Behavior Books.

19. Morris, E. 1979. *The rise of Theodore Roosevelt*. New York: Coward, McCann & Geoghegan, Inc., p. 13.

20. Tufte, E. R. 1983. *The visual display of quantitative information*. Cheshire, CT: Graphic Press, p. 1.

21 Ho, C. Y., Powell, R. W., & Liley, P. E. 1974. Thermal conductivity of the elements: A comprehensive review. *Journal of Physical and Chemical Reference Data* 3:1–244.

22. 2003. Science and engineering visualization challenge. *Science*, 12 September:1472–1477. See also, www.sciencemag.org/feature/data/vis2003.

23. Sullivan, J. J. 1988. Financial presentation format and managerial decision making. *Management Communication Quarterly* 2 (2):194–215.

24. Comstock, T. 1974. *New dimensions in dance research: Anthology and dance*. New York: Committee on Research in Dance, p. 226.

25. McConnell, M. 1987. *Challenger: A major malfunction*. Garden City, NY: Doubleday, p. 229.

26. Kimmel, A. J. 2004. *Rumors and rumor control*. Mahway, New Jersey: Lawrence Erlbaum Associates.

27. Pace, W., & Boren, R. 1973. *The human transaction*. Glenview, IL: Scott, Foresman, p. 137.

28. McKinnon, S. M., & Bruns, W. J., Jr. 1992. *The information mosaic*. Boston: Harvard Business School Press, p. 15.

29. Easterby-Smith, M., Crossan, M., & Nicolini, D. 2000. Organizational learning: Debates past, present and future. *Journal of Management Studies* 37 (6):783–796.

30. Alavi, M. & Tiwana, A. 2003. Knowledge management: The information technology dimension. In *Handbook of organizational learning and knowledge management*, edited by M. Easterby-Smith & M. A. Lyles (pp. 104–121), p. 109. Malden, MA: Blackwell Publishing.

31. Watson, J. D. 1968. *The double helix*. New York: New American Library.

32. Judson, H. F. 1979. *The eighth day of creation*. New York: Simon & Schuster, p. 113–114.

33. Note: In recent years Rosalind Franklin's role in this discovery has been re-examined and she has been granted more credit than in the past. See Maddox, B. 2002. *Rosalind Franklin: The dark lady of DNA*. New York: Harper Collins.

34. Freydkin, D. 2003. Doctored cover photos add up to controversy. *USA Today*, 17 June:3D.

35. Churchill, W. S. 1931. *The world crisis*. New York: Scribners, p. 673.

36. O'Reilly, et. al., op. cit., p. 612.

37. Loveman, G. 2003. Diamonds in the data mine. *Harvard Business Review* 81 (5):109–113.

38. Clampitt, P. G., & DeKoch, R. J. 2001. *Embracing uncertainty: The essence of leadership*. Armonk, NY: M.E. Sharpe.

39. Wurman, op. cit., p. 45.

40. Bronowski, J. 1973. *The ascent of man*. Boston: Little, Brown & Co., p. 247.

41. Wriston, op. cit., p. 66.

42. Granovetter, M. 2003. Ignorance, knowledge, and outcomes in a small world. *Science*, 8 August:773–774, p. 773.

43. Cross, R., Nohria, N., & Parker A. 2002. Six myths about informal networks—and how to overcome them. *MIT Sloan Management Review* 43 (3):67–75, p. 70.

44. Cross, R., Davenport, T. H., & Cantrell, S. 2003. The social side of performance. *MIT Sloan Management Review* 45 (1):20–22. See also, Cross, R. & Prusak, L. 2003. The political economy of knowledge markets in organizations. In *Handbook of organizational learning and knowledge management*, edited by M. Easterby-Smith & M. A. Lyles (pp. 454–469). Malden, MA: Blackwell Publishing.

45. Soo, C., Devinney, T., Midgley, D., & Deering, A. 2002. Knowledge management: Philosophy, processes, and pitfalls. *California Management Review* 44 (4):129–150.

46. Cross, R. & Prusak, L. 2003. The political economy of knowledge markets in organizations. In *Handbook of organizational learning and knowledge management*, edited by M. Easterby-Smith & M. A. Lyles (pp. 454–469), p. 468. Malden, MA: Blackwell Publishing.

47. Dodds, P. S., Muhamad, R., & Watts, D. J. 2003. An experimental study of search in global social networks. *Science,* 8 August: 827–829.

48. Kontzer, T. 2003. The need to know. *Informationweek,* 18 August:34–44.

49. Doyle, A. C. 1978. *Sherlock Holmes.* Secaucus, N.J.: Castle Books, p. 13.

50. Clark, R. W. 1971. *Einstein.* New York: Avon Books.

51. 1984. Interview: The Macintosh design team. *Byte,* February:58–80, p. 60.

52. Nutt, P. 1999. Surprising but true: Half the decisions in organizations fail. *Academy of Management Executive* 13 (4):75–90, p. 75. See also, Nutt, P. C. 2002. *Why decisions fail: Avoiding the blunders and traps that lead to debacles.* San Francisco: Berrett-Koehler.

53. Cohen, H. B. 1998. The performance paradox. *Academy of Management Executive* 12 (3):30–40, p. 30.

54. Pfeffer, J., & Sutton, R. I. 1999. Knowing what to do is not enough: Turning knowledge into action. *California Management Review* 42 (1):83–109, p. 87.

55. Pfeffer, J., & Sutton, R. I. 1999. Knowing 'what' to do is not enough: Turning knowledge into action. *California Management Review* 42 (1):83–108.

56. Davenport, T. H. 1997. *Information ecology.* New York: Oxford University Press, p. 18.

57. Heaton, L., & Taylor, J. R. 2002. Knowledge management and professional work. *Management Communication Quarterly* 16 (2):210–236

58. Wenger, E., & Synder, W. 2000. Communities of practice: The organizational frontier. *Harvard Business Review* 78 (1):139–146.

59. Storck, J., & Hill, P. A. 2000. Knowledge diffusion through "strategic communities." *Sloan Management Review* 41 (2):63–74, p. 73.

60. Hayes, N., & Walsham, G. 2003. Knowledge sharing and ICTs: A relationship perspective. In *Handbook of organizational learning and knowledge management,* edited by M. Easterby-Smith & M. A. Lyles (pp. 54–77). Malden, MA: Blackwell Publishing.

61. Plaskoff, J. 2003. Intersubjectivity and community building: Learning to learn organizationally. In *Handbook of organizational learning and knowledge management,* edited by M. Easterby-Smith & M. A. Lyles (pp. 161–184). Malden, MA: Blackwell Publishing.

62. Panksepp, J. 2003. Feeling the pain of social loss. *Science,* 10 October: 237–239.

63. Prokesch, S. E. 1997. Unleashing the power of learning: An interview with British Petroleum's John Browne. *Harvard Business Review* 75 (5):146–168, p. 168.

64. The notions were adapted from a study by McKinnon & Bruns, op. cit., p. 132–133.

65. Birkinshaw, J., & Sheehan, T. 2002. Managing the knowledge life cycle. *MIT Sloan Management Review* 44 (1):75–85.

66. Calhoun, M. A., & Starbuck, W. H. 2003. Barriers to creating knowledge. In *Handbook of organizational learning and knowledge management,* edited by M. Easterby-Smith & M.A. Lyles (pp. 473–492). Malden, MA: Blackwell Publishing.

67. Sutcliffe, K. M. & Weber, K. 2003. The high cost of accurate knowledge. *Harvard Business Review* 81 (5):74–82, p. 78.

7

Providing Performance Feedback

Feedback is one of the fundamental facts of life and ideas of science, yet only in the last fifty years have we recognized its all-pervasive presence. The idea is simple: A feedback mechanism registers the actual state of a system, compares it to the desired state, then uses the comparison to correct the state of the system. Feedback is goal-oriented. . . . Movement is the essence of feedback. It implies purpose and progress. Like a walker on a high wire, it continually achieves balance in order to achieve something beyond balance. It can never rest.

Horace Freeland Judson

What if there was no feedback? What if feedback not only rested but also took a Rip Van Winkle sojourn? Cells would not know when to stop multiplying. The economy would fly out of kilter. Without feedback, the world as we know it would not exist; the high wire walker would fall. No system can survive without feedback.

Chapter 7: By the Numbers

19%
of senior managers believe their companies remove low performers quickly and effectively

60%
of employees are dissatisfied with the performance feedback system

20%
of employees are unsatisfied with information about their job requirements

43%
of employees are unsatisfied with information about how they are judged

90%
of employees favor the concept of a formal evaluation

80%
of U.S. companies use some form of merit pay

Yet, many employees feel that they are expected to do just that. Performance feedback has surfaced as a problem area in every organization in which my colleagues and I have conducted communication assessments. For example, over 60% of the employees in our database expressed dissatisfaction with the performance feedback system.[1] In interviews with employees, many made comments such as, "Performance evaluations don't really exist here. If they do, I don't know what they look like. It's like pulling teeth." In short, there is probably no more pervasive and perplexing difficulty than how to effectively provide feedback to employees about their performance.

The cynic might ask, "So what"? Does performance feedback actually make any difference? Indeed, I mentioned to one vice-president that employees felt they did not get adequate feedback. He responded, "They get their paychecks every two weeks, don't they?" Researchers have a more critical view. Performance feedback has a high correlation with job performance and satisfaction. In fact, employees indicated that performance feedback had a greater impact on their performance than every other communication variable, including the communication climate, co-worker communication, and even supervisor–subordinate relationships.[2] In one study, employees were asked to recall a specific incident that caused their productivity to increase. Over 65% of the employees mentioned some kind of feedback from management, such as a written note of praise from the company president or an extra bonus for effectively completing a challenging task.[3] In short, employees like to know how they are doing. For some, feedback serves as a reward or motivation; for others, it provides useful information to correct behavior or a way to build self-esteem. Meeting these sometimes divergent needs requires a sound feedback system and skillful managers. These issues are the focal points of this chapter.

Foundational Principles

The following four principles provide a solid foundation for the more specific discussion about creating an effective feedback system.

1. Everyone, Whether They Acknowledge It or Not, Has Standards of Performance

In every task, duty, and decision, employees assess their own level of effectiveness. If deemed satisfactory, they seek to maintain it. If they fall short, they make changes. After cyclist Lance Armstrong won his fifth grueling Tour de France by only sixty-one seconds, he admitted he was not in optimal condition and vowed to train harder in pursuit of an unprecedented sixth title.[4] These are very high standards, indeed. There are, of course, other people who are happy to work to minimal standards and just hope not to get fired. Regardless of where on the spectrum our performance standards lie, they are a nonoptional part of the human experience; they guide our behavior, determine our aspirations, and ultimately define our essence. Therein lies a manager's challenge.

2. High Performance Standards Foster Employee Development and Organizational Viability

Employees generally benefit from high performance standards. Those who are challenged to achieve their potential tend to be more satisfied and productive. "Self actualization," the term Abraham Maslow made famous in his theory of the hierarchy of human needs, places this assertion on firm theoretical grounds. The thoughtful philosopher and poet, Jacob Bronowski, beautifully expressed it:

> The most powerful drive in the ascent of man is his pleasure in his own skill. He loves to do what he does well, and having done it well, he loves to do it better. You see it in his science. You see it in the magnificence with which he carves and builds, the loving care, the gaiety, the effrontery. The monuments are supposed to commemorate kings and religions, heroes, dogmas, but in the end the man they commemorate is the builder.[5]

Most people aspire to fulfill their potential. Companies should not frustrate this desire but seek to encourage it by offering challenging tasks and high standards. To sustain performance in this demanding atmosphere, employees' efforts and accomplishments must be acknowledged, supported, and rewarded.

When not properly challenged, employees lose their motivation and organizations lose their viability. A company will eventually lose market share if a competitor can make a better product faster and/or cheaper. It happens all the time. For example, even highly admired companies like IBM find it difficult to compete with companies like Dell in the personal computer market. Service-oriented organizations face a similar challenge. Wal-Mart, for example, has driven any number of local competitors out of the market because they offer more products that customers want at cheaper prices. When organizations have lower standards of reliability, performance, and service than their competition, the results are inevitable and often terminal. Companies and managers need have no apologies for high performance standards.

3. All Employees "Receive"
Feedback About Their Performance

Even if employees do not receive explicit feedback, they will make inferences about the acceptability of their work. From the organizational context, employees extract messages and come to conclusions such as, "No news is good news," or "I haven't heard any complaints, so I must be doing OK." When employees fail to receive explicit feedback, they infer it and continue to perform at levels they deem acceptable to themselves. Or to put it another way, a manager cannot *not* "give" performance feedback.

Unfortunately, this inferential method of feedback often encourages employees to make inaccurate speculations. Consider, for example, managers who sugarcoat their feedback by over-emphasizing the positive and downplaying the negative.[6] Employees may assume the best, in which case true problems go undetected and uncorrected. On the other hand, employees may assume the worst, in which case anxiety and undue stress are the likely results.

4. The Ideal Feedback System
Drives Employees to Identify, Perform, and
Commit to the Evolving Performance Standards

Employees and managers do not always share the same standards. New employees often have quite different standards than their managers because of their different backgrounds, training, and experiences. Indeed, researchers have shown managers have the greatest impact on their employees' standards, values, and expectations during the initial training period.[7] After that, employees tend to be more influenced by their co-workers and other organizational factors. As seen in Figure 7.1, if proper selection procedures have been utilized, employees will share, to some extent, the performance standards of their managers. The training process should result in a more complete sharing of expectations, therefore increasing the degree of overlap. The standards may be altered as situations change, the manager matures, and the employee develops. Yet, the objective endures: close the gap between the standards of the employee and the manager.

The employee must not only know the standards but also must perform as expected and be committed to these standards. For example, a professor may set a standard for professionalism in writing, which might include not having any spelling errors on reports. Clearly the professor can encourage proper writing but exhortations are useless unless the students actually turn in papers of this quality. In the long-term, however, each student must recognize the importance of correct spelling and be committed to this level of professionalism. The professor aims for knowledge, performance, and commitment. Ideally, each student learns the appropriate standards, turns the

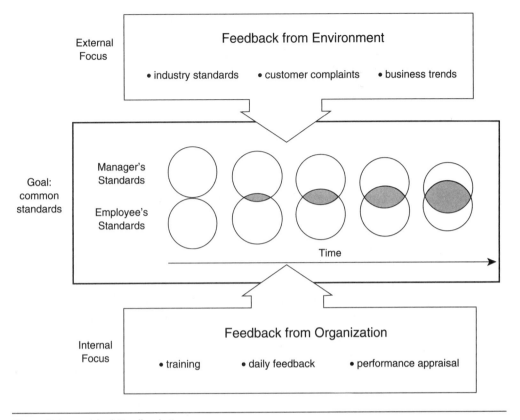

Figure 7.1   Ideal Feedback Process

knowledge into action, and transforms the action into resolve. Ultimately, effective managers want their employees to internalize the standards instead of depending on external commentary by others.

Even as employees seek to perform up to the standards, new standards will emerge. Why? Because the competitive environment changes, technology improves, and organizational needs evolve. Thus, managers naturally need to reconsider the usefulness of the current performance standards (see Figure 7.1). Are the present standards sufficient to meet corporate goals? To be competitive? Have the employees suggested any new standards? These are the kinds of questions that must be regularly asked to ensure the viability of the standards.

Implementing a Successful Feedback System

The principles previously discussed provide a useful background for developing an effective feedback system. There are many systems and methods for providing employees with feedback. Yet, ultimately the success of any system hinges on four basic questions.

1. Do employees know their job responsibilities?

2. Do employees know the standards of evaluation?

3. Do employees receive useful informal feedback?

4. Do employees receive useful feedback from performance appraisals?

There cannot be a weak link in the chain. The answer to each of these questions must be affirmative for the feedback system to work.

1. Do Employees Know Their Job Responsibilities?

Dynamic organizations tend to experience the most difficulties in this area. Our research in over thirty companies revealed that almost 20% of the employees felt unsatisfied with information about their job requirements. Clearly, if employees do not know their job responsibilities, they are probably not doing their job.[8] The reasons for this are many. Employees may have never read their job descriptions. Or, the situation may have changed so much that the job descriptions are outdated. Additionally, the employee may get conflicting messages about the actual job duties from co-workers and the supervisor. As a result, effective managers set up some kind of formal mechanism—either in the appraisal interview or in a separate discussion—to ensure that employees understand their job duties and expectations. Either way, employees learn how they are expected to add value to the organization.

2. Do Employees Know the Standards by Which They Are Being Evaluated?

Research suggests that 43% of the employees are unsatisfied with information about how they are being judged.[9] For example, one manager at a bank said: "I know my job, my manager knows I know my job, but I haven't a clue how he evaluates me." An employee may know her job is to troubleshoot for an engineering division but may be completely unaware of how her performance will be judged. Is it the number of problems she solves that counts? Does the complexity of the problem matter? These are questions about standards of evaluation, not about job duties. Employees need to see the yardstick.

In almost every job, there are at least a few quantifiable criteria, which can be discussed with employees. As one performance criterion, a bank teller may have to establish a designated number of new IRA accounts. But there are also qualitative aspects of every job that are equally important. Bank tellers must be concerned with effective customer relations. Some overly enthusiastic behavioral psychologist might argue that even this can be quantified. A few businesses, for instance, insist that the employee smile at the customer a designated number of times while conducting a transaction and conclude with a canned, "Have a nice day." These dictates may work for robots but they quickly wear thin with employees and clients. Thus, I do not share in the behaviorist's mad rush to quantify everything that can be counted. Harry Levinson, a noted management psychologist and clinical professor of psychology at the Harvard Medical School, perceptively commented, "The greater the emphasis on measurement and quantification, the more likely the subtle, non-measurable elements of the task will be sacrificed. Quality of performance frequently, therefore, loses out to quantification."[10]

Consequently, effective managers use a combination of quantitative and qualitative measures in evaluating an employee's performance. Still many managers resist having discussions of their criteria. Why? *First, some feel that specifying criteria inhibits their flexibility in evaluating employees.* So what? The manager's flexibility should be less important than creating a high-performing work climate. Moreover, flexibility usually emerges in the qualitative criteria. *Second, some managers feel ill-equipped to discuss criteria, especially qualitative measures.* Clearly these discussions are not easy. They may be unable to articulate their expectations and their intuitive sensibilities that are honed by experience. They may also have to commit to a series of discussions with employees rather than a single meeting. Yet, effective managers willingly accept these challenges because they know how energizing and important well-defined yardsticks can be to employees and their organizations.

3. Do Employees Receive Useful Informal Feedback?

In the long run, the day-to-day "pat on the back" or reprimand may have a greater impact on employee performance than any other communication event. Regrettably, most employees are not satisfied with the daily feedback they receive and can relate to an airline employee who said, "[Giving] specific, positive reinforcement is management's worst problem. They can't seem to praise anyone. You'd think it was costing them money." The problem pervades organizations across the spectrum, from service-oriented companies to manufacturing firms. Indeed, over 40% of the employees in our databank were dissatisfied with the extent to which their efforts were recognized by the organization. There are two primary reasons for this problem.

Many managers do not take the time to give regular feedback. The inherently different perspectives of employees and managers compound the difficulty. For example, assume that a manager of a twenty-person department decides to spend three minutes every week giving honest feedback to each employee. The manager invests one hour each week in this process. Yet to the employee three minutes a week is a mere commercial break. Thus, managers almost always overestimate, at least from the employees' perspective, the amount of daily feedback they communicate.

Many managers simply do not notice employee performance unless there are difficulties. Managers get more credit for problems solved than problems avoided. No wonder they are quick to comment when employees fail but slow to praise a job well done. Employees want to be recognized, and they bemoan the "I only hear when things go wrong" managerial philosophy.

Despite these inherent difficulties, the effective manager allocates time to providing routine feedback. In the long run it may actually save managerial time. Why? Corrective feedback can stop small problems from growing into larger ones, thus the routine pat on the back can be amplified into major successes.

4. Do Employees Receive Useful Feedback From Performance Appraisals?

Much ink has been spilled over the issue of performance appraisals. Business journals, periodicals, and books are filled with discussions on how to more effectively conduct the performance review. And with good reason; there is probably no greater area of employee dissatisfaction. In fact, although most organizations maintain a formal performance process, few achieve their objectives.[11] This disgruntled employee expresses the sentiments of many:

> My immediate supervisor felt it was her duty to give me my evaluation as required once a year. It was handed to me with, "I'll discuss it later." When I asked her, "Why not now?" she said, "I don't have time." This was my year's work and it was no big deal! *It was to me.*

Other complaints abound. Unfair rating scales, lack of objectivity, and lack of specific examples to back up the evaluation are just a few of the ones frequently mentioned.[12] But this does not mean that employees want to avoid the formal appraisal. Employees want this kind of feedback. In fact, in spite of problems, one survey found that 90% of employees reacted favorably to the concept of a formal evaluation.[13] There are a variety of reasons for problems with appraisal systems but three are particularly noteworthy.

Many managers resist the appraisal process because it is used to accomplish multiple goals that are sometimes incompatible (see Table 7.1). One airline we investigated used the appraisal process to simultaneously provide feedback about employees' past job performance, as well as to determine their promotional potential and make salary adjustments. Many of the managers felt the variety of goals encouraged distortions, such as inflated ratings, and overly positive comments. Some managers did not want to hurt employees' long-term promotion opportunities, so they made vague general comments. Others were less virtuous. One manager took a Machiavellian approach, giving a troublesome employee high marks to promote him out of his department. That is, of course, one way to get rid of a problem—give it to someone else.

Table 7.1   Potential Objectives of Appraisal Systems

Objective	Concern
Make salary adjustments	Salary decisions are rarely based solely on performance. Factors such as market conditions, length of service, and corporate economic outlook affect the decision.
Determine promotion potential	An employee may perform one job with a high degree of competence, but be unsuitable for greater responsibility.
"Grade" past performance	At times a "grade" may not motivate employees. It may also fail to uncover important reasons for performance levels.
Motivate	Many managers leave out the "bad news" when trying to motivate employees.
Improve performance	Sometimes, managers are so "problem-oriented" they fail to effectively and specifically praise employees.

Many managers feel compelled to inflate ratings. It might be called the *Lake Wobegon Phenomena*, "where everyone is good looking and all the employees are above-average." Part of the problem lies in the natural competition between different departments. Many managers feel that other department managers rate their employees highly, and if they do not do the same, then their employees will be penalized in the long run. Another part of the problem lies in the meanings attached to the numbers or categories typically used in appraisal forms. In one study we asked a group of managers from the same company to respond to a series of precise questions about what they meant when they used terms such as "above-average," "average," and "below-average" on their appraisal forms. We found many discrepancies. One of the more striking was the meaning of the word, "average." Over 60% of the managers believed it meant "the employee completed all jobs satisfactorily," whereas 37% felt it meant that "performance was uneven, some above-average and some below."[14] Clearly such discrepancies can lead to uneven evaluations.

Third, many managers resist the appraisal process because they feel that they are "playing God." Douglas McGregor expressed it eloquently:

> Managers are uncomfortable when they are put in the position of "playing God." The respect we hold for the inherent value of the individual leaves us distressed when we must take responsibility for judging the personal worth of a fellow man. Yet the conventional approach to performance appraisal forces us not only to make such judgments and to see them acted upon but also to communicate them to those we have judged. Small wonder we resist![15]

Understandably, managers try to avoid situations involving the deity-to-sinner kind of relationship. Yet, in many cases, this fear of "playing God" masks a deeper problem of an inability or unwillingness to face conflict.

Regardless of the actual reason for the reticence, managers are destined to "provide" some kind of feedback. That changes the question from "Should I provide feedback?" to "What kind of feedback is useful? "Or more specifically, "Did my feedback contribute to the employee's growth?" Furthermore, providing objectively based judgments need not imply a divine verdict of a person's worth. The alternatives are worse. Harold Mayfield put the matter in perspective:

> Is there one of us who has not kicked himself for some inglorious episode in our human relationships? This risk I believe to be one of the prices we must pay for any attempt at serious communications. Against it, we must weigh the cost of silence. It, too, leaves scars.[16]

Communicating Performance Feedback

Providing effective informal and formal performance feedback may well be the singular characteristic distinguishing the merely adequate manager from the superior one. The skillful manager addresses two essential aspects of this vital communicative task: the method and the message.

The Method

Effective managers carefully hone their feedback to employees. They strategically incorporate the following in the appraisal process.

Utilize self-appraisal and task-inherent feedback. Commission salespeople are inherently aware of their level of sales. In this case, a supervisor may not need to comment on the discrepancy between goal and performance level. Rather, the supervisor's role becomes more of a coach and counselor. In fact, researchers have isolated five potential sources of feedback and ranked their utility to employees. The most important, in order, are: oneself, the task, supervisors, co-workers, and the organization.[17] Employees are more likely to accept feedback from those who have directly experienced their work and who they deem objective and credible. No wonder self-appraisal and task-inherent feedback top the list. So the wise course for a supervisor would be to create mechanisms that encourage employees to conduct self-appraisals based on feedback from the task itself. Researchers, for example, have determined that computer-generated performance feedback often improves production worker effectiveness more than supervisory feedback.[18] Such methods are a subtle way to augment the appraisal process.

Seize every opportunity to provide employee feedback. The *One-Minute Manager* has dominated the best-seller lists much longer than the title might suggest. The premise is simple. "Catch" employees doing the right things and tell them. Admonish them on the spot when you find them doing the wrong things. The timing and informality are critical because these one-minute discussions provide helpful feedback in a nonthreatening environment. Corrections can be made quickly and core company values can be specifically reinforced. In fact, several one-minute chats may do more good than the most carefully planned appraisal interview. This may explain why the one-minute manager's advice endures over time.

Decide on a useful technique to formally assess employee performance. Essay evaluations, rating scales, ranking methods, and critical-incident techniques are just a few of the options.[19] The specific objectives of the system should dictate the type of approach (see Table 7.2). If the organization wants to encourage employee growth, then written essays about employee performance would prove useful. To promote a competitive spirit within a sales force, for example, ranking employees may work best. The most widely used approach, rating scales, can be useful in most situations.

In recent years, 360-degree reviews have gained popularity. The employee at the hub of a 360-degree review receives feedback from every angle—up, down and all around.[20] This may prove invaluable because subordinates, peers, or even customers may be in a better position than supervisors to provide useful feedback about certain issues such as leadership. Moreover, the employee cannot easily dismiss criticism independently garnered from a number of different sources. On the flip side, 360-degree reviews are time-consuming and potentially confusing to the employee. When used widely in organizations, they may encourage gamesmanship with such behind-the-scenes deals as "I'll rate you high, if you rate me high." It is difficult to be both peer and judge, so many organizations use the 360-degree review for developmental purposes, separating it from the salary review process.[21]

Even if managers don't "have a say" in the choice of evaluation methods, it is important that they are aware of the limitations and advantages of the various options. The wise manager can then supplement the mandatory system with other "homegrown" measures.

Regardless of the method used, the organization needs to commit to provide training for the appraisers. This helps ensure that practice harmonizes with purpose. It also cultivates more uniformity and fairness in the rating process by limiting distortions that may emerge from "political games" in the organization. Importantly, training can protect the organization from a potential legal minefield (see Table 7.3). For instance, McDonnell Douglas was sued for laying off an employee who believed that age, not performance, was the determining factor. The court sided with the company because appraisal records showed that her performance was consistently and objectively rated below her peers.[22] In short, successful organizations, just like the courts, recognize the value of well-conceived and executed performance appraisals.

Discuss with employees the exact purpose of appraisal interviews. At the outset of the interview, every employee should be reminded of the appraisal's purpose as well as how the information will be used. This helps new employees

Table 7.2   Appraisal Techniques

Method	Strengths	Weaknesses
Rating Scale	• Allows comparison between employees without forcing distinctions. Easy to use.	• Might be disagreement over meanings of the numbers.
Essay	• Allows appraiser flexibility to uniquely characterize each employee.	• Is difficult to compare employees. • Might have variances between raters in level of specificity.
Rank Order	• Creates clear distinctions between employees. Often used for salary purposes.	• Forces unfair or artificial comparisons between employees.
Critical Incidents	• Focuses on employee behavior. • Avoids appraisals of employee personality. • Provides specific evidence.	• Takes time to record every incident. • May cause manager to delay daily feedback. • May encourage an overemphasis on the peaks and valleys of performance, rather than typical performance.
360-degree	• Provides various points of view. • Underscores the importance of all the relationships an employee must effectively manage.	• Is time-consuming. • May encourage "gamesmanship." • May be potentially confusing to employee.

Table 7.3   Minimizing Potential Legal Challenges

Action	Rationale
Train appraisers to focus on behavioral, observable, and objective evidence.	Training increases perceived fairness in the process and should curtail more subjective evaluations. The courts will not support terminating someone because of a personality conflict.
Use consistent standards and apply them fairly to all employees.	The courts frown on a seemingly aberrant review to justify termination. A history of documented problems is very helpful to support the organization's case.
Encourage employee participation in the process.	Participation encourages dialogue that could be used to correct misperceptions and misunderstandings that may occur in the process.
Allow employees to respond to reviews.	Distortions in the review process are bound to occur for any number of reasons. Providing the employee the ability to respond in writing acts as a safety valve for the process.
Document the process and review.	Written evidence carries greater weight than a supervisor's memory.

determine what type of information is appropriate to share. Even though this may become a bit repetitive over the years, it helps ensure that employees are continually focused on the objectives. Setting a specific time and place for the interview sends a powerful secondary message that the interaction has great significance. Interruptions, like phone calls, should be avoided. These may sound like small matters but they often prove significant to employees.

Assign employees specific preparations for the appraisal process. Many organizations provide appraisal forms for both the manager and the subordinate, which are parallel in format. The manager rates the employee's performance in designated areas and the employee rates his or her own performance on a similar form. These documents are to be completed before the actual appraisal interview and should include task-inherent measures. This step reinforces the importance of the process, while ensuring that employees come to the meeting fully prepared. The two documents can serve as a stimulus for focused discussion on the employee's performance. No topics are skirted out of fear or anxiety.

The Message

The right method is just one part of the equation. Wise managers also think seriously about the message and tone because they recognize how both influence employee reactions. These issues are discussed in this section.

Contemplate and capitalize on the employee's unique abilities, qualities, and motivations. Traditionally, managers "motivated" employees by rewarding or punishing specific performance behaviors. These behavioral techniques encourage the repetition of the desired behavior. However, repetition may actually become dysfunctional because situations change and novel contingencies arise. There is a better, more strategic approach. Character qualities such as thoughtfulness, attentiveness, flexibility, discretion, sensitivity, thoroughness, and diligence profoundly impact the quality of organizational life. Any opportunity to reinforce these values should be seized by the manager. But that first requires that managers discern the unique capabilities of each employee.

Great statesmen, like great managers, seem to have special insights into the uniqueness of those with whom they work closely. They have an extraordinary grasp of the essential and fundamental qualities and abilities of the person. Winston Churchill, one of the greatest leaders of all time, wrote of his rival, friend, fellow cabinet minister, and eventual Prime Minister:

> (Lloyd George) possessed two characteristics that were in harmony with this period of convulsion. First, a power of living in the present, without taking short views. Every day for him was filled with the hope and the impulse of a fresh beginning. He surveyed the problems of each morning with an eye unobstructed by preconceived opinions, past utterances, or previous disappointment and defeats. In times of peace such a mood is not always admirable, nor often successful for long. But

in the intense crisis when the world was a kaleidoscope, when every month all the values and relations were changed by some prodigious event and its measureless reactions, this inexhaustible mental agility, guided by the main purpose of Victory, was a rare advantage. His intuition fitted the crisis better than the logical reasoning of more rigid minds.[23]

This is the kind of praise the wise manager gives. It is based on keen observation and shows deep thought into the person's uniqueness. Employees perceive this type of praise as sincere and motivated by the manager's thoughtfulness. It demonstrates insight into an individual's character.

This is not enough, however. Otherwise, all biographers would be great statesmen. Leaders must also have the ability to transform insight into action. In addition to Churchill's extraordinary discernment into Lloyd George's qualities, he also demonstrated an amazing perceptiveness into situations in which the Prime Minister would be most effective. Herein lies the essence of world-class management.

Effective managers are sensitive to the natural motivators of their employees, but also know how to link the motivators to critical objectives.[24] In the appraisal interview in Figure 7.2, the manager fails to pick up on the fact that the employee is highly motivated to provide quality service to the customer. The manager could have linked "customer service" to the problem areas of "organization" and "selling Individual Retirement Accounts (IRAs)." The manager might have said: "I'm impressed by your commitment to quality customer service. By being organized you can better service the customer. For instance, you will be able to find vital information more quickly, which will translate into speedier service for the customers." Such linkages may be difficult to execute but they reap great dividends.

Link specific behaviors to valued qualities and abilities. The employee who submits an insightful proposal that has anticipated numerous potential objections could be praised for an "excellent report." Such a comment might encourage future reports of this type. But more could be said: "Your report is remarkable. It shows a quality of thoroughness and insightfulness that we value in this organization." The manager reinforces a specific behavior (report writing), but, more important, highlights the quality of thoroughness and insightfulness. Linking the specific behavior to the character qualities encourages employees to not only continue writing quality reports but also to find other novel situations in which to exhibit the desired qualities. The charm of a character quality, like "thoroughness" and "insightfulness," lies in its ambiguity. It can be applied in so many different situations that even the wisest manager could not anticipate all the possible applications (see Figure 7.3). Such an approach brings to bear the naturally motivating creative instincts in people. It has the indelible mark of the human touch.

In fact, the most frequent problem with management's effort to praise employees lies in the level of specificity.[25] Every manager must be able to confidently answer this question: Can I prove my assessment? The problem

Speak	Dialogue	Commentar
MANAGER:	Hi Chris. Welcome. Please sit down.	
EMPLOYEE:	Thank you.	
MANAGER:	As you know, this is the regularly scheduled performance appraisal that I conduct with each employee. The purpose of this talk is to review your performance during the past year. Actually, there should be few surprises because I've tried to keep you informed throughout the year. You've read over my report, I assume, so I want to spend our time discussing some critical areas and answer any of your questions.	
EMPLOYEE:	Fine, that sounds good because I do have some questions.	
MANAGER:	I'd like to start with the positive areas. Let me just list your greatest strengths: 1. You seem to be able to handle the cash drawer without assistance or errors. 2. You have the ability to explain savings products effectively to customers. 3. Your general attitude toward the job is quite positive. In general, I'm impressed by your abilities after being here only nine months.	
EMPLOYEE:	Well thanks—I've really tried hard. I enjoy working here and that really helps. My co-workers are really a joy to work with—they make it easy.	
MANAGER:	Now I'd like to explore with you three areas of improvement. First, I've rated you average in organizational abilities. At times, you seem unorganized.	
EMPLOYEE:	Well, I just try to do so much—sometimes I don't take time to keep things organized. I mean, I try to keep my papers straight and stuff—but my priority is on customer service.	
MANAGER:	Oh, but I still think some improvement is needed here.	

Figure 7.2   Sample Appraisal Interview

(Continued)

169

Figure 7.2 (Continued)

Speaker	Dialogue	Commentary
EMPLOYEE:	I've always had this problem and frankly, it seems more important to serve customer needs.	
MANAGER:	The second area that I'd like to see improvement in is cross-selling. We set a goal of cross-selling seven IRA accounts. You actually sold five IRA accounts. I'd like to see that up to par next year. You know this is a high priority in the business.	
EMPLOYEE:	I know I've kind of failed in that area, but sometimes it's so hard—I feel kind of awkward mentioning it—I just try to be friendly. I don't want to offend the customer. I feel like I really do service the customer effectively.	
MANAGER:	Well, you do, but I'd still like to see more cross-selling. The third area is bringing in new customers. We set a goal of ten new customers—I have only five new customers credited to your efforts this year.	
EMPLOYEE:	You know that goal is practically impossible—all my friends are already customers, and I just don't know what to do.	
MANAGER:	I understand—this isn't really criticism. Overall, you're doing a fine job—I want to emphasize that! For only being here nine months, I'm impressed. Really!	
EMPLOYEE:	So you think I'm doing a good job!	
MANAGER:	Yes, basically, yes. You are making progress—I'm pleased. Do you have any questions?	
EMPLOYEE:	No, it's basically what I expected—I mean you always tell me I'm doing a good job. Thanks.	
MANAGER:	Well, there are some areas of improvement.	
EMPLOYEE:	Yes, I know, but basically, I'm doing a good job. I mean I like my job and the people I work with. Is that all?	
MANAGER:	Yes, I guess so, except I need you to sign this form.	

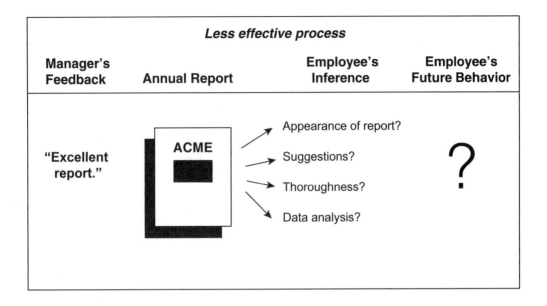

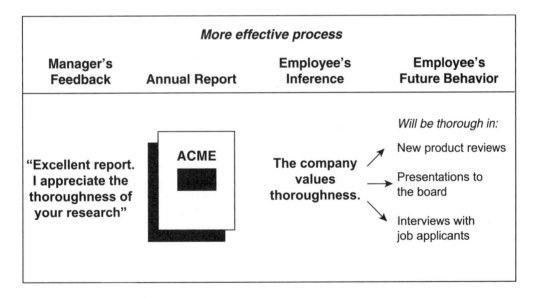

Figure 7.3   Linking Praise to Attributes

usually does not occur on the negative items but surprisingly with the positive issues. Typically praise runs along these lines: "Good job," "Way to go," or "At-a-boy." This kind of ambiguous praise tends to be more evaluative than descriptive. Descriptive praise tends to be more effective.[26] For example, instead of saying, "You really are effective with customers," a more useful and descriptive comment might be, "You really have an ability to communicate effectively with customers. The way you smile and ask pertinent questions shows your sensitivity to their needs." These remarks show that the manager pays attention to the employee's performance and recognizes the employee's unique contribution.

Criticize tactfully and develop a plan for improvement. Criticism needs to be handled with equal finesse. Successful critics must clearly state the problem while preserving the relationship.[27] Certainly it should be done in private, with an emphasis on behavioral corrections.[28] Managers should distinguish between personality traits, which are most often treated as non-changeable aspects of an individual, and character qualities that anyone can develop. Indeed, criticism of a specific behavioral problem could be couched in terms of acquiring a certain character quality. Students may be encouraged to spell correctly and use grammar properly by exhorting them to become more professional and show attentiveness to detail. Thus, specific writing skills are related to two qualities useful in a wide variety of settings.

Employees are naturally defensive if they feel their personality is under attack. Yet, if managers deeply ponder the matter, they will often recognize that some basic behaviors are at the root of performance problems. Someone, for instance, might remark: "You are a very stubborn individual." The insightful manager comments on a specific behavior:

> During meetings you need to listen more carefully to others' ideas and suggestions. You could look at people while they talk and even try to restate their opinion rather than your objections. I personally appreciate the way you stand by your convictions. This is admirable but this could be balanced with a greater sensitivity to others. It is important to be a person of conviction, but it is equally important to know when to use this quality. Now, let's discuss some action steps. . . .

The employee still might bristle at those comments, but they do focus on behavior while attempting to preserve the employee's self-esteem and set a path forward. These are extremely delicate situations as Buck Rodgers, who served as a marketing director at IBM, noted:

> I never thought it necessary to let others know that someone in my department didn't do his job properly. . . . I entered each of these private conversations with the assumption that both of us wanted to accomplish the same thing: perform our job with the highest degree of excellence possible. And, with a minimum of bruised feelings, correct our mistakes and get on with the job.[29]

Notice that Rodgers links his criticism to a larger positive context. He structures the criticism so that it's maximally informative and minimally evaluative.[30] Additionally, people react differently to criticism. Employees who are confident and have a high need for achievement react more positively. They may even actively seek negative feedback in order to improve their performance. Employees with lower self-esteem and achievement needs may become disheartened and discouraged.[31] Clearly, the wise leaders, like Buck Rodgers, adapt to these different contingencies.

Carefully consider how interpersonal needs influence the feedback process. Managers often avoid giving negative feedback unless severe problems have been recognized. Moreover, because they do not wish to appear judgmental, they frequently distort their feedback in a positive direction.[32] For example, in the appraisal interview in Figure 7.2, note how the manager says, "This isn't really criticism. . . . Overall you are doing a fine job." On the other hand, employees seek to maintain a positive self-esteem and typically see negative information as more positive than it actually is.[33] They often attribute problems to factors beyond their control. Moreover, poor performers actively try to short-circuit criticism by seeking out positive comments.[34] Note, for example, how in Figure 7.2, the employee implies that there is simply not enough time to be organized. In other words, Chris denies personal responsibility.

Poor performers may even build the excuses into their inquiries or ask leading questions about their performance.[35] Notice that Chris's final remarks end with a question that almost begs the manager for confirmation of an overly glowing assessment. Therefore, the manager and employee, by virtue of their predispositions, co-create a process in which each party inevitably draws seemingly reasonable but decidedly warped impressions. Employees "may hold positively inflated views of their organizational performance."[36] But managers frequently have an equally skewed view and feel that employees have a clear understanding of the areas of improvement, when in fact, they do not. Certainly, that happened in Figure 7.2 and the end result was that the employee's performance never improved. Wise managers are aware of these powerful forces at work in the appraisal interview. They seek to control the process so employees have an unclouded view of their performance, while carefully avoiding needless damage to self-esteem. Charles Ames, the former CEO of three companies including Uniroyal Goodrich Tire Company, summarized the manager's responsibility best:

> There is nothing kind about glossing over weaknesses that could be corrected if the individual were aware of them. Nor is there anything kind about deluding someone into thinking that he or she is doing well or has greater opportunities than is actually the case. Failure to be completely honest can easily hurt someone's chances of becoming an effective contributor. And it may even jeopardize the person's career. No manager has the right to do that. And if the manager can't get up the nerve or confidence to talk straight about this, that manager shouldn't remain a manager—because that person isn't.[37]

Finally, use past performance as a bridge to the future. While part of the feedback process should be dedicated to an evaluation of the past, managers ought to look forward as well. New contingencies brought on by the inevitable changes in the organization and the competitive environment can be discussed as a focal point for new standards and goals. Skillful managers learn to link employees' past accomplishments to future challenges. In the end, the employee, regardless of the course of the appraisal, should be offered the most basic of all human needs—hope.

While at a conference in Philadelphia, I noticed a building a few blocks from my hotel that was being torn down to make way for a new structure. A massive crane with a huge wrecking ball pounded into the building and slowly ripped apart the structure. For five days this enormous crush of iron on brick went on, and still, the small ten-story structure was only partially demolished. What a contrast to the instantaneous destruction of much larger buildings by the careful placement of dynamite charges at strategic points. In a matter of seconds, even a fifty-story building can be toppled. Unfortunately many managers thrash into their employees with salvo after salvo of criticism like this massive wrecking ball. They fail to notice employees' unique abilities and motivations, focus on personality characteristics, and do not link past accomplishments to future challenges. The result: The problems remain and the new structure cannot be built. A wise manager, like a demolition expert, discerns those strategic points and quickly removes the offending behaviors, building in the same spot a new foundation for personal and organizational growth

Conclusion

In the long run, the effective feedback system seeks to improve employee performance to increase organizational performance. As one thoughtful scholar put it, "Stripped of all jargon it is simply an attempt to think clearly about each person's performance and future prospects against a background of this total work situation."[38] Yet, a number of factors can inhibit the clarity of the manager's thinking (see Table 7.4).[39] It takes effort, insight, and dedication to overcome these barriers, but the rewards to managers, employees, and the organization alike are many-fold.

Several years ago we conducted a communication assessment in which the company scored considerably below-average on every feedback question. Upon arriving at the company to present the results, we walked past an isolated cluster of brown, brittle, and dying shrubbery in front of the company's office. At the time, I thought what a perfect symbol for this company's management philosophy! The company watered and cared for those bushes about as well as they gave feedback to their employees. The employees had no job descriptions, they had no idea how they were being evaluated, they were never praised, and appraisal reviews had not been conducted in years. The end results were predictable: low job satisfaction, poor motivation, uneven performance, and a host of other communication difficulties. Most companies are not in such severe shape. But every company could pay much closer attention to its feedback system. As any horticulturist knows, this can be done only day-by-day and with the utmost of care.

Table 7.4   Responses to Common Appraisal Biases

Bias	Explanation The propensity to . . .	Response
Leniency	give overly favorable ratings, even when actual performance lags.	Recognize that the appraisal should focus on employee development.
Severity	give overly negative ratings, even for effective performers.	Be aware of how interpersonal needs impact perceptions of feedback.
Halo	allow highly favorable ratings in one area to influence evaluations in other areas.	Keep accurate records of employee performance and review before providing feedback.
Similarity	give positive ratings to those who have similar personal characteristics as the appraiser (e.g., race, gender, age, etc.).	Distinguish between evaluating personality and performance.
Central tendency	give average ratings on performance items regardless of actual performance	Consider how the appraisal impacts employee motivation levels.
Primacy	allow first impressions to influence ratings.	Assign employee-specific preparations for the appraisal. Keep accurate records of employee performance and review before providing feedback.
Recency	allow most recent events to overly influence performance evaluation.	Assign employee-specific preparations for the appraisal. Keep accurate records of employee performance and review before providing feedback.

*Based on London, M. 2003. Job feedback: Giving, seeking, and using feedback for performance improvement. New Jersey: Lawrence Erlbaum Associates.

Notes

1. Downs, C. W., & Hazen, M. 1977. A factor analytic study of communication satisfaction. *Journal of Business Communication* 14:65–74.

2. Clampitt, P. G., & Downs, C. W. 1993. Employee perceptions of the relationship between communication productivity relationship: A field study. *Journal of Business Communication* 30:5–28.

3. Ibid.

4. Anderson, K. 2003. Tour de Lance. *Sports Illustrated*, 4 August:50–53, p. 53.

5. Bronowski, J. 1973. *The ascent of man.* Boston: Little, Brown, p. 116.

6. See, for example, Cusella, L. P. 1987. Feedback, motivation, and performance. In *Handbook of organizational communication,* edited by F. Jablin, L. Putnam, K. Roberts, & L. Porter (pp. 624–678). Newbury Park, CA: Sage.

7. Jablin, F. M. 2001. Organizational entry, assimilation, and disengagement/exit. In *The new handbook of organizational communication,* edited by F. M. Jablin & L. L. Putman (pp. 732–818). Thousand Oaks, CA: Sage.

8. Clampitt & Downs, op. cit.

9. Clampitt & Downs, op. cit.

10. Levinson, H. 1970. Management by whose objectives? *Harvard Business Review* 48 (4):125–134, p. 127.

11. Lopez, F. M. 1968. *Evaluating employee performance.* Chicago: Public Personnel Association.

12. Laird, A., & Clampitt, P. G. 1985. Effective performance appraisal: Viewpoints from managers. *Journal of Business Communication* 22 (3):49–57.

13. Mayfield, H. 1960. In defense of performance appraisal. *Harvard Business Review* 57:80–85.

14. Laird & Clampitt, op. cit.

15. McGregor, D. 1972. An uneasy look at performance appraisal. *Harvard Business Review* 50 (5): 133–138, p.134.

16. Mayfield, op. cit., p. 83.

17. Hanser, L. M., & Muchinsky, P. M. 1978. Work as an information environment. *Organizational Behavior and Human Performance* 21, 47–60.

18. DeNisi, A. S., & Kluger, A. N. 2000. Feedback effectiveness: Can 360-degree appraisals be improved? *Academy of Management Executive* 14 (1):129–138.

19. London, M. 2003. *Job feedback.* New Jersey: Lawrence Erlbaum Associates.

20. Ibid.

21. Peiperi, M. A. 2001. Getting 360-degree feedback right. *Harvard Business Review* 79 (1):142–149.

22. Martin, D., Bartol, K, & Kehoe, P. 2000. Legal ramifications of performance appraisal: The growing significance. *Public Personnel Management* 29 (3):379–406.

23. Churchill, W. S. 1931. *The world crisis.* New York: Scribner, pp. 688–689.

24. See, for example, Pinder, C. C. 1984. *Work motivation.* Glenview, IL: Scott, Foresman.

25. Larson, J. R., Jr. 1986. Supervisors' performance feedback to subordinates: The effect of performance valence and outcome dependence. *Organizational Behavior and Human Decision Processes* 37:391–408.

26. Downs, C. W., Johnson, K. M., & Barge, J. K. 1984. Communication feedback and task performance in organizations: A review of the literature. In *Organization communication abstracts,* edited by H. Greenbaum, R. Falcione, & S. Hellweg (pp. 13–47). Newbury Park, CA: Sage.

27. Tracy, K., VanDusen, D. & Robinson, S. 1987. "Good" and "bad" criticism: A descriptive analysis. *Journal of Communication* 37 (2):46–59, p. 46.

28. Arvey, R. D., & Ivancevich, J. M. 1980. Punishment in organizations: A review, propositions, and research suggestions. *Academy of Management Review* 5:123–132.

29. Rodgers, F. G. 1986. *The IBM way.* New York: Harper & Row, pp. 40–41.

30. Downs, C. W., Smeyak, G. P., & Martin, E. 1980. *Professional interviewing.* New York: Harper & Row.

31. McFarlin, D. B., & Blascovich, J. 1981. Effects of self-esteem and performance feedback on future affective preferences and cognitive expectations. *Journal of Personality and Social Psychology* 40 (3):521–531.

32. Fischer, C. D. 1979. Transmission of positive and negative feedback to subordinates: A laboratory investigation. *Journal of Applied Psychology* 64:533–540.

33. Ilgen, D. R., Fischer, C. D., & Taylor, M. S. 1979. Consequences of individual feedback on behavior in organizations. *Journal of Applied Psychology* 64:349–371.

34. Larson, J. R., Jr. 1989. The dynamic interplay between employees' feedback-seeking strategies and supervisors' delivery of performance feedback. *Academy of Management Review* 14 (3):408–422.

35. Ibid.

36. Cusella, op. cit., p. 653.

37. Ames, B. C. 1989. Straight talk from the new CEO. *Harvard Business Review* 67 (6):132–138, p. 138.

38. Mayfield, op. cit., p. 27.

39. London, M. 2003. *Job feedback: Giving, seeking, and using feedback for performance improvement*. New Jersey: Lawrence Erlbaum Associates.

8 Communicating Across Organizational Boundaries

I can hardly consider specialization, in itself, evil. On the other hand, I am thoroughly convinced that much of the evil of our times is related to specialization and that we desperately need to develop an attitude of suspicious caution toward it. I think we need to treat specialization with the same degree of distrust and safeguards that we bring to nuclear reactors.

M. Scott Peck

The final memo was terse but lacked the previous punch, like a boxer's weary jab at the end of a long bout: "You guys just can *not* get it right, the lid still leaks." What began as a routine and friendly exchange of memoranda between the research and marketing departments was ending more like a slugfest with the heavyweights trading insults as if they were punches. Marketing wanted a plastic lid for their new frosting mix. And the research department dutifully developed one that, quite frankly, they were proud of

Chapter 8: By the Numbers

10–20%
of all U.S. managers sent
abroad return early because
of job dissatisfaction or
difficulty adjusting to the
new country

65%
of organizations experience major
interdepartmental communication
problems

40%+
of cross-border strategic business
alliances between Central and
Eastern Europe fail

80%
of the world's electronic databases
and communication networks are
in English

46%
of companies are satisfied with
outsourcing arrangements

because it was both inexpensive to produce and structurally sound. So the new plastic lid was ceremoniously sent off to the marketing department to be tested on the cans of frosting mix. The research team was soon to be disappointed.

Two days later, the research team received memo one:

Good work guys! The lid looks great and is plenty sturdy, but it leaks! Our delicious white frosting turns brown after a few hours with the lid on it. There must be something in the lid that leaks out. Can you check it out?

The tone of the memorandum was pleasant enough but it was greeted with a mixture of puzzlement and disbelief. Despite their obvious predilections, the researchers tested and retested the lid. The results: negative. The lid did not, and indeed, *could not* leak. In due course, the research team drafted an equally magnanimous memorandum to the marketing department suggesting that something might be wrong with the frosting.

The second round was not long in starting. Suddenly "greats" became "terribles," "the lid" became "*your* lid" and the friendly tones were replaced with hostile ones. The researchers chose not to respond in kind but proceeded to conduct still more tests. Again, nothing. They sent an appropriate, though less congenial note, to marketing providing the "final" results of their tests. Unfortunately, marketing did not choose to respond with such restraint and a three-month battle ensued in which neither side demonstrated a great deal of wisdom or professionalism.

Skirmishes like this occur in countless organizations between an ever-changing variety of departments, divisions, and suppliers. Indeed, about 65% of the organizations we have surveyed had significant problems with interdepartmental communication. The trend toward greater job specialization, outsourcing, and globalization will only enhance the importance of effective boundary spanning. This chapter explores the nature of boundary spanning and concludes by providing strategies and tactics to address these issues. Incidentally, the mysterious "leaking lid" controversy was resolved. More on that later. A little hint, though: A key part of the message involved the use of the term "leaking."

The Nature of Boundaries

Humans are boundary creators, maintainers, and defenders. We create boundaries in our homes to separate activities, to provide privacy, and to foster ownership. Organizations create boundaries to separate functions, to develop expertise, and to generate efficiencies. Nations create boundaries— thereby separating people, cultivating pride, and perpetuating cultures. Boundaries may be drawn in a seemingly arbitrary manner but once the line has been legitimized, people define themselves in terms of their relationship to the line—on one side are kindred spirits, and on the other side are the "outsiders."

This "us versus them" mindset can be beneficial. Henry Ford must have instinctively known this. Before mass production, cars, like most products, were built one at a time. Henry Ford's production techniques exploited the advantages of boundaries by creating more rigid departmental lines in the factory. For example, using old technology, it took eighteen minutes to assemble a flywheel magneto, but by using the moving assembly line, the time was cut to five minutes. This change greatly affected production levels: In 1909 the company manufactured about fourteen thousand cars; by 1914 production rose to two hundred and thirty thousand per year.[1]

Obviously, tremendous benefits have been reaped through the use of mass production techniques. Efficiency has improved. Expertise has grown. Production has increased. And profits have soared. Yet, as with any change, there are certain benefits of the old order left by the wayside. Ironically, the production efficiency gained through simplicity and standardization decreased the efficiency of communication by creating complex networks. Throw into the mix that some divisions are located in separate countries, and the difficulty of the task increases exponentially. Think about a few of the potential boundary-spanning activities of today's manager:

- Working in cross-functional teams.
- Coordinating specifications with suppliers.
- Supervising units in different nations or cultures.
- Meeting with customers.
- Executing a joint operation with another department or division.
- Negotiating agreements with off-shore partners.

Boundaries inherently create communication challenges that effective managers need to understand and master. We turn to these issues next.

Potential Problems of Boundaries

Lack of coordination creates difficulties in dance studios as well as in organizations. In essence, boundary spanners coordinate the activities of those separated by the boundary. Failure to do so can spawn the kind of problems discussed next.

Investment Losses

How could an organization unwittingly vaporize a $125 million investment on Martian soil? NASA had to answer that very question about the Mars Climate Explorer spacecraft that was designed to conduct scientific experiments in the Martian atmosphere. After a 9 ½ -month journey to the red planet, the spacecraft unexpectedly crashed into the surface, destroying the data dreams of planetary researchers. The cause of the calamity was as simple as it was troubling:

> Lockheed-Martin, the company controlling the day-to-day operations of the spacecraft, was sending out data about the thrusters in Imperial units, miles, feet and pounds-force to mission control, while NASA's navigation team was assuming . . . that they were receiving their instructions in metric units. The difference between miles and kilometers was enough to send the craft 60 miles off course on a suicidal orbit into the Martian surface.[2]

The confusion over the measurement standards was the visible manifestation of a boundary-spanning failure.

Likewise, how could a business unwittingly relinquish a 100% market share to competitors? Answer: by not listening to the ideas of boundary spanners. When Procter & Gamble first introduced disposable diapers in Japan, it totally dominated the market. Managers from the Japanese subsidiary who actually produced the diaper made numerous suggestions to P & G about how to better serve the market. For instance, they suggested adjusting the size of the diaper to better fit Japanese babies. However, the company did not act on the recommendations; soon competitors moved in and seized market share. The result: P & G's market share dropped by 70%. This was one of the events that triggered an initiative to improve boundary spanning at the company.[3]

Customer Service Failures

Boundary-spanning failures can also engender customer dissatisfaction. In one analysis of an airline's communication networks, we found that customers would frequently call the reservations agents and ask about new fares, only to be informed that the fare did not exist. Upon further investigation we found that the marketing department would send out advertising about new rates to customers and the media. Yet, marketing belatedly informed the reservation agents of the changes, and in some cases, failed to inform them at all. Marketing perceived their primary function as communicating to the public; communicating to departments internally was a secondary responsibility. Clearly the department fulfilled their primary responsibility at the expense of the broader and more important concern: customer relations. For some very obvious reasons, the net result was that customers chose other airlines. Amazingly, marketing was bewildered as to why the company lost customers when they offered such low fares. Thus, the internal communication problems were reflected in the external image of the company.

Unmotivated Employees

"I just do what I'm told." A comment like this often signals a "silo" mentality where employees are only concerned with their own narrow departmental issues. They are unmotivated to span boundaries and seize opportunities to better meet organizational goals. Employees learn to cope with conflict, disconfirmation, and rejection by retreating to the confines of their silos. For example, at the airline previously discussed, one individual reported this intriguing incident:

> During the first part of February, the scheduling and information services departments spent several man-hours developing a computerized method to analyze aircraft seating capacities. When ready to implement the changes, we discovered that most of these changes had already been handled in a manual mode. Thus, all of our efforts were negated. One hand did not know what the other was doing.[4]

Such incidents demoralize and frustrate employees. In these organizations, workers learn to avoid questioning procedures and policies. They know better because the response is always the same: "That's company policy." Employees naturally respond by working to minimal standards and reason, "I can't see why we do things the way we do, so why try?"

Clearly many organizations unwittingly discourage boundary spanning, resulting in a poor working climate. But what happens when different units *must* work together? One creatively designed study answered this question by examining how employees tended to handle conflict during *intra*departmental as opposed to *inter*departmental conflicts.[5] The researchers found that conflicts between departments (silos) were highlighted by strategies that were more confrontational and controlling, which can lead to greater antagonism. In one sense, such expression might be useful if critical issues surfaced in the discussion. More often, such arguments strain relationships even further. As a result, the departments may take a myopic view of the problem in a win/lose frame of mind. While one department might "win," ultimately the organization, as a whole, loses.

Contributing Factors _____

A number of conditions tend to accentuate the inherent problems associated with organizational boundaries. The factors discussed next create even greater barriers, like adding a hedge of thorns to a fence already separating two homes.

Language Differences

Even today the haunting Biblical story about the Tower of Babel can provide insight.[6] The tale records that God wanted to ensure that his people did not dishonor him by building a monument to themselves:

> Now the whole world had one language and a common speech. . . . But the Lord came down to see the city and the tower that the men were building. The Lord said: "If as one people speaking the same language they have begun to do this, then nothing they plan to do will be impossible for them. Come, let us go down and confuse their language so they will not understand each other." So the Lord scattered them from there over all the earth, and they stopped the city.[7]

The instrument used to stop the building was not some divinely ordered thunderbolt or meteor shower or even a ghastly plague. Rather it was a singularly effective and powerful tool: compelling the people to speak different languages. Equally, though less deliberately, language dissimilarities prohibit modern organizations from effectively spanning boundaries.

Something always seems to be missing in the translation. Consider these purported English translations of critical messages in other lands:

- "Our wines leave you nothing to hope for." (on a menu in a Swiss restaurant)
- "We take your bags and send them in all directions." (in a Copenhagen airline office)
- "Teeth extracted by the latest Methodists." (in a Hong Kong dentist office)[8]

Translation problems may be humorous, but they also reveal something significant about the communicators. Namely, speakers of different languages often have different views of the world. Arabic, for example, has three thousand words for "camel" and is deeply influenced by the poetic style of the Koran. One scholar suggested that "because of the love of language, the Arab is swayed more by words than by ideas and more by ideas than by facts."[9] Even when communicators share a language, they may not share meanings. People in the United States, for instance, have a different understanding of the words "freedom" and "democracy" than do those in the one hundred or so other countries where English is widely spoken as an official, semi-official, or popular language. Indeed, George Bernard Shaw once quipped, "England and America are two countries separated by a common language."[10]

Experts of all kinds cultivate their own linguistic exclusivity. Accountants speak of debits, credits, liquidity, and yield. Computer programmers have their own vocabulary of bytes, bits, CPU, hardware, and software. They use different jargon, acronyms, and even describe the same things in different ways. The expert has more specific knowledge and makes more precise distinctions than the novice. "Horsebreeders have various names for breeds, sizes, and ages of horses; botanists have names for leaf shapes; interior decorators have names for shades of mauve; printers have many different names for different fonts, naturally enough."[11] In a literal sense, experts see things that non-experts do not see.

Purchasing agents face an unusual challenge in this respect. They are constantly ordering materials that have an almost infinite variety of peculiarities. One agent, for instance, received a memo from the engineering department requesting ten 3/4-inch screws because the 7/8-inch screws "didn't work." Sounds simple—or at least it did to the engineers. Now consider the purchasing agent who has to thumb through an assortment of catalogs, select a vendor, and answer these kinds of features: a) left or right twist; b) tolerance/strength; c) flat head, round head, or hex; d) length; e) type of alloy; f) designed for metal, wood, or plastic; and g) head type. The engineers in this particular company simply had no idea about the degree of specificity needed to order a seemingly "simple" item. To the engineers, a "screw" represented a single concept. To the purchasing department, a "screw" was a multidimensional concept.

Language conventions, jargon, acronyms, and specialized meanings for words typically facilitate effective and efficient communication within the community. The problems occur when trying to communicate to employees outside the community. Perhaps this Czech proverb best summarizes the challenge, "Learn a new language and get a new soul."

Culture

Cultural barriers on a macro and micro scale can also inhibit boundary spanning. Macro-cultural issues come into play when organizations communicate across national boundaries, such as international firms working with divisions in various countries, or a U.S. firm arranging to outsource its IT services to India. On the other hand, micro-cultural issues focus more on the unique corporate culture developed in particular units, such as in a finance or engineering department.

Intercultural communication scholars, who typically study macro-cultural issues, often compare cultures on twenty-two dimensions, such as orientation to nature, time, space, action, authority and community.[12] The four dimensions reviewed in Table 8.1 appear to be the most important and help explain the following situations:[13]

- Why do Westerners often grow uneasy with silences and conversational pauses when talking to managers from China, Japan, and Korea? Managers from these Asian countries value pithiness, succinctness, and understatement. Low-context cultures value explicitness, which may be perceived by high-context cultures as verbosity (high vs. low context).
- What do Vietnamese managers mean when they say, "It's complicated" or "It's not the right time" during an intense negotiation? They use these expressions to signal rejection of a proposal or plan. The culture values indirectness, which may be totally misunderstood by Americans[14] (direct vs. indirect orientation/meaning making).
- Why are Westerners often befuddled by the unenthusiastic reactions of Russians to long-term strategic planning? Most Russians are "actually not interested in planning and consider it useless" despite years of living in a "planned economy"[15] (short-term vs. long-term orientation).
- Why do employees in some countries provide "input" and those in others do not? Some cultures, such as Malaysia, Panama, and India, stress obedience to those in authority whereas Austria, Israel, and Denmark do not (high power vs. low power).

Table 8.1   Cultural Communication Dimensions

Dimension	Explanation	Example
High vs. low context	Meanings emerge from the situation (high) versus from the words (low)	High context: Japan, China, Korea Low context: United States, Germany, Nordic states
Direct vs. indirect	Meanings are explicit (direct) versus implied (indirect)	Direct: United States, Great Britain, Italy Indirect: Japan, China, Vietnam
Short-term vs. long-term	Orientation focuses on immediate results versus the long-term	Short-term: Pakistan, Nigeria, Philippines Long-term: China, Hong Kong, Taiwan
High power vs. low power	Great deference is shown to those in authority positions (high power) versus more collegial relations (low power)	High power: Malaysia, Panama, Mexico Low power: Austria, Israel, Ireland

Note: For more information on country rankings, see Hofstede, G. 2001. *Culture's Consequences: Comparing values, behaviors, institutions, and organizations across nations (2nd edition)*. Thousand Oaks, CA: Sage.

Learning the tendencies of different cultures on these dimensions can help facilitate communication. A note of caution: These are merely "sophisticated stereotypes" that vary from person-to-person in the culture. Clearly we need to modify our characterizations based on personal experiences.[16]

Similar concerns occur when dealing with micro-cultures. The accounting department, for instance, has different sensibilities, standards, and perceptions than the HR department. These cultural biases emerge from an amalgam of recruitment practices, professional training, and information sources. Problems occur when employees from one department assume that others will view an issue in a similar way. For instance, although the HR manager might find it perfectly acceptable to factor intuitions into a decision, the accounting professional might frown on such practices. Consequently, conflict, misinterpretations, misattributions, and strained relationships often emerge in these situations. Neither party recognizes that the problems are rooted in different cultural mindsets that encourage them to perceive and respond to situations differently. The difficulties are all the more befuddling when the factions ostensibly share a similar language and macro-culture. Such are the frustrations of assuming similarity rather than difference when spanning boundaries.

Location

Even in the age of high-tech communication, location may well create the subtlest barrier to boundary spanning because it subconsciously restricts natural communication impulses. Winston Churchill once said, "We shape our buildings, after that they shape us." Office design influences who has access to whom by creating barriers to some departments and bridges to others. In some fascinating research at MIT, Thomas Allen revealed that people more than ten meters apart have only an 8 to 9% probability of communicating at least once a week, versus a 25% chance at five meters[17] (See Figure 8.1). For example, the telemarketing department of a company was so physically separated from other departments that the telemarketing reps would not talk to other employees for weeks. Despite having a joint lunchroom, employees from different departments huddled around their individual tables. The telemarketing reps vividly characterized the situation: "There is zero communication between 'upstairs' and 'downstairs.' 'The Great Stairwell' separates us. We up here can't bother them downstairs."

For centuries, the Great Wall of China separated China physically, culturally, and intellectually, from the rest of the world. In much the same way, "The Great Stairwell" separated telemarketing from the other departments. The office design was sound for maximizing functionality within the departments, but the layout failed to consider some significant interpersonal communication issues. Such design decisions, whether intentional or not, unfolded into some rather disquieting implicit messages to employees and contributed to the difficulties between the departments.

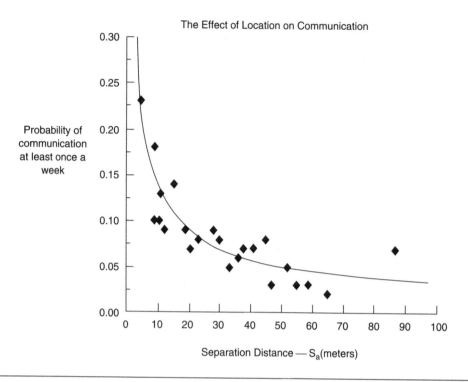

Figure 8.1

Structure of Rewards and Punishments

Generally, there are few direct rewards or punishments associated with communicating across boundaries. As a result, the communication may lack the urgency of other messages. Consider Pat, an engineer in a large manufacturing firm. He simply refused to share technical information with Sean, an engineering colleague in another department. Why? Because Pat felt that Sean would take credit for developing new, more efficient techniques. Only when Pat's boss asked for the requested information did Pat comply. Meanwhile, valuable time had been lost. Moreover, Pat was not even cautioned about his lack of collegiality. Even when the organization has a more positive communication climate, employees often view sharing information across divisions as a favor to a colleague. In many cases this leads to a dysfunctional pattern of information bartering.

The Arithmetic/Geometric Factor

When an organization *adds* departments, it *geometrically increases* the number of communication linkages. The implications of this are profound.

For instance, a company that has two departments has only one communication link between the departments. When the company adds another department, the communications linkages increase to three. Add a fourth department, and the linkages increase to six. Figure 8.2 shows the dramatic increase in linkages that occur when only one more department is added to the organization.

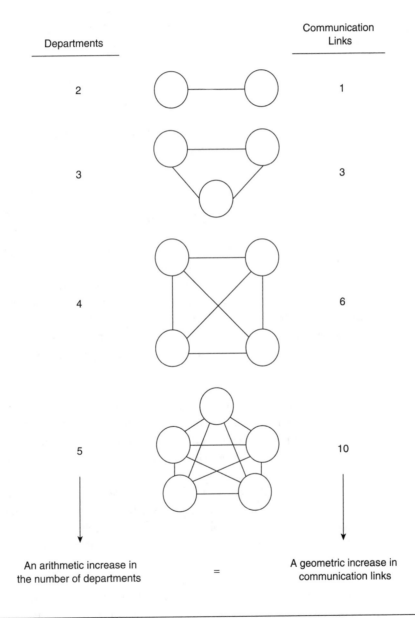

Departments		Communication Links
2		1
3		3
4		6
5		10

An arithmetic increase in the number of departments = A geometric increase in communication links

Figure 8.2   Relationship of Number of Departments and Communication Links

Many executives mistakenly see the addition of a single department as a small structural change, without recognizing the dramatic increase in linkages. Instead of just adding one more department to coordinate with, the company dramatically increases the number of linkages needed to coordinate their activities. How do executives respond to the unwieldy number of communication links? Some might set up rigid policies designed to control contact across boundaries; others might open up the system, like the free market, and let each department fend for itself. Information overload, office politics, and information bartering are often the results of this extreme. Thus, by failing to take into account the linkages factor, many top administrators unwittingly create structures that hinder effective boundary spanning.

What to Do?

Diagnosed problems are not solved problems. How can managers encourage more effective boundary spanning? Consider the strategies and related tactics reviewed in this section.

1. Select and Train the Right People

Boundary spanners require a very special skill set. They must be proficient at developing and maintaining relationships, skilled at seeking out information and persuading others, and comfortable with uncertainty and conflict.[18] As few people naturally possess all these skills, managers must select those employees who are willing and able to develop the skill set (see Table 8.2). Training employees, particularly those spanning national boundaries, requires a special orientation discussed in the following tactics.

Create awareness of one's personal culture. Employees who take an objective look at their own culture establish the basis for working with those in other cultures. Employees can become aware of their assumptions about time, human nature, and cause–effect relationships. Americans, for instance, learn how the customer service orientation of business sets in motion expectations about fast service and decision making. Further reflection reveals the complexity of the culture. After all, there are venues where deliberateness trumps speed, such as in the U.S. court system. As employees become aware of the assumptions and complexity of their own culture, they develop the analytical tools and emotional distance necessary to understand those on the other side of the boundary.

Focus on values and the communicative style of the other culture. Boundary spanners rarely acquire the innate sensibilities of those who actually live in the culture. Because cultures are too rich and complex to be easily comprehended, would-be boundary spanners need to develop cognitive shortcuts in

Table 8.2   Skills of Boundary Spanners

Skill	Rationale
Develop relationships	Interpersonal relationships are the gateway to information sharing and mutual understanding across boundaries.
Maintaining relationships	Boundary spanners must continually update others on important changes or new perspectives on problems.
Seeking information	Boundary spanners seek out information to meet the needs of the various groups they serve.
Persuading others	Boundary spanners need to convince various groups to change perspectives or behaviors in order to better coordinate their activities.
Managing uncertainty	Boundary spanners must often operate without clear plans or objectives. They must rely on their intuitions to guide their sense making.
Resolving conflict	Boundary spanners must often resolve disputes between various groups.

the form of generalizations that apply in *most,* but *not all,* situations. Studying the history of a culture can cultivate sensitivity to the underlying values. Examining communicative differences based on the four dimensions reviewed in Table 8.1 can help the boundary spanner properly interpret and make sense of conversations, rituals, and symbols.[19]

Developing such sensibilities encourages decision makers to develop the tolerance to modify even seemingly sacrosanct symbols. For instance, the pink Cadillac has been the trademark incentive for Mary Kay salespersons based in the United States. But that had to change when the company launched its doorbell campaign in Eastern Europe. In Poland the cosmetic superstar salespersons drive silver BMWs.[20] A note of caution: Even if two cultures share communicative styles and values, there can still be important differences.[21] For example, even though Poland and the United States have a similar orientation to time (short- versus long-term) they clearly have different automotive preferences.[22]

Foster an anthropological mindset. Think about how Margaret Mead studied the primitive youth of Samoa.[23] She immersed herself in the culture, assumed little, and observed before formulating and testing her hypotheses.[24] This same mindset should pervade the boundary spanner. Note that she did not try to understand every culture; she focused on one at a time. Managers cannot expect employees to successfully span every boundary; depth usually trumps breadth. Likewise, notice her methods for conducting the study. Two scholars with extensive experience in cross-cultural training summarize the method:

Approach learning another culture more like a scientist who holds conscious stereotypes and hypotheses in order to test them. One of the key differences between managers who were identified by their fellow MBA students as the "most internationally effective" and the "least internationally effective" is that the former changed their stereotypes of other nationalities as they interacted with them while the latter did not.[25]

In short, the anthropological viewpoint encourages boundary spanners to become skilled and efficient learners. In essence, they learn *how* to learn about another culture.

2. Implement Error Correction Processes

Most scientists are awestruck with the beauty and simplicity of the DNA replication process. The fidelity of this communicative process must be of the highest order. And it is. As one scholar put it, the "Quality control process, in which the pairing of bases is chemically proofread, keeps the error rate in DNA replications to only about one in ten billion."[26] Any scientist knows that error detection and correction are essential when transmitting information.[27] Likewise, boundary spanners should find mechanisms to check for errors that correct misperceptions and coordination problems. The first tactic discussed addresses the former issue, whereas the second focuses on the latter.

Use quizzes. One organization that was experiencing some rather dramatic turf wars asked a consultant for some help. The consultant assembled all the department heads and asked them to describe their core responsibilities. No problem. Then he inquired if there were any surprises in the meeting thus far. There were none. Then he asked, "How healthy are relationships between departments?" Silence. In one-on-one interviews, they would quickly reel off a dozen complaints about other departments, but in a group setting they conspired in their silence. At least they demonstrated they could work together—even if it was unintentional.

In a flash of insight, the consultant thought of a way to break through the silence. He asked all the department heads to write down five things everyone in the room should know about his or her unit. He then said to the assembled silent conspirators, "I'm going to put all these facts together into a questionnaire. How many of you are going to get 90% or better on this quiz?" Everyone's hand quickly shot up. The next week they took the thirty-item quiz. The result: their collective confidence was completely shattered. The average score was barely above 50%. This proved to be the crucial event that turned their silence into genuine dialogue about the turf wars. Interestingly, almost 90% of the items on the quiz dealt with how long it took to complete certain tasks. Amazingly, these basic facts had never been clearly communicated. In short, the quiz provided a much needed educational experience. Similar tactics can facilitate boundary spanning. For example, one company includes in every newsletter a ten-item true/false quiz highlighting facts about a particular department.

Track organizational processes. What would happen if you stapled yourself to a purchase order in your organization? From this vantage point, you might gain a deeper understanding of how boundary-spanning conflicts occur. In fact, several of Harvard Business School's finest proposed this very activity as a way to better serve customers, seize business opportunities, and improve organizational performance. Their research yielded the following conclusions:

> In field visits to eighteen different companies in vastly different industries, we invariably found a top marketing or administrative executive who would offer a simple, truncated—and inaccurate—description of the order flow. The people at the top couldn't see the details of their OMC (Order Management Cycle); the people deep within the organization saw only their own individual details. And when an order moved across departmental boundaries, from one function to another, it faded from sight; no one was responsible for it or the customer.[28]

My associates and I replicated their study in a number of organizations, reaching similar conclusions. But we added a twist. We used the results to improve boundary spanning by creating a dialogue with all those who helped construct the OMC diagram. Often the group realized that the procedure could be simplified by taking out steps. At other times, the group recognized that adding a particular piece of information could greatly speed up the process. In every case, the group gained a greater understanding of the entire process and the constraints of other departments.

3. Encourage Activities That Promote Shared Experiences and Common Goals

Effective boundary spanners build personal relationships with others. Relationships provide a means to resolve the vexing problems of role ambiguity and conflict that most boundary spanners experience. Role ambiguity often occurs because of the peculiar position of the boundary spanner. Consider the typical problems a union employee experiences when asked to become a manager in the unit in which she works. Her former colleagues wonder, "Is she one of them or one of us?" And her new managerial colleagues might ask the same question. Any boundary spanner must deal with issues like this because people find comfort in putting others in categories of "us" or "them." Yet, both the boundary spanner's utility and anxiety emerge from this precarious position. Researchers have clearly shown that creating relationships in the crucible of shared experiences can help ease these concerns.[29]

Bruce Moorhouse, Manager of Corporate Communications at 3M, clearly articulated the strategic challenge:

> People think either holistically (simultaneous thinking) or in a linear way (sequential thinking). The challenge for us as leaders is to get orga-nizations that are full of sequential thinkers to think more holistically across departments and divisions. We want them to ask, "What is best for the organization as a whole?" not "What is best for me, or my department, or my division?"[30]

Common goals or values provide a flag that all departments can rally around, thus transcending organizational boundaries. Customer service often fits the bill. Competitors can also become a source of inspiration, as in, "At Avis, we try harder." Turf battles usually occur because departments fight over scarce resources, prestige, and any number of other factors. But who really wins? Usually executives must raise the flag and bring together the troops. Then the departments can fight battles worth winning.

On a tactical level, leaders should consider the ideas discussed in the cor-porate culture chapter. In addition, they might consider the following tools.

Hold company-wide seminars. A company-wide seminar that involves first-line employees as well as top management personnel can provide a rich and unique opportunity to highlight a unifying theme for employees from any department or venue. Many topics are of interest to personnel at all levels of the organization, such as conflict resolution or basic communication skills. Skillful seminar leaders can help bring out the perspectives of the various departments, organizational levels, and various cultures in such a way that everyone develops greater sensitivity to the big picture. If the seminar involves some sort of case study or group project, the wise seminar leader would encourage people to work together who would normally not get the opportunity to do so.

For instance, a basic communication skills workshop was conducted for all personnel at a financial institution. In each session there were employees from various departments, representing tellers as well as top-level man-agers. This was one of the few opportunities for employees from across the organization to get together. One employee reported that such seminars allow time to develop a "lingo link" that helps bridge departmental barri-ers. Although not one of the major objectives, a pleasant benefit of the seminar was that top management became aware of a particular issue that tellers were facing on a day-to-day basis. Changes were made that may not have been considered had the tellers' concerns been forwarded through normal channels. Additionally, management, by their presence, was subtly communicating that they valued training of this type and that they were still learning, right along with their employees.

Host brainstorming sessions. Many times other units can provide useful insights into difficulties that another department or division experiences.

Setting up sessions between divisions in which each unit shares its problems can be a creative experience. The agenda need not be formal. For instance, the marketing department of a plastics research firm noted that the plastic carriers used to transport cats and dogs on airplanes often chipped and broke on the corners. They recognized the marketing possibilities and mentioned this to the research department in a brainstorming session. Subsequently, they designed a new and elegantly simple animal carrier that created quite a success in the marketplace. Normally, project ideas did not surface in this manner. In this case, the communication pattern was altered—and with convincing results. Such meetings also spur commitment to common goals shared by every division.

Develop links between role counterparts. Employees face a special challenge when they are asked to build an alliance with another organization or coordinate plans with an overseas unit. Encouraging communication between role counterparts in the other organization or division (i.e., lawyers to lawyers, production managers to production managers) can facilitate developing relationships across these boundaries. These kinds of relationships are more easily nurtured because these employees are more likely to have similar conceptual models, professional sensibilities, and role expectations. These similarities can be used as a bridge to build personal relationships, understanding, and trust. As a result, one study concluded that this "Web of interpersonal connections expedites communication, conflict resolution, and learning."[31]

Consider the boundary-spanning problems between physicians and medical insurers. Newspaper headlines routinely exploit tales of greed and denial of service. The core problem often revolves around who has the patient's best interest in mind. In many cases, when a physician requests a test or procedure that seemingly violates the insurance provider's protocol, the physician negotiates with a faceless regulation "enforcer" who has limited medical training. But not at Blue Cross of California Worker's Compensation Managed Care Services. As medical director, Dr. Theodore Blatt engineered a successful boundary-spanning initiative that linked role counterparts. Thus, the practicing physician negotiates with a physician representing the insurance company to jointly work out an agreement. The result: a negotiated alternative treatment plan that provides a basis for a more productive working relationship built on mutual respect.[32]

Elevate the voices of boundary spanners. Expatriates, non-citizens working in a foreign country, are by definition, boundary spanners. Theoretically they should be the perfect bridge between two national cultures. In practice, though, few decision makers actually use the bridge and the chasm remains. Two scholars explained the problem:

> Even well-respected expatriates who have been sent from the home country can become marginalized by their physical absence from the corporate office. Ironically, people on the margins of organizations

sometimes have a more accurate view of events and circumstances than central decision makers . . . An organizational norm becomes established that discourages either seeking information from the marginal members, or from granting much attention when such people volunteer information.[33]

Norms like this drove Toyota to resist the recommendations of U.S. managers to manufacture an eight-cylinder pickup truck. Company President Fujio Cho acknowledged the missed opportunity and has made efforts to break the grip of the culturally driven conventions.[34]

Of course, it helps immensely when senior leaders elevate the voices of the boundary spanners. But furthers steps are needed. In particular, the norms can be re-shaped by developing a critical mass of boundary spanners, who have developed special sensitivity to the critical role of "outsider" knowledge. Some companies create this climate by instituting job rotation. This year's production manager was the personnel manager three years ago, and this year's marketing manager was the previous production manager. And so it goes. "At Canon, critical people move regularly between the camera business and the copier business and between the copier business and the professional optical-products business."[35] As a result, the company strategically brings together organizational knowledge in order to develop or enhance products and services.[36] This kind of program provides managers and employees with an amazing amount of detailed knowledge about functions of departments and the company as a whole. Beyond sensitivity, managers develop a commitment to the company instead of to their specialty. It may seem that employees in rotated jobs might experience more ambiguity about their roles than those who do not rotate, but researchers found exactly the opposite.[37] Perhaps, by knowing more about the big picture, employees know more about their specific role in the organization. More important, the program breaks tacit, but powerful, norms that marginalize one group in favor of another.

Encourage co-authoring of articles. At a chemical research firm, a member of the marketing division co-authored an article with the researcher who developed the product. The article was published in a trade journal. Both individuals reported a renewed respect for the other's expertise. Furthermore, the marketing department now had an important advocate within the research department who was able to explain a marketing perspective. The article was the tangible result, but the intangible and more lasting outcome was the influential relationship the process cultivated.

Show-and-tell. Most school children eagerly look forward to show-and-tell day. What new electrical gizmo will Johnny bring to class? Will Martha's cat really dance? Many organizations would do well in reviving this tradition. Recall the plastic lid case at the beginning of this chapter. After the research department was thoroughly disgusted with marketing and vice versa, they decided to have one final bout. Each brought their respective documents to show how the other side was wrong and misguided. Predictably, the arguments that had hitherto been expressed in other forums were vented in the face-to-face encounter. At one point, someone from marketing pulled out a can of frosting, removed the vacuum-sealed aluminum covering, and placed the plastic lid on the can. The meeting concluded indecisively with both sides claiming victory and neither admitting defeat.

As often occurs, messages unpersuasively transmitted with statistics and arguments can be vividly and convincingly communicated with one simple demonstration. By happenstance, the research department took the can of frosting back to the office. Lo and behold—it turned brown overnight. The very next day, research had the answer. What happened was that the lid was porous to air molecules and the air had interacted with the frosting, causing it to discolor. Research was right; the lid did not "leak." Marketing was right; there was a problem with the lid and frosting. Yet, both were wrong. Neither department attacked the problem in the most effective manner. One simple but powerful demonstration could have resolved the difficulty without needless strife, frustration, and wasted time. So it was the grade school diversion of show-and-tell that stopped the adults from arguing like little children.

4. Integrate Boundary Spanning Into the Structure of the Organization

For over twenty-five years, Dr. Barry Usow practiced medicine, treating thousands of patients on a variety of urological matters. Like most physicians, he practiced medicine on a case-by-case basis, prescribing medicine for some patients, and performing surgery on others. Instinctively he approached his new job as Chief of Staff at St. Luke's Hospital in the same way. An organizational problem would arise and he would address it. Another conflict would occur and he would deal with it. Soon he learned that the managerial world was not at all like the medical world. He revealed:

> You can't make much progress working case-by-case; you can't schedule hospital problems like patient visits. There would be an emergency every minute of the day. I eventually surmised that by setting up mission-driven committees staffed with the right people, different departments naturally learned to work together more effectively. My role was to make sure that the right organizational structure and processes were in place, not to try to resolve every problem.[38]

In short, healing rifts across boundaries usually requires patience and the right environment, not radical surgery. Of course, strategic clarity does not guarantee tactical competence. So, the effective manager considers which of the following tactics best fit the situation and can be successfully implemented.

Build boundary spanning into job descriptions. Few organizations have boundary spanning built into job descriptions. Honda is one exception. In their Maryville, Ohio plant, there are only two job classifications: assembly and maintenance. Honda workers perform many different tasks, which is inconceivable in other auto factories that have up to one hundred classifications.[39] This approach permeates everything Honda does. Job descriptions are left purposely vague:

> My boss gave me the best advice I've ever received. During my first week, I commented on how difficult it was for me to understand what my actual job was. He looked at me silently for a few seconds and then said in a low voice, "Your job is everything." That was it! Not another word and he walked away. It took me a while to realize what he meant and how right on target he was.[40]

Such job descriptions may induce some degree of anxiety, but they are unlikely to create departmental blinders. Typically, job descriptions are narrowly confined to departmental responsibilities, not corporate-wide ones. In sum, job descriptions may send the clearest message to employees about the organization's commitment to effective boundary spanning.

Support job switching and job shadowing. In some situations, temporary job switches or job shadowing can cultivate meaningful relationships. The basic premise is that employees from various departments switch jobs for several days to experience and understand another person's job. Or they follow and observe a fellow worker during the workday. Then employees can see first-hand how their actions impact another department. For instance, an industrial laundry experienced considerable tension between the plant workers who cleaned customers' linens and loaded them onto the trucks, and those who delivered the clean laundry to clients. Management stepped in to solve the ongoing conflict of getting the plant workers to load the trucks for efficient delivery. Instead of issuing an edict demanding better cooperation, they decided to institute a job-shadowing program. In particular, they asked plant workers to ride along with the drivers who delivered the linens to customers. After only five of the sixty plant workers participated in the program, some dramatic changes occurred. In fact, the shadowers emerged as advocates for the drivers and the tension between the departments slowly dissipated. Amazingly, without any explicit appeal, the plant workers started arranging the linens in the trucks in way to make it easier for the drivers to do their job. The power of such quick and vivid first-hand experiences can replace hundreds of rules, exhortations, reports, and countless hours of training.

Use cross-functional teams. When members of a closely knit departmental team put off communicating with the rest of the organization, they prevent others from understanding the design principles that guide their decision making. Cross-functional teams try to circumvent this natural organizational problem by bringing together people from different departments to manage a project. Researchers have found that these teams can dramatically cut costs, decrease product development time, and get products or services to the marketplace sooner than their competitors.[41] Cross-functional teams also have been used successfully in a wide variety of other situations ranging from purchasing computers to resolving factory problems.[42]

A note of caution: Cross-functional teams are not a panacea; they require special leaders with superb interpersonal communication skills. Diverse work groups tend to experience greater conflict, higher turnover, elevated stress levels, more communication problems, less trust, lower cohesion, and less job satisfaction.[43] Overcoming these tendencies requires special effort and training. Finding and exploiting points of similarity between group members can provide the basis for cultivating useful interpersonal relationships and trust that can bridge other gaps.[44] For example, leaders can highlight similarities in age, hobbies, or tenure with the company. These activities may not seem vital to the task at hand but effective managers know that interpersonal relationships provide the cohesiveness necessary to accomplish cross-functional goals.

Redesign the physical environment. Whether intentionally or unintentionally, office design fosters certain communication events and discourages others. The telemarketing company that had some interdepartmental communication problems (aided and abetted by the "Great Stairwell"), could not take out the stairwell or change the physical environment. Yet there was one saving grace: All employees ate in the same lunchroom. But, even here the office design conspired in the downfall. The lunchroom had twenty small round tables that sat four or five people each. Guess who sat with whom? The telemarketing reps sat with telemarketing reps; the marketing personnel sat with marketing personnel; upstairs employees sat with upstairs employees; and downstairs employees sat with downstairs employees. The "Great Stairwell" was still intact even in a common lunchroom. Solution: put in longer tables, like long picnic benches, and stagger lunch hours so employees would have to eat lunch with people in other departments. Informing the employees about the purpose of this change, accompanied with the development of a strong communication policy, proved successful.

The CEO of Viant, Bob Gett, also believes in the power of architecture. When competing against the likes of McKinsey and Andersen Consulting, his company needs every advantage it can get. "Gett believes that up to 50% of breakthroughs on projects—'bursts of brilliance'—occur when people run into one another and begin talking."[45] What to do? Viant's offices were designed to create "knowledge accidents," those wonderful times when experts bump into one another, solving a critical problem in some novel way. But "accidents don't just happen"; you can engineer them by minimizing walls, eliminating offices, and creating handy conference rooms for those spur-of-the-moment meetings. Through these efforts and others, Gett has created one of the hottest, most integrated, and most successful consulting businesses in the world.

Incorporate parallel development cycles. Traditionally, departmental relations were set up to run like a relay race—one department finishes its job and

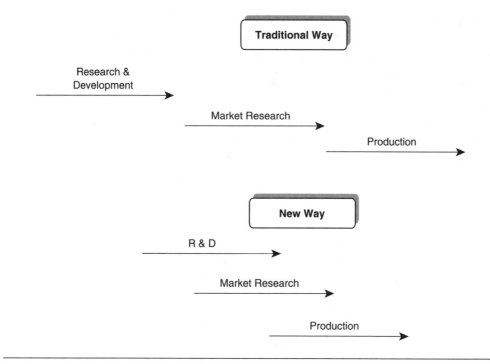

Figure 8.3   Ways of Organizing Work Processes

hands off the project to the next group. If there were problems, the race would start all over again at the beginning of the process (see Figure 8.3). More recently, innovative companies like Toyota and Microsoft have set up concurrent or parallel processes.[46] For instance, the marketing and engineering departments might work on a project at roughly the same time.[47] Or different design teams might work concurrently on different parts of a major software project such as Microsoft Word.

The benefits of this approach are more rapid innovation, greater flexibility in product designs, and an improved ability to quickly respond to marketplace changes. Making this process work requires some special communication plans. Microsoft uses what has been aptly named the "synch-and-stabilize" strategy:

> The essence is simple: Continually synchronize what people are doing as individuals and as members of teams working in parallel on different features, and periodically *stabilize* the evolving product features in increments as a project proceeds, rather than once at the end of a project. Microsoft people refer to their techniques variously as the "milestones," "daily build," "nightly build," or "zero-defect" process. The term "build" refers to the act of putting together or "integrating" partially completed or finished pieces of a software product during the development process to see what functions work or what problems exist. . . . [48]

These routine communication cycles between teams or departments foster solid relationships. The speed of the feedback cycles helps ensure that misunderstandings and incompatible assumptions are quickly discovered. Naturally, daily conflicts will occasionally emerge from such a process. However, such conflict beats starting over an entire project because departments either infrequently or inadequately communicated. In short, the company wins the race to the consumer by eliminating the hand-offs altogether; everyone arrives at the finish-line at approximately the same time.

Conclusion

Most organizations, to some degree, have difficulties with boundary spanning that can be resolved by the strategies and tactics in Table 8.3. Unfortunately, the problem is frequently overlooked and, even when recognized, often the symptoms are treated instead of the causes. To a large extent the problems are unavoidable in business because of the penchant for rigid segmentation. Decreasing conflict, improving performance, and seizing opportunities are compelling reasons for taking active measures to boundary spanning. Yet, one question remains: Are there any dangers in encouraging boundary spanning? Yes. An overly integrated organization may increase uncertainty and slow decision making. Frankly, the benefits outweigh these potential problems.

Table 8.3   Summary of Boundary-Spanning Strategies and Tactics

Strategy	Tactics
Select and train the right people.	• Create awareness of one's personal culture • Focus on values and the communicative style of the other culture • Foster an anthropological mindset
Implement error-correction processes	• Use quizzes • Track organizational processes
Encourage activities that promote shared experiences and common goals	• Hold company-wide seminars • Host brainstorming sessions • Develop links between role counterparts • Elevate the voices of boundary spanners • Encourage co-authoring of articles • Show-and-tell
Integrate boundary spanning into the structure of the organization	• Build boundary spanning into job descriptions • Support job switching and job shadowing • Use cross-functional teams • Redesign the physical environment • Incorporate parallel development cycles

In a sense, communicating across boundaries resembles taking a voyage into an unknown land. Daniel Boorstin in his magnum opus, *The Discoverers,* writes passionately about the real goal of the "discoverers":

> The ability to come home again was essential if a people were to enrich, embellish, and enlighten themselves from far-off places . . . Getting there was not enough. The internourishment of the peoples of the earth required the ability to get back, to return to the voyaging source, and transform the stay-at-homes by the commodities and the knowledge that the voyagers had found over there.[49]

Likewise, the boundary spanner seeks to enrich, embellish, and enlighten the lives of individuals throughout the company. The frontier these days is not geographical, but rather technical, informational, and managerial. Yet a trek into another's cognitive landscape, like any other journey into an unknown land, often proves unsettling, baffling, and thrilling.

Notes

1. 1999. The businessman of the century. *Fortune,* 22 November:111.

2. Barrow, J. D. 2002. *The constants of nature.* New York: Pantheon Books, p. 6. Ouchi, W. 1981. *Theory Z.* Reading, MA: Addison-Wesley, p. 199.

3. Taylor, S., & Osland, J. S. 2003. The impact of intercultural communication on global organizational learning. In *Handbook of organizational learning and knowledge management,* edited by M. Easterby-Smith & M. A. Lyles (pp. 212–232). Malden, MA: Blackwell Publishing, p. 226.

4. 1988. Personal and confidential communication.

5. Putnam, L. L., & Wilson, C. E. 1982. Communicative strategies in organizational conflicts: Reliability and validity of a measurement scale. In *Communication yearbook 6,* edited by M. Burgoon (pp. 629–673). Beverly Hills, CA: Sage.

6. In Hebrew, the word "Babel" sounds like the word for confused.

7. 1978. *Holy bible: New international version.* Grand Rapids, MI: Zondervan Bible Publishers.

8. www.transperfect.com/tp/eng/badxlate.html.

9. Ibid., p. 154.

10. Shaw, G. B. Find at www.miketodd.net/encyc/lingo.htm under "Inside the American Language" tab.

11. Pullum, G. K. 1991. *The great Eskimo vocabulary hoax and other irreverent essays on the study of language.* Chicago: The University of Chicago Press, p. 165.

12. Osland, J. S., & Bird, A. 2000. Beyond sophisticated stereotyping: Cultural sensemaking in context. *Academy of Management Executive* 14 (1):65–79, p. 66. See also, Stohl, C. 2001. Globalizing organizational communication. In *The new handbook of organizational communication,* edited by F. M. Jablin, & L. L. Putman (pp. 323–375). Thousand Oaks, CA: Sage.

13. Taylor, S., & Osland, J. S. 2003. The impact of intercultural communication on global organizational learning. In *Handbook of organizational learning and knowledge management,* edited by M. Easterby-Smith & M. A. Lyles (pp. 212–232). Malden, MA: Blackwell Publishing, p. 220.

14. Borton, L. 2000. Working in a Vietnamese voice. *Academy of Management Executive* 14 (4):20–29, p. 25.

15. Michailova, S. 2000. Contrasts in culture: Russian and Western perspectives on organizational change. *Academy of Management Executive* 14 (4):99–112, p. 107.

16. Osland & Bird, op. cit., p. 67.

17. Allen, T. J. 1967. Communication in the research and development laboratory. *Technology Review,* October–November. See also, Ornstein, S. 1989. The hidden influences of office design. *Academy of Management Executive* 3 (2):144–147.

18. Druskat, V. U., & Wheeler, J. V. 2003. Managing from the boundary: The effective leadership of self-managing work teams. *Academy of Management Journal* 46 (4):435–457. See also, Finet, D. 1993. Effects of boundary spanning communication on the sociopolitical delegitimation of an organization. *Management Communication Quarterly* 7 (1):36–66.

19. Osland & Bird, op. cit.

20. Brown, H. 2003. The eastern front. *Forbes,* 27 October:60.

21. Zaidman, N. 2001. Cultural codes and language strategies in business communication: Interactions between Israeli and Indian businesspeople. *Management Communication Quarterly* 14 (3):408–441.

22. Hofstede, G. 2001. *Culture's Consequences: Comparing values, behaviors, institutions, and organizations across nations (2nd edition).* Thousand Oaks, CA: Sage.

23. Mead, M. 2001. *Coming of age in Samoa: A psychological study of primitive youth for western civilization.* New York: Perennial.

24. Bateson, M. C. 2001. *With a daughter's eye: A memoir of Margaret Mead and Gregory Bateson.* New York: Harperperenntial Library.

25. Osland & Bird, op. cit., p. 75.

26. Dozier, R. W., 1992. *Codes of evolution: The synaptic language revealing the secrets of matter, life, and thought.* New York: Crown Publishers, p. 77.

27. Mezard, M. 2003. Passing messages between disciplines. *Science,* 19 September:1685.

28. Shapiro, B. P., Rangan, V. K., & Sviokla, J. J. 1992. Staple yourself to an order. *Harvard Business Review* 70 (4):113–122, p. 115.

29. Nygaard, A., & Dahlstrom, R. 2002. Role stress and effectiveness in horizontal alliances. *Journal of Marketing* 66 (2):61–82.

30. Moorhouse, B. 2000. Personal communication. January 12.

31. Hutt, M. D., Stafford, E. R., Walker, B. A., & Reingen, P. H. 2000. Case study: Defining the social network of a strategic alliance. *Sloan Management Review* 41 (2):51–62, p. 59.

32. Blatt, T. 2003. Personal communication. November 23.

33. Taylor & Osland, op. cit., p. 218. See also, Salk, J. E., & Simonin, B. L. 2003. Beyond alliances: Towards a meta-theory of collaborative learning. In *Handbook of organizational learning and knowledge management,* edited by M. Easterby-Smith & M. A. Lyles (pp. 253–277). Malden, MA: Blackwell Publishing.

34. Bremner, B., & Dawson, C. 2003. Can anything stop Toyota? *Business Week,* 17 November:114–122.

35. Prahalad, C. K., & Hamel, G. 1990. The core competence of the corporation. *Harvard Business Review* 90 (3):79–93, p. 91.

36. Hamel, G. & Prahalad, C. K. 1994. *Competing for the future.* Boston: Harvard Business School Press.

37. Keller, R. T., & Holland, W. E. 1981. Job change: A naturally occurring field experiment. *Human Relations* 34 (12):1053–1067.

38. Usow, B. 2000. Personal communication. January 15.

39. Koepp, S. 1986. Honda in a hurry. *Time,* 8 September:48–49.

40. Shook, R. L. 1988. *Honda.* New York: Prentice Hall Press, p. 129.

41. Maccoby, M. 1999. Building cross-functional capability: What it really takes. *Research Technology Management* 42 (3):56–58; Jassawalla, A. R., & Sashittal, H. C. 1999. Building collaborative cross-functional new product teams. *The Academy of Management Executive* 13 (3):50–63.

42. Avery, S. 1998. Purchasing leads desktop PC buy team to success. *Purchasing* 125 (7):104; Bernhardt, G. 1999. Goals, teams and letting go. *Textile World* 149 (4):13.

43. Ayok, O., Hartel, C., Fisher, G., & Fujimoto, Y. 2004. Communication competence in cross-cultural business interactions. In *Key issues in organizational communication,* edited by D. Tourish & W. Hargie (pp. 157–171). London: Routledge.

44. Keller, R. T. 2001. Cross-functional project groups in research and new product development: Diversity, communications, job stress, and outcomes. *The Academy of Management Journal* 44 (3):547–556.

45. Welles, E. 1999. Mind gains. *Inc.,* December:112–124, p. 116.

46. Sobek, D. K., Ward, A. C., & Liker, J. K. 1999. Toyota's principles of set-based concurrent engineering. *Sloan Management Review* 40 (2):67–84.

47. Iansiti, M., & MacCormack, A. 1997. Developing products on internet time. *Harvard Business Review* 75 (5):108–117.

48. Cusumano, M. A. 1997. How Microsoft makes large teams work like small teams. *Sloan Management Review* 39 (1):9–20, p. 11.

49. Boorstin, D. 1983. *The discoverers.* New York: Random House, p. 158.

9

Communicating About Change

. . . There is nothing more difficult to carry out, nor more doubtful of success, nor more dangerous to handle, than to initiate a new order of things. For the reformer has enemies in all those who profit from the old order, and only lukewarm defenders in all those who would profit from the new order, this luke warmness arising partly from the incredibility of anything new until they have had actual experience of it.

Machiavelli

Failure is never fatal, but failure to change might be.

John Wooden

Most organizations are far more adept at evaluating their financial position than they are at measuring the effectiveness of their change efforts. Perhaps executives find it easier to manage budgets and measure rates of return than they do to manage and evaluate the rate and degree of acceptance of a change effort. Regardless of the reason, this is an area that is ripe with opportunities for improvement.

Take your pick of managerial buzzwords: empowerment, lean manufacturing, reengineering, Six-Sigma, or e-commerce. Each notion implies a change and requires a major communication effort. Employees do not just accept an idea because it sounds progressive. For example, an underlying assumption of empowerment is that employees want to be empowered. Yet, we have interviewed numerous employees who freely admit that they would prefer to be told exactly what to do. Often major organizational changes require employees to take on new or different duties. How are they convinced to do so? In short, regardless of the organization's motive for implementing change, leaders need to properly communicate this motive. Ironically, almost all the founders of these movements recognize the importance of communication but few develop a systematic communication plan.

Approaches to Change

Chapter 9: By the Numbers

80–90%
of a change leader's time is devoted to planning communication tactics vs. strategy

50%
of senior managers have experienced major business changes in the past 5 years

4%
of senior managers claim they are "very well" prepared for changes in the next decade

#1
ranked characteristic of top employers in the biotechnology and pharmaceutical industry is "top leadership makes changes needed to keep organization on track"

52%
of employees think their colleagues are overwhelmed by the degree of change in the organization

All organizations, either explicitly or implicitly, have an orientation to change that defines for employees who can suggest, institute, and act on a new idea. Three typical patterns emerge: top-down, bottom-up, and integrative.

Top-Down

Traditionally top management assesses the need for change and dictates implementation through the chain of command. Arrow managers take this approach. The assumption is that those in leadership positions are in a better position to recognize the need for change, to know what needs to be changed, and to know how the change should be implemented.

Some organizations, out of necessity, adopt this approach because of a turbulent business environment or rapidly changing conditions. For example, after the tragedy of September 11, President Bush and leaders of Congress reorganized and realigned various government agencies to form the Office of Homeland Security. Change may also be instigated at the top when a CEO or a manager has a bright, new vision of where the organization can be in the future. Former Secretary of State, Henry Kissinger, perceptively wrote on statesmanship:

A nation and its leaders must choose between moral certainty coupled with exorbitant risk, and the willingness to act on unprovable assumptions to deal with challenges when they are manageable. I favor the latter course. . . . The statesman's duty is to bridge the gap between his nation's experience and his vision. . . . The qualities that distinguish a great statesman are prescience and courage, not analytical intelligence. He must have a conception of the future and the courage to move toward it while it is still shrouded to most of his compatriots.[1]

Likewise, some prescient executives see beyond the sights of the colleagues and predict with astonishing regularity the future trends while leading the company in that direction. A.P. Giannini of Bank of America was such a man. As the corporate founder, he was one of the first to introduce advertising by banks, bankcards, and a host of other novel ideas. By leading the way, visionaries ensure the organization has a stake in the future.

Yet, an overly zealous top-down style can be problematic. It may stifle the innovative spirit of employees and at times, "visionary leadership" can go awry. For example, researchers have found that less than 50% of mergers and acquisitions actually end up adding value as intended.[2] Visions do not always translate into reality; they may be mere delusions.

Bottom-Up

With the bottom-up orientation, ideas for changes and innovations percolate up through the organizational hierarchy.[3] Employees are encouraged to have input into changes and methods of implementation. This approach assumes that employees are in the best position to suggest changes. Leaders who use this approach often find it highly motivating because employees who participate in the decision-making process are more likely to wholeheartedly accept, understand, and implement the change. Circuit managers favor this approach.

Advocates of this approach recognize that lucrative opportunities may be lost when employee ideas are ignored. A kind of collective blindness can occur with an excessively top-down orientation. Ralph Lauren, for example, tried for years to sell his superiors and colleagues on his unique fashion concept. He failed. But he struck out on his own, becoming one of the most successful retailers in the world. Not only has he created the distinctive "Polo look" in clothing, but he has also branched out into home furnishings.[4] The voice of a solitary prophet in the wilderness may be more trustworthy than the chants and choruses of the multitudes.

Many effective and useful changes can be initiated at the grassroots of the organization. However, all changes cannot be initiated at this level of the organization. The very element that makes grassroots change so uniquely enlightening also acts as a conceptual blinder. Employees with a grassroots viewpoint usually focus on grassroots problems, which often preclude a clear understanding of changes needed at other organizational levels. For example, the supervisor of a print shop may have excellent suggestions about how to improve the efficiency and effectiveness of that department. However, the supervisor's boss, who manages the printing, purchasing, and maintenance departments, may ask a more fundamental question: Can the organization as a whole function more effectively by having material printed by an outside vendor? Few print shop supervisors would recommend this change. Indeed scholars studied this issue and found that when personnel specialists were asked to suggest changes in their own jobs, the specialists typically came up with fewer than thirty minor changes.[5] Yet, their managers came up with a list of over one hundred ideas involving substantial change to enhance the personnel job.

Integrative Approach

The critiques of the two previous approaches suggest a third and more appropriate choice for managing change. Effective leaders avoid focusing exclusively on *who* champions the change. Instead they determine if the situation (e.g., who, what, when and where) warrants a top-down approach, bottom-up approach, or some combination of the two. There is no one best strategy for coping with change, just as there is not one best form of transportation. It all depends on *who* you are traveling with, *what* you intend to do, *when* you plan to leave, and *where* you intend to go. Likewise, thoughtful managers do not ask, "What is the best approach"?

Labeling this approach "integrative" is not incidental. Both approaches are needed in an organization. Successful leaders integrate the two approaches in a logical and meaningful way, just as our left eye compensates for the distortions of the right eye. Employees need to understand why certain changes are appropriately and necessarily made at different levels of the organization. There is an added bonus: binocular vision, which produces depth perception. And almost every organization could benefit from a deeper and clearer vision.

Types of Change

All changes are not of equal magnitude. Effective managers create unique communication strategies based on the degree of change. Changes can be described on a continuum from routine to non-routine. For instance, financial institutions routinely change their interest rates and airlines regularly change their rates. On the other end of the continuum are changes such as major reorganizations, mergers, new product lines, plant closings, or new corporate strategies.

But everyone does not share the same perspective about the magnitude of change. Figure 9.1 illustrates how the change initiator's and receiver's perspectives interact to create different communication scenarios. Effective managers avoid under- or over-communicating.

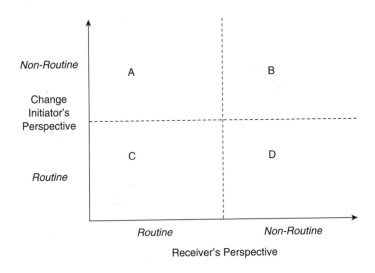

Figure 9.1   Perspectives on Change

Under-Communicating

Frequently those instituting changes underestimate the impact that the change will have. For instance, upgrades in software may cause organizational havoc because the programmers see the changes as relatively minor, but users have a decidedly different view (see Quadrant D of Figure 9.1). Consider another common situation. A committee might devote weeks studying a new office procedure. Committee members become familiar with all the arguments and counterarguments for various perspectives through an almost countless number of iterations of talk back and forth. Unconsciously they transition through various difficult reaction stages, leading to the proposal's acceptance. Yet, they will devote little time communicating about those matters and instead, only communicate the final proposal.

Over-Communicating

Occasionally, employees will over-communicate and provide their colleagues with more information than they desire (see Quadrant A of Figure 9.1). Unfortunately, the ease of forwarding e-mail encourages those who fail to understand others' priorities and information needs. More information does not necessarily equal better communication.

Ideally, change initiators understand the perspectives of their intended audiences. Routine changes would be treated as simple information-sharing situations and conform to the principles discussed in Chapter 6 about managing data, information, knowledge, and action (see Quadrant C of Figure 9.1). Non-routine changes would be seen as a time for strategic communication and conform to the principles discussed in the remainder of this chapter (see Quadrant B of Figure 9.1).

Reactions to Change

Major changes almost always involve at least a temporary loss of employee productivity. As seen in Figure 9.2, there are two dimensions of the drop: the depth of the drop (a) and the duration of the drop (b). An effective communication strategy seeks to minimize both the depth and duration of the loss.

In fact, employees also often experience a loss of a different sort, more akin to bereavement. Few scholars know more about this process than Elisabeth Kubler-Ross. Her keenly perceptive work, *On Death and Dying*, presents a theory about the psychological stages that terminally ill patients go through in learning to cope with their impending death:[6]

Stage 1 - Denial and Isolation

Stage 2 - Anger

Stage 3 - Bargaining

Stage 4 - Depression

Stage 5 - Acceptance

Her approach focuses on easing the natural pain, stress, and trauma of the situation by using communication strategies that are compatible with the patient's stage in the coping process. Such efforts require a deep sensitivity to the patient's unique psychological makeup. There are no pat answers, only some general principles to follow (see Table 9.1). Moreover, Kubler-Ross makes the important point that how well a patient handles the situation depends, to a great extent, on how effectively the doctors, nurses, and family members communicate.

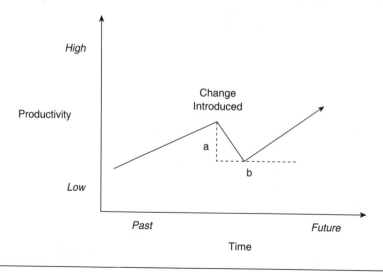

Figure 9.2   Impact of Change on Productivity

Table 9.1   Communicating Change at Different Reaction Stages

Stage	Identifying Actions	Appropriate Actions	Inappropriate Responses
Denial	• Not showing up for meetings • Being overly busy with routine tasks • Less socializing • Procrastinating	• Discerning actual points of resistance • Discussing positives and negatives of change • Legitimizing concerns • Discussing rationale of the change	• Ignoring the resistance • Ridiculing the person's denial
Anger	• Being irritable • Contemplating sabotage • Being confrontive • Appearing "short-fused"	• Staying calm and professional • Clarifying the details of the change • Showing understanding of the anger while firmly emphasizing need for change • Allowing some ventilation	• Escalating into a relationship conflict • Threatening others • Blaming others for the change • Taking anger personally • Ignoring anger
Bargaining	• Trying to make deals • Trading favors • Promise making	• Being flexible with inconsequential items • Being firm with the basic position • Focusing on long-term benefits	• Rejecting suggestions briskly • Giving into employee demands • Giving impression of agreement
Depression	• Being untalkative • Appearing apathetic • Missing work • Appearing listless • Looking somber	• Showing concern • Providing "space" • Encouraging discussions with others who have fully accepted change	• Pressuring for full acceptance • Jesting about feelings • Being overly happy or giddy
Acceptance	• Fully implementing change • Returning to normal atmosphere	• Encouraging auxiliary suggestions • Resuming "normal" communication • Giving praise	• Saying, "I told you so" • Joking about previous reactions

When faced with major changes, many employees will go through similar, although less severe, stages of reactions. The manager's skill in guiding employees through this process greatly affects the smoothness of the transition, limiting the depth and duration of productivity loss. Sensitive managers discern the stage of employee reaction and communicate accordingly.

In *Denial and Isolation (Stage 1),* employees often react with comments such as, "Oh no, not here"; "It can't happen like that, not with my job." In the denial stage, the manager should communicate clearly and calmly the particulars of the change while providing as much factual material as necessary. An employee may react emotionally but the manager should realize that this is a normal reaction and allow the denial to take its natural course. Upon encountering initial emotional reaction, some managers unwisely back off or sugarcoat the change, resulting in not fully informing employees of the change. Others try to browbeat or ridicule employees into acceptance. Either approach undermines the change-acceptance process.

Stage 2, *Anger,* involves a kind of anger over the "whys" of the change: "Why did this happen to me? At this time?" Little incidents can set off major emotional outbursts. Employee behavior may seem inexplicable. Managers should avoid taking the anger personally and exacerbating the difficulties. A pattern of "mutual pretense" might emerge in which the manager and employee play a game: "I know that you know, but I won't talk about it because it might upset you. And you won't talk about it because it will upset me." The net result: a conspiracy of silence with resentment simmering underneath the veneer of civility. Then interpersonal conflicts further heighten the problems. Effective managers acknowledge the anger, while gently guiding the employees' attention to the real source of anger and helping them work through it.

Bargaining, Stage 3, occurs when employees may attempt to make various exchanges to forestall the impending change. Creativity abounds when faced with an unpleasant alternative. Employees attempt to make deals as they seek to alter the course of events. They may attempt to make deals outside the normal chain-of-command structure, in essence behind the manager's back. But making such machinations only prolongs the matter and puts off the inevitable. Resolution and perseverance are the manager's tools at this point.

In Stage 4, *Depression,* employees display signs of listlessness and depression but they begin to accept the inevitable. Just allowing the employees to voice their concerns or feelings at this point can be helpful. At other times, sensitive silence or a gentle touch may be most effective. Sharing sadness with someone who can empathize can be amazingly therapeutic. An insensitive, "Hey, it's not that bad," can have the opposite impact.

In the *Acceptance* stage (Stage 5), employees accept the situation by endorsing the change. Managers should show respect for the employees and not chide them for their initial reactions. Even seemingly innocent verbal jousting may be deeply but secretly wounding. The wise manager preserves employee dignity.

This may sound like a fairly drawn out process. But these reactions can take place in the span of hours or extend over several months, as in the case reviewed in Table 9.2. Doubters, such as the Arrow manager, may even question whether an employee really goes through those reactions. Circuit managers may become overly sympathetic and actually delay acceptance. Effective change agents recognize that they are often at a different stage in the process than their employees. They realize, for example, that a manager who has accepted the change should avoid "cheerleading" those in the depression stage into the acceptance stage. They also know how to strategically

Table 9.2   Case Study: Reaction Stages to a Change

<u>Situation</u>: Smith's Solid Waste, a small family-owned disposal company, is being bought out by B.L. Disposal, a larger disposal company. Smith's owner and two managers are aware of the pending sale. They are preparing to tell the employees about this change in ownership. The owner and two managers plan to stay on as supervisors, but there will be some changes in the operations. More office staff will be hired and the way records are kept will change. Drivers will be required to keep more accurate records and submit more reports to the office staff. In the past, very few records were kept and drivers had a lot of freedom about how they ran their routes.

<u>Chronology of events</u>

Day 1:	Mr. Smith calls a meeting for all drivers and announces the sale of Smith's Solid Waste to B.L. Disposal. All drivers will be required to reapply for their jobs with B.L. Disposal. He distributes the applications and tells the drivers to turn them in within one week so he can send them to B.L. Disposal.
Days 2–10:	No activity
Day 11:	Mr. Smith notices that no one has turned in an application. He asks all the drivers why he has not received any of their applications. They respond, "We were unsure if we had to. We didn't think you were really going to sell." Mr. Smith replies, "B.L. Disposal is buying this company. I will still be your direct supervisor. However, you must reapply for your jobs within the next week; B.L. will not wait for these applications forever. I will be handing over whatever applications I have in one week."
Analysis:	*Employees are clearly denying that the company is going to be bought out, and avoiding anything that would dispel the myth. It is the game of "mutual pretense." Mr. Smith's response might seem appropriate because it gives employees maximum flexibility and avoids conflict. But it fails to deal with the reasons for the denial. Moreover, all the aspects of the change have not been fully explained. The abruptness of the supervisor's comments on Day 11 creates added tension.*
Day 18:	Workers tell Mr. Smith, "If you want to sell out, you should just tell the owner of B.L. that we are all good workers and if he doesn't agree to keep us, we'll all quit. Then he'll have no workers."
Analysis:	*The anger stage is clearly in full swing. Providing a rationale for why the applications need to be filled out as a formality is a little late at this stage and should have been done earlier. Furthermore, Mr. Smith still has not explained how this sale will affect the drivers. He assumes the workers should not be concerned because he will still be their direct supervisor. The threats only exacerbate the situation until it builds into an interpersonal conflict.*
Day 20:	Mr. Smith and B.L. Disposal's vice president agree to meet with employees to discuss how the change will affect them and to answer any questions.
Day 21:	Employees want guarantees that everyone will keep their same job and responsibilities. The new owners assure them that they will all keep their jobs if they turn in their applications. But new workers will be brought in, as well, mainly to do administrative work in the office. The workers are happy to hear they will keep their jobs but confused about why office workers are needed.

(Continued)

Table 9.2 (Continued)

Analysis:	*This is a textbook example of the negotiation or bargaining stage. The workers are promised their jobs if they turn in their applications.*
Day 24:	The drivers ask Mr. Smith why more office help is needed. He tells them that they (the drivers) will need to complete more detailed route reports so the business can bill and manage time more effectively. Additional office workers are needed to process these reports. The drivers are furious that they will have less freedom than before with these new responsibilities. The result: They do not turn in their applications.
Analysis:	*They revert back to the anger stage. The drivers still feel lied to and do not trust the new owners.*
Day 26:	Mr. Smith and B.L inform the drivers that if their applications are not submitted in one week, they will begin to hire new drivers.
Days 28–36:	Hesitantly, the drivers turn in their applications. The drivers will not talk to Mr. Smith or other managers because they feel betrayed. They barely talk to each other.
Analysis:	*The depression stage has set in. Most likely, employees are silent because they are bitter. Mr. Smith may have done the wise thing, given the current situation.*
Day 36-50:	The name, "B.L. Disposal," begins to show up on the dumpsters and on the customers' invoices. The drivers are given the new forms they must complete and hand in every day to the office staff. Everyone begins talking again and slowly relationships return to normal.
Analysis:	*Acceptance, finally. Maybe not wholehearted acceptance, but acceptance, nevertheless.*
6 months later:	All the drivers are filling out the correct forms.
1 year later:	In the break room, drivers discuss how easy it is to do the route sheet and how much less customers complain about mistakes on their billing statements.

communicate about major changes to hasten employee acceptance and boost productivity. Doing so requires a thoughtful analysis of the situation as suggested by the model reviewed in the next section.

The Iceberg Model

Most of an iceberg's bulk lies below the surface. Ships that ignore the ice below the water are in mortal danger. Likewise, organizational change efforts may flounder because of a lack of strategic communication planning—the "below the water-line" issues (see Figure 9.3). This model outlines a strategic approach to communicating change based on four levels of planning:

- Contextual Analysis (Level 1)
- Audience Analysis (Level 2)
- Strategic Design (Level 3)
- Tactical Preparations (Level 4)

The model is fluid, focusing on asking the right questions in the proper order. The specific action plan emerges from the dynamic interplay of critical communication principles and the answers to these core questions. These questions are presented in Table 9.3.

Most companies spend 80–95% of their time and resources dealing with issues such as:

- Should we publish a brochure or issue a company-wide e-mail?
- What day of the week should we release the announcement?
- Who should communicate about the change?

These are the "above the water-line," tactical issues concerned with determining the content of a message, timing, channels, and spokespeople. These

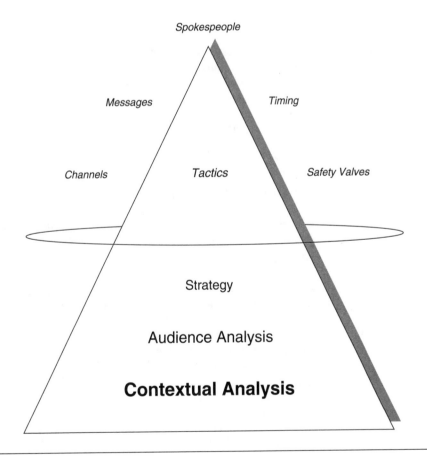

Figure 9.3   The "Iceberg" Model

are all legitimate questions but they are really secondary. They are, in fact, indicative of a *tactical* rather than a *strategic* approach to communicating change. My experiences suggest that resources should be allocated in precisely the opposite direction. Between 70–80% of resources should be devoted to the first three levels of planning: contextual analysis, audience analysis, and strategic design. Once these issues are resolved, the tactical decisions are usually fairly simple and straightforward.

Contextual Analysis

(Gravity beats a rocket every time. Eventually rockets run out of fuel and succumb to gravitational fields. In a similar way, a great message will always succumb to the employees' field of experience. If change initiators fail to understand the context, the change effort may be crushed by the weight of the status quo.)The background knowledge about the organization serves as a base for understanding how the change might be perceived. Planners must know about the written and unwritten organizational rules of the organizational culture. These historical communication patterns set the context

Table 9.3   Thought Process for a Strategic Communication Plan

Contextual Analysis	1. How have employees assimilated other changes?
	2. How congruent is the change with the culture?
	3. How non-complex and manageable is the change?
	4. How advantageous is the change over past practices?
	5. What benefits will be readily observable?
	6. How will key relationships be impacted?
Audience Analysis	1. What are the major groups of employees that will be affected by the change?
	2. How will each group be impacted by the change?
	3. What are the most likely points of resistance of each group?
	4. What are the communication or channel preferences of each group?
	5. What does each group know or think they know about the change?
	6. Who are the key opinion leaders ("the lions") of each group?
Strategic Design	1. What are the tentative communicative objectives for each of the audiences?
	2. What are the common objectives shared by all the audiences?
	3. What is a unifying theme that energizes and motivates employees?
	4. Based on the audience analysis, how should the communication resources be allocated?
	5. What should be the general sequence of stages or phases for achieving the objectives?
Tactics	1. What channels should be used?
	2. What are the key messages?
	3. What are the "safety valves"?
	4. What should be the timing of the various communications?
	5. Who should communicate the messages?

of interpretation for employees. In fact, one researcher has shown that employee reactions to change can be traced back to an organization's founding conditions. The company's origin somehow deeply imprints employees, even those subsequently hired.[7] As Sir Winston Churchill put it, "The longer you look back, the farther you can look forward. This is not a philosophical or political argument—any oculist can tell you it is true."[8]

The president of a small manufacturing firm related the following story. He was concerned about the rough financial times his company was experiencing and decided to implement some cost-saving measures. The president considered himself a moral and straightforward person. Therefore, he felt he had an ethical obligation to inform his employees of the news. In due course, he called a meeting of all employees to discuss some of the difficulties ahead as well as the requisite changes involved. In good faith, he mentioned that there were no plans for layoffs and employees would be dealt with "as fairly as possible under the circumstances." So far, so good. Or so it seemed.

Within a few days the entire plant was buzzing with rumors about an impending plant closing and wage reductions. In fact, there was not a bit of truth in either rumor. The president was completely bewildered. He felt he had told the employees the truth and was honest about the situation. How could such vicious rumors spring from such noble of intentions? Weeks of meetings took place in order to quell fears. Still, for months, morale and productivity suffered.

Upon deeper probing and a year's worth of hindsight, it became abundantly clear why employees came away from the meeting with precisely the opposite message that the well-intentioned president had so sincerely sought to communicate. The president had never before held a company-wide meeting to discuss *any* issue, much less this kind of anxiety-producing news. Hence, they legitimately, although incorrectly, reasoned that "things must be really bad" if the president "had to" call a meeting of this type. There was the feeling that management "must not be telling us all they know." Like a virus in an unhealthy body, rumors and inaccurate inferences naturally flourish under such conditions. Had meetings like this been held on a regular basis, the possibility of such an interpretation would have been minimized. The context of the situation spoke louder than the actual message. The president was bewildered because he focused on the inner message—his actual words—and had no understanding of the context in which employees interpreted the words. Both the employees and the president erroneously focused on only one part of the actual communication event. Pure intentions do not always guarantee perceptions of integrity.

The moral of the story is that when instituting a change, managers must carefully consider the context in which employees interpret the message. This incident also demonstrates why effective managers continually update employees on corporate news. Furthermore, it may mean that in order to institute a change with full employee support, management may need to apologize for past errors in failing to communicate effectively. A successful future can only be built on the firm foundation of the past. Rosabeth Moss Kanter, a strategy professor at Harvard, noted, "If the foundations will not support the weight of what is about to be built, then they must be shored up before any other actions can take place."[9] Thus, contextual analysis focuses the change initiator's attention on possible resistance points. We use the following questions to guide the discussion of the contextual issues.[10]

How have employees assimilated other changes? The previous scenario clearly demonstrates how history impacts the speed with which changes are assimilated. Organizations that have successfully assimilated past changes tend to more efficiently absorb new ones. Why? The employees have learned how to effectively manage the change process with all its emotional strains and setbacks. Without that kind of history, employees need to assimilate the change as well as learn about the change process; doubling the duty, but clearly not doubling the fun. If the organization has not readily responded to other change efforts, then change initiators often find that they must slow down the process by taking smaller steps and train employees about change management.

How congruent is the change with the culture? Changes seen as an extension of the culture are more likely to be embraced. Those that are not congruent will create more resistance. For instance, the terms "lean manufacturing" or "process improvement" may induce resistance because employees see this as a radical departure from the "way we do things around here."[11] But if the planners use another label—one more in line with the culture—resistance might be minimized. In one situation we renamed a lean manufacturing project as "Our House" because employees recently became partial owners of the company. If employees see changes as alien to the culture, change initiators would do well to reconsider the endeavor or at the very least, find ways to make the change more hospitable to the culture.

How non-complex and manageable is the change? More complex changes are often resisted. Even if the changes are perceived as complex, there are ways to break down the task and make it appear more manageable and attainable. These tactics include the use of planning charts, outlines of key project phases, and scaled-down models of new products or processes.

How advantageous is the change over past practices? Change initiators find this one of the more difficult questions for two reasons. First, they must deal with employees who may feel that any change represents an indictment of their past work practices. In a manufacturing plant, we helped introduce a major structural change of reporting relationships that created more accountability. One of the consistent refrains was, "We made the numbers in the past, we're achieving our goals now, why do we need to change?"

Ironically, the very managers who said this were those who had consistently complained about the general lack of accountability at the plant. Their lament was basically, "If it ain't broke, why fix it?" Even the verbally skilled have a difficult time effectively communicating what often appear as contradictory messages:

a. In the past, the systems worked effectively.

b. Yet, now the situation has changed and new practices are needed.

However, this may be the exact message that needs to be relayed to employees.

The second problem involves differing perspectives. Who benefits from the change? The employee? The organization? All too often changes are introduced as benefiting the organization at the expense of certain employees. Sending work off-shore to workers in another country may add to the company's bottom-line, but what about the current employees' job security? Thus, change initiators need to carefully consider how to balance these sometimes competing perspectives.

What benefits will be readily observable? Many advantages are conceptual in nature and often prove the least persuasive to employees. Instead, they need to see tangible and visible evidence that the change will provide benefits. Therefore, change initiators may have to provide a physical demonstration of the benefits. Advertisers tend to be skillful in demonstrating readily observable benefits to consumers. Change initiators might think about how their favorite infomercial spokesperson or product endorser would communicate the benefits of the change. If this proves exceedingly difficult, then in all likelihood the organization will not fully embrace the change.

How will key relationships be impacted? One of the least discussed resistance points involves changes in social relationships. Changing the physical layout of an office may alter interpersonal relationships. Those employees who routinely see one another for casual conversations may not have such opportunities with a new office plan. Organizations that are moving to "virtual offices" often find this issue impinging on the ultimate success of the venture.

A strategy will begin to emerge as these questions are discussed. The responses may indicate that small modifications in the change initiative, such as renaming it, need to be made to facilitate acceptance. In other cases, more aggressive responses might need to be initiated to address the concerns. For instance, organizations that are heavily reliant on telecommuting may create quarterly retreats for those employees "residing" in their virtual offices. This could be a mechanism to overcome concerns about alterations in personal relationships or "feeling disconnected."

Audience Analysis

What one person finds persuasive, another may not. This is the fundamental principle of audience analysis. Change planners should start the analysis by isolating key groups of employees that may be directly and indirectly affected by the change. But, all the groups affected may not be readily apparent. This is a special challenge, because not identifying all who will be affected may lead to serious repercussions. For instance, many downsizing efforts have failed to reach long-term productivity goals because organizations have not planned the communication to the "survivors," those employees left after the cutback. These employees often have deep fears about their future security, which may decrease their effectiveness.

Determining the key groups of employees will vary with the type of change. There are a lot of ways to slice the pie. When an organization alters a benefits package, age may be the key variable. With a job redesign issue, the critical variable will most likely be job classification. A flextime proposal might affect employees with children differently than those without children.

After the key groups have been isolated, five critical questions need to be answered:

How will each group be impacted by the change? The final Halloween of the last millennium was scarier than usual for Hershey Foods. They didn't deliver enough Hershey Bars and Peanut Butter Cups treats to their regional suppliers. How did this happen? Hershey couldn't pull off the ultimate trick of successfully integrating a $112-million computer system into their operations. It was supposed to modernize and expedite the entire order and distribution process, but it did not. There were technical problems. But there were also communication problems.[12] Hershey failed to understand the implications of the change for their various audiences, and neglected to ask critical questions, such as "How would the new computer system affect suppliers? Distributors? The ultimate consumer?" Wise managers anticipate how different groups are likely to interpret the change, by asking "What will it mean to them in terms of their job duties, as well as their emotional well-being?"

What are the most likely points of resistance of each group? Employees are often willing to discuss their concerns. Typically, they will discuss generic issues such as economic loss, inconveniences, and workload shifts.[13] But they are often hesitant to bring up the other concerns that are more emotional in nature, such as perceived loss of status, social disruptions, reduction in influence, anxiety over the unknown, or insecurities such as "Can I really do this new job?" These concerns may surface in a dysfunctional way in the form of vicious rumors. Change initiators cannot assume that employees will be able to identify and articulate all of their own concerns. Wise planners take this into account.

What are the communication or channel preferences of each group? Different groups may prefer to receive their information in different forms or through different channels. Introverts, for instance, like to study documents before responding, whereas extroverts prefer discussing issues face-to-face. Statistics might prove a proper way to make an argument for employees in the finance department, but those in the marketing department may be more persuaded by stories or critical incidents.

What does each group know or think they know about the change? During times of change, misinformation, rumors, and speculation pervade organizations. This mishmash of impressions greatly influences employee interpretations. Change initiators must be prepared to counter both misconceptions and pent-up emotions. Thus, successful change initiators describe the beliefs each audience has about the change, no matter how silly, odd, or misguided they may be. For example, during one cost-cutting initiative the change planners recognized that a small but vocal group felt that "The company already makes enough money." At this point in the planning process, the planners are *describing,* not *evaluating* beliefs.

Who are the "lions"? The lions rule the tropical! as well as the organizational jungles. Influence is unequally distributed in an organization and is not necessarily tied to job titles. Often the viability of a change will rest on the reactions of key opinion leaders. Therefore, change initiators should identify the "lions" and think about how best to influence them. The "lions," once convinced, will in turn influence others. On a practical level, this means creating a list of the lions for each group and developing related tactics for each of them.

Strategic Design

The well-known military historian, B.H. Liddell Hart, once wrote that, "In strategy, the longest way round is often the shortest way home."[14] Communication strategies are no different. Planning a strategic communication process takes both time and effort; it is the "long way round." This section discusses five steps that increase the probability of successfully implementing a major change.

Step 1: Develop Tentative Communicative Objectives for Each of the Audiences

Figure 9.4 provides a worksheet we use to summarize the audience-analysis phase and start the strategy-making phase. The resistance points and knowledge base of each group naturally lead to the development of specific communicative objectives.

MetaComm Strategic Change Analysis Planning Guide

Audiences (groups)	How will the group be impacted?	What will be the group's likely resistance points?	How intense will the resistance level be? (*High, Med., Lo*)	What is the channel choice of the group?	What does the group "know" about the change?	Who are the "lions" in the group?	Objectives for the group

Figure 9.4   Planning Worksheet

Consider the following situation. A small medical clinic with seven branch offices decided to update its phone system. Under the old system patients called a specific office, and any available employee answered the phone. It often took several iterations before the patient was connected to the appropriate person. The new system would allow patients to call a single clinic number, answered by a dedicated operator, who would then connect the caller to the appropriate personnel. This was designed to improve office efficiency and provide more convenient patient care. We anticipated that not everyone would see it that way. Therefore, we split the audience pie into the affected, unequally sized groups and created unique objectives for each audience. Table 9.4 presents a shortened version of the planning document. Note that although we identified unique objectives for each audience, some overlapped, which nicely leads to the next step.

Table 9.4   Example of an Audience Analysis

Audience	Concerns	Objectives
Older patients	• "Will I have the same access to care?" • "Will I be able to adapt to the new phone system?" • Will this group be able to break out of their old habits?	• Provide reassurances that care will be the same or improved. • Demonstrate the ease of the new phone system. • Restore confidence in their ability to handle changes. • Show how the new phone system is more convenient by providing them quicker and more direct access to the desired staff.
Younger patients	• "Will I have the same access to care?" • "Will this make scheduling office visits more efficient?"	• Provide reassurances that care will be the same or improved. • Underscore the efficiency of the new system.
Medical Staff	• "Will I be able to get my job done more efficiently and effectively?" • "Will the transition to the new system be burdensome?" • "How will this impact patient care, particularly for the elderly?" • "Will I be able to learn the new phone system?"	• Demonstrate the efficiency of the new system. • Highlight the employee's role in the transition. • Describe specific benefits and potential concerns for elderly patients. • Discuss the training that will be provided.
Physicians	• "Will I be able to get my job done more efficiently and effectively?" • "Will the transition to the new system be burdensome?" • "How will this impact patient care, particularly for the elderly?" • "Will I be able to learn the new phone system?"	• Demonstrate the efficiency of the new system. • Underscore the support system for the change. • Describe specific benefits and potential concerns of elderly patients. • Discuss the training that will be provided.

Step 2: Determine Common
Objectives that are Shared by all the Audiences

Typically, a deeper analysis of the objectives for each group reveals a global, common set that applies to most of the audiences. In the case of the medical clinic, the global objectives of the communicative campaign were fairly obvious:

- Provide reassurance that medical care will remain the same or improve.
- Demonstrate the ease and efficiency of the system.

These objectives, in turn, suggest a starting point for making all the tactical decisions about what to communicate, how to inform people, and when to do it. The objectives also set up the next strategic step.

Step 3: Develop a Unifying theme
that Energizes and Motivates DEmployees

The objectives need to be shaped into a memorable and inspiring theme. The leadership team of the clinic decided on "Challenge 2005" because it a) nicely suited all the audiences, b) implied technological progressiveness and cutting-edge medical care, and c) linked to one of core clinic values. After all, what patient, young or old, would not want physicians "on top" of the most recent advances?

Consider this legendary case. When Stanley C. Gault became the CEO of Rubbermaid, he took the company from modest success to "superstar" status. He did it by becoming the "No. 1 quality controller." He constantly talked to consumers about Rubbermaid's products and was known to order the redesign of a product based on one customer's complaint. He had a reputation for becoming absolutely "livid" about poor-quality workmanship or as he boasted, "On quality I'm a sonofabitch." Yet, as one observer put it, "Ultimately it's Gault's infectious pride in Rubbermaid's products, rather than his wrath, that motivates his troops. When it comes to encouraging quality, passion at the top counts as much as engineering precision at the bottom."[15] In order for employees to buy into an initiative, they must see a vision of the future, even a slightly hazy one. They must know the global goals, the possibilities, and hopes implicit in the change. In short, they must be collectively inspired by the change.

Employees should find the unifying theme engaging, significant, inspirational, and achievable. Catchy slogans are not enough, as one company discovered when it launched a human resources initiative designed to improve career options and training. The change initiators chose "Career Pathing" as the moniker for this endeavor. Think about how the terminology limits, and perhaps ostracizes, certain audiences. What about employees who are happy with their current job and do not want to "move up"? Are they considered less valuable than those on a particular path? This was not the message the company wanted to send, but many employees made that inference. So eventually the company started using a new term, "Career Enhancement," that was more inclusive and motivated all employees to improve their skills, even those not on a "path." As this example illustrates, effective change leaders contemplate the potential inferences drawn from the theme. They realize that employees need to personally relate to the theme in a way congruent with strategic objectives.

Step 4: Allocate Communication Resources According to the Audience Analysis

In order for change to be sustained, three questions must be answered affirmatively:[16]

- Is there a *need* for the change or initiative?
- Is this the appropriate *remedy?*
- Have the major *drawbacks* to the initiative been resolved?

Because audiences have limited attention spans, choices need to be made about what issues to emphasize. If their concerns are not met fairly quickly, the initiative could stall at the denial stage. Consider a company concerned about the rising cost of health care. They may want to change the benefit package, while employees are satisfied with the status quo. In this case, the change strategist must first establish a *need* and alert employees to the staggering financial burden of the existing medical plan. In another case when employees are already convinced of the need, the focus of the communication should be on the *remedy*—the choice of new plans available—and how *potential obstacles* have been resolved.

In practice, applying this simple notion can prove challenging. For instance, the change strategist might discover that five groups do not believe any changes are needed, three groups recognize the need for change but are concerned about the remedy, and several other groups are focused on how to resolve the inherent drawbacks in the initiative. What to do? These are matters of process considered in the next step.

Step 5: Formulate a General Sequence of Stages or Phases

Persuading employees is a process. One "persuasive" mass e-mail or cleverly designed brochure will not be enough. Employee "buy-in" emerges over time and after many communicative actions. Expect this to be a rather helter-skelter and messy enterprise. As previously discussed, employees have a fairly standard set of reactions to change, starting with denial and ending with acceptance. Moreover, different employees and groups may be experiencing those emotions at various times during the change process. Thus, change leaders must be highly flexible in approaching the various groups.

Setting up the appropriate stages of the communication plan requires tenacity, insight, and creativity. The change initiators should take into account the communicative objectives established in Steps 1 and 2, the core messages or themes (Step 3), and resource allocations for the groups (Step 4). They should also consider how the groups exert influence on one another. How do change leaders integrate all these pieces? To be sure, the task challenges even the most astute leader. Consider this question as a starting point, "In what order should we pursue the objectives gleaned from Step 2?"

Often a natural progression of objectives will emerge. For example, in some cases, we discovered that objectives could be grouped into three fairly distinct phases: alert, analysis, and proposal. In the *alert* phase, the major objective is to convince employees of the necessity for the change or initiative. Change theorists might characterize the specific objectives at this stage as "building awareness," "raising dissatisfaction," or "questioning tradition."[17] The *analysis phase* focuses on convincing key audiences that the issue has been properly analyzed. Change leaders need to let others understand their thinking. How was the need detected? How was the situation analyzed? What are the alternatives? Once these questions are sufficiently answered, the change initiators can move onto the *proposal phase,* and discuss the specific proposal. This phase presents a special challenge because many employees will still be skeptical of the underlying need for the change. *In fact, many change initiators are astonished at how frequently they must repeat the rationale for the change, thus returning to the alert stage.* Thus, change initiators should be prepared to till that soil one more time. But cultivation pays off. This phased strategy increases the odds that the change will develop deep roots in the organization.

A more difficult issue involves planning the roll-out to various groups that have different concerns about the initiative. Ideally, the communication messages would be rolled out to all groups at the same time in order to prevent the spread of misinformation. But that may not be possible or even wise. Some groups have sway over others. Some will be more resistant than others. Therefore, change leaders should plan the strategic phases with various groups in mind. Successful change strategists build momentum, working with groups that will more quickly "buy-in" and can be used as leverage over other groups. President George W. Bush, for example, sent the Secretary of State to various countries to garner support for the war against terrorism. Convenience or happenstance did not dictate the order of visits. Any successful strategist knows that.

Tactical Preparation

The tactics are the "how-to's," the operational plans that emerge from the strategy. There are five areas to consider in developing tactics. Some standard rules of thumb in developing each tactic are highlighted below.

Channels

There are several principles that enhance the effectiveness of using communication channels.

It is usually more effective if change leaders use multiple channels in communicating the change. There are several reasons for this. The use of multiple channels increases the probability that employees will hear about the change. Additionally, each media has its strength and excels at presenting different aspects of a change. For example, oral channels can be more useful in fielding employee questions, whereas a print medium can better show a new office design. Finally, the redundancy helps to continually remind employees of the vision behind the change.

Change leaders should try to use rich channels for communicating non-routine changes. Rich channels, such as face-to-face meetings, allow for rapid feedback and quick adaptation to employee concerns. Assume a company announced a major initiative via a memo (a lean channel) sent to employees' homes, and did not use any follow-up communication. How could change initiators ascertain the reaction stage of employees? Eventually responses might filter through other avenues, but by then, opinions and conclusions may have hardened into deep resistance. Rich channels encourage a more fluid dynamic that allows change initiators to help employees move more rapidly through the reaction stages.

This principle also holds for large organizations with employees in many locations. I helped change leaders at one Fortune 500 company grapple with this problem. We wanted to build feedback into the process but were constrained by the number of sites impacted by the major announcement. So we eventually opted for a two-stage process. First, the executive team used a video-conference to make the announcement to the thousands of employees at all sites. (We used all the principles discussed throughout this chapter when making the "announcement." For instance, executives discussed the need for the initiative, proposed a remedy, and discussed potential drawbacks.) Second, the executive team made a commitment to fly to all the sites within the week to review the initiative and answer employee questions face-to-face. In fact, the very expense of this process sent a powerful symbolic message that management cares about effectively communicating with employees.

Message

Professional communicators use many principles in constructing messages but several are particularly noteworthy at this juncture.

Try to link messages to the audience's pre-existing thinking routines. For example, when leaders at one company discussed the need to reduce costs in the company health care plan, they compared the situation to a family managing its personal finances. The leaders oriented their communication around this analogy, "As a parent, what would you do if your children were in the habit of buying clothing from an expensive store if you knew that they could shop elsewhere to get similar clothing less expensively?"

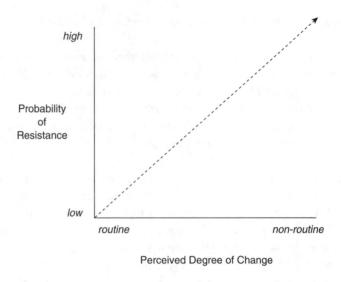

Figure 9.5   Probability of Resistance to Change

Most employees could easily relate to this comparison. This proved particularly persuasive because the audience analysis revealed that most of the
employees had teenagers and their leisure activities were oriented around
family matters.

Always discuss the upside and downside of the change. Some change leaders
oversell the change by only stressing the benefits. However, in the long
run, a reasonable discussion of the downside proves useful. Why? Because it
provides a more realistic assessment of the change and allows employees to
adjust their expectations. Also, by communicating the downside, employees
may be in the perfect position to solve some of the potential problems.
Communicating the downside also demonstrates that the change leaders have
devoted some time to thoroughly studying the issue. Sharing these concerns
builds confidence in the decision-making process and cultivates a climate of
trust. As scholars have documented, this approach expedites the process of
moving from denial to acceptance and eases the pains of implementation.[18]

Directly address likely resistance points. The more non-routine employees
perceive the change, the greater the probability that there will be some
resistance (see Figure 9.5). Although management often initiates change,
only employees can sustain it.

One note of caution: The issues *perceived* by management as possible
concerns may not be the *actual* concerns of employees. In fact, employees may
not even mention the real source of their angst. The generic employee concerns
include job security, job stability, loss of wages, social disruptions, inconveniences, and anxiety over the unknown.[19] Some scholars have identified

Table 9.5   Resistance Points at Organizational Stages

Organizational Stage	Identifying Characteristics	Possible Resistance Points
Birth and early growth	• Emphasis on entrepreneurship • Heavy influence of "founding fathers"	• Uncertainty about CEO's reaction • Diminished CEO control • Change of corporate vision
Maturity	• Creation of standard operating procedures • Institutionalized vision • Solidified departmental responsibilities	• Interdepartmental differences • Protection of "turf" • Control of resources
Decline or redevelopment	• Downturn in competitive environment • More bureaucratic structure • Quest to reshape corporate vision	• Employee indifference and lethargy • Concern over impact on established careers • Change in power relationships • Employees need crisis to propel action

another set of potential resistance points (see Table 9.5). They argue that organizations, like nations, go through various developmental stages and that different organizational impediments occur during each period.[20] Therefore, the wise manager anticipates these various issues and develops appropriate responses to each concern.

Change leaders should consider responding to each potential objection point-by-point. The CEO of a small marketing firm used this approach in announcing a plan to change the marketers' responsibilities. In one part of his speech he said:

> Some of you may be concerned about wages under the new system. This is a legitimate concern. But let me assure you that there will be no wage reductions under this new plan. In fact, our projections show, with the added revenues, your salaries will actually increase. Others of you may be concerned about layoffs. This has never even crossed my mind. In every single change we've instituted in this company's twenty-year history, we have always ended up adding personnel.

Note that the CEO accomplished four important objectives in this excerpt. First, he clearly identified the potential resistance points, which legitimized the employees' anxieties. Second, he categorically denied each one. Third, he not only denied them but also said exactly the opposite would happen. Finally, he provided some kind of evidence to back up each of his claims. The speech must have worked, because the CEO reported that this was the most smoothly implemented change in the company's history.

In a variation on this theme, some companies issue a "Frequently Asked Questions" document about the initiative and then provide answers to each item. Both approaches counteract resistance and build support for a change.

Remind employees that not "everything" is changing. Employees often panic if they perceive the "entire world is turning upside down." They may even start behaving like victims. Employees need anchors of stability and a sense of personal control. Mooring or linking the change to established organizational values, customers, or mission statement helps. So does reminding employees that they have sailed in these kinds of waters before. Employees, like sailors, seek inspiration from their past successes.

Publicize initial successes. Change initiators who demonstrate success early in the process persuade others to jump on the bandwagon. It doesn't take much—an article in the newsletter, a phone call to a key person, or a kind word in the hallway—any little nudge of encouragement. These simple acts signal that change initiators are building a coalition to institute the change while whispering to the bystanders, "Get on board."

Safety Valves

No matter how persuasively the initiative has been advocated, employees will have some doubts and will probably voice some dissent regarding parts of the plan. Change initiators should harvest the dissent, which means proactively soliciting worker concerns about the change in a supportive environment. If management does not harvest the dissent, others will. In one dairy plant, the plant manager announced major policy changes on bulletin boards and in plant-wide meetings. He was perplexed that "Nothing I say ever gets done." The reason for this was that he never harvested the dissent—he would not entertain any significant questions to the new policy. This was a perfect opportunity for a few malcontent union workers to harvest the dissent themselves—in a non-constructive manner—and stymie change efforts.

Therefore, effective change leaders include safety valves in the process and allow employees to express their concerns. Consider this simple but powerful technique that change leaders can implement: 1) Ask employees to voice their concerns in a meeting. 2) Record the concerns in a non-evaluative fashion on a flip chart. 3) When all issues have been recorded, lead a discussion or debate on the most important ones. 4) Transform the list and discussion into a "Question and Answers" (Q & A) document. 5) Distribute the Q & A document to all employees in a timely manner.

This process limits misunderstandings and creates a vehicle by which employee concerns can be managed. The result: employees' concerns are legitimized, de-personalized, and de-emotionalized. So what? This helps move employees out of the denial stage, limits the role of emotion in forming opinions and encourages thoughtful inquiry. Change initiators, inspired by their visions, often resist this seemingly sloppy enterprise because it appears to tarnish their conception. Yet, wise change leaders do not seek kudos; rather, they focus on garnering quick acceptance of the new vision.

Timing

Timing may be the least studied and understood facet of effective communication. When making timing decisions, change leaders need to rely on their intuitions and the following guidelines.

Take into account the other initiatives the organization is pursuing at the time. In a deeply insightful article, David Nadler and Michael L. Tushman suggest:

> Successful long-term changes are characterized by a careful self-discipline that limits the number of themes an organization gives its employees. As a general rule, managers of a change can only initiate and sustain approximately three key themes during any particular period of time. The challenge in this area is to create enough themes to get people truly energized, while limiting the total number of themes. The toughest part is having to decide not to initiate a new program—which by itself has great merit—because of the risk of diluting the other themes.[21]

These theorists suggest that change leaders might be best advised to delay an important initiative while the organization digests other changes.

Develop a schedule or method so that most employees are informed about the initiative during a similar time frame. Why? It creates an impression of fairness and partially limits destructive grapevine activity. It also signals that everyone has an important role in the change process.

Allow time to harvest and respond to dissent in a meaningful way. Harvesting dissent involves actively soliciting employee concerns about initiative. Typically, announcing a major initiative on the last day of a work week or before a major holiday inhibits meaningful dialogue. Employees will naturally want to talk to others in order to make sense of the announcement. Family members and friends may provide comfort but they do not have all the facts to engage in meaningful dialogue about the initiative. And these are precisely the people that employees will turn to on the weekend or during the holidays. Ideally, change leaders create opportunities for discussions about employee concerns on the day after a major announcement.

Schedule follow-up communications. These may take the form of small group meetings, brochures, mass e-mails, or surveys assessing the general organizational climate. Redundancy and repetition facilitates the acceptance process. Moreover, follow-up communications allow for mid-course corrections in the strategy or message. Remember that a single communication event may grab employee attention, but it rarely persuades—just ask any advertiser.

Spokespeople

Who communicates the change may be as important as what they say. Those perceived as more credible are more persuasive. Therefore, change initiators need to carefully select who will announce and sponsor changes. In a medical clinic, we asked all the physicians to be involved in the announcement of an organizational change. They were not all equally skilled presenters. However, demonstrating solidarity among the physicians was more important than oratorical performances. We arranged for the physician with the greatest charisma to begin the presentation. A physician who was very precise and detail-oriented explained the actual process and stages of the change. We unexpectedly discovered that this multi-speaker approach allowed us to address the rational and emotional components inherent to the change.[22] The charismatic physician attended to the emotional concerns, while the others were more adept responding to the rational issues.

In other strategic situations, different choices might be made. A professor of Business Strategy at INSEAD, Quy Nguyen Huy, theorized that different types of change require different sorts of change agents.[23] An organizational restructuring might require a "commander" as change agent, whereas redesigning work processes might call for an "analyst" as a change leader. Likewise, a "teacher" advocate might be suited for communicating about changing the corporate culture, whereas a "facilitator" might be most appropriate for changing social relationships. The implications are clear—select spokesperson(s) based on the type of change. A commander, for instance, will probably do more harm than good advocating changes in the social structure. In sum, effective communication emerges from a sound strategy but it must be executed by those best suited to the task.

Conclusion

From personal experience I have learned that change advocates often feel as if they are living through a nightmare. They frequently encounter resistance, wild speculation, emotional tension, political gamesmanship, and personal attacks. But skilled change leaders realize that this is all part of the process of creating acceptance. They hasten that process along by thoroughly planning a communication strategy that emerges from the contextual and audience analyses. Then they assist on the tactical level by crafting compelling messages, selecting the proper channels and spokespersons, developing thoughtful time tables, and creating safety valves. Consequently, the obstacles slowly fade into hindsight, as the initiative progresses from one person's vision to *our* collective commitment to the "way it always was" or "should be." What will eventually be seen as inevitable can only begin as an inconceivable dream.[24]

Notes

1. Kissinger, H. 1982. *Years of upheaval.* Boston: Little, Brown, p. 169.

2. Ashkenas, R. N., & Francis, S. C. 2000. Integration managers: Special leaders for special times. *Harvard Business Review* 78 (6):108–116, p. 108.

3. Pinchot, G. 1985. *Intrapreneuring.* New York: Harper & Row.

4 Trachtenberg, J. A. 1988. *Ralph Lauren: The man behind the mystique.* Boston: Little, Brown.

5. Paul, W. J., Robertson, K. B., & Herzberg, F. 1969. Job enrichment pays off. *Harvard Business Review* 47 (2):61–78.

6. Kubler-Ross, E. 1969. *On death and dying.* New York: Macmillan.

7. Boeker, W. 1989. Strategic change: The effects of founding and history. *Academy of Management Journal* 32:489–515.

8. Manchester, W. 1983. *The last lion: Winston Spencer Churchill.* Boston: Little, Brown, p. 12.

9. Kanter, R. M. 1983. *The change masters.* New York: Simon & Schuster, p. 283.

10. Rogers, E. M. 2003. *The diffusion of innovations* (5th ed.). New York: Free Press.

11. Deal, T. E., & Kennedy, A. A. 1982. *Corporate cultures.* Reading, MA: Addison-Wesley.

12. Nelson, E., & Ramstad, E. 1999. Hershey's biggest dud has turned out to be new computer system. *Wall Street Journal,* 29 October:A1, A6.

13. Whipp, R. 2003. Managing strategic change. In *The Oxford handbook of strategy: Volume II: Corporate strategy,* edited by Faulkner, D. O. & Campbell, A., (pp.237–266). New York: Oxford University Press.

14. Hart, B. H. L. 1967. *Strategy.* London: Faber & Faber Ltd., p. 5.

15. O'Reilly, B. 1990. Quality of products. *Fortune,* 29 January:42–43, p. 43.

16. Debaters will recognize these as the key stock issues known as need, remedy, and disadvantage.

17. Whipp, op. cit.

18. Miller, K. I., & Monge, P. R. 1985. Social information and employee anxiety about organizational change. *Human Communication Research* 11 (3):194–203.

19. Lawrence, P. R. 1969. How to deal with resistance to change. *Harvard Business Review* 47 (1):4–8.

20. Gray, B., & Ariss, S. S. 1985. Politics and strategic change across organizational life cycles. *Academy of Management Review* 10 (4):707–723.

21. Nadler, D. A., & Tushman, M. L. 1989. Organizational frame bending: Principles for managing reorientation. *Academy of Management Executive* 3 (3): 194–203, pp. 199–200.

22. Fox, S. & Amichai-Hamburger, Y. 2001. The power of emotional appeals in promoting organizational change programs. *Academy of Management Executive* 15 (4):84–94.

23. Huy, Q. N. 2001. Time, temporal capability, and planned change. *Academy of Management Review* 26 (4):601–623.

24. This chapter is based on the following article, which discusses other case studies: Clampitt, P. G., & Berk, L. R. 1996. Strategically communicating organisational change. *Journal of Communication Management* 1 (1):15–28.

10

Cultivating the Innovative Spirit

Everything that can be invented has been invented.

Charles H. Duell, Director of U.S. Patent Office, 1899

Loyalty to petrified opinion never broke a chain or freed a human soul.

Mark Twain

He was like so many innovators who yearned for change and looked to the future with a wide-eyed eagerness. He was young, energetic, a bit brash, and had an infectious enthusiasm for life. He had a favorite saying that inspired not only him but also those around him, "Some men see things as they are and say, why? I dream things that never were and say, why not?" This is the spirit of innovation. And it was that spirit which emboldened the thousands who supported him. Tragically, his life was cut short at the hand of an assassin.

Yet, even in the anguish and despair of that moment there was a glimmer of hope. The vision—his vision—still lived. Even today, there are those who dream dreams and have the courage and tenacity to bring them to reality. Robert F. Kennedy never had that chance. But he would cheer on those who did. He understood the innovative process and how to foster the spirit of innovation, which provides the focus for this chapter.

Misconceptions

Chapter 10: By the Numbers

15%
the amount of work time some 3M employees can devote to their own innovative ideas

50%
of new ideas at P & G come from outside the company

80%
of all new products fail or fall significantly short of their profit forecast within six months of their introduction

2.4 to 1
is the estimated ratio of innovations per employee in small businesses vs. large ones

5–10%
of the success of an innovation is owed to the idea generation phase

---

In order to understand the innovation process, we must first deal with the following pernicious myths.

Myth 1 - Innovation Is Risky

Managers and organizations often resist innovation because of a fear of the unknown. Innovative practices, by definition, are not tested, tried, and proved; they are not traditional. Results cannot be guaranteed. There can, in fact, be "failures." The safe course appears to continue to do what the organization does well. Thus, managers often assume that tampering with past successes can incur unnecessary risks. Why change if everything is going well? Yet, this pseudo-argument begs the question; the answer is implicit in the question. Logically, one could just as easily ask, why not change? After all, the successful company or manager has the economic and political wherewithal to experiment.

In the long run, organizations risk more by *not* innovating than they do by innovating. Consider the near collapse of the U.S. steel industry. For years, major U.S. manufacturers took a pass on the mini-mill technology while competitors embraced the innovations. The result: Today mini-mills produce most of the rods, bars, and structural beams in North America.[1] In fact, scholars have analyzed the financial results of firms that heavily invest in research and development efforts. They discovered that those companies recognized for being on the cutting-edge significantly outperform other, less innovative competitors in terms of stock prices, earnings, and productivity.[2] Consider, for example, Denmark's Bang & Olufsen, a manufacturer of high-end consumer electronic equipment. The CFO, Peter Thostrup, increased investment in new products because he believes that innovation provides a way of out of recession.[3]

But the risks of not innovating go beyond the domination of a particular market. The survival of our economic system depends on innovation. Around 1909, Bell Telephone conducted a study of how many telephone operators would be needed if telephone usage continued to increase at the rate of the time. They concluded that between 1925 and 1930, every female in the United States between the ages of 17 and 60 would have to become a telephone operator.[4] That scenario, of course, was untenable. Yet, within two years, automatic switching devices were developed. In short, the perceived risks of innovating quickly faded upon deeper examination.

Myth 2 - Innovations Spring From Revolutionary "Big" Ideas or Grand Schemes

Although some innovations, such as the Wright Brothers' airplane, are revolutionary, most are not. The "little" ideas, the minor modification or the addition of a feature, are the greatest sources of innovation. Here's a sampling:

- During the 1950s, Allen Grant, the president of Glen Raven Mills, asked his wife, Ethel, "What would happen if we made a pair of panties and fastened the stockings to it?" She thought it was a grand idea. The result: pantyhose.[5]
- Howard Shultz dreamed of building a company that treated ordinary people, like his father (who was an unskilled worker), with dignity. He was also bold enough to believe that consumers would pay a premium to drink a superior cup of coffee. The result: Starbucks, a highly profitable company, which is widely respected for its personnel policies.[6]
- An employee at a small paper converting plant suggested that someone begin work one-half-hour early to warm up the cutting machines. The result: An increase in efficiency by eliminating 5 working hours each week (and the addition of 5 hours of idle time for that division).

In each case, these seemingly minor innovations reaped huge dividends.

Likewise, many of the greatest scientific discoveries were the product of the seemingly inconsequential. For instance, Louis Pasteur became intrigued by an experiment that had gone "bad" when his calcium tartrate solution became turbid because of some mold. "Most chemists would have poured the liquid down the sink, considering the experiment as entirely spoiled."[7] Not Pasteur. He used such a seemingly trivial event to launch into his prodigious innovations of pasteurization and immunizations for contagious diseases. Pasteur once reflected on "the infinitely great power of the infinitely small" in the world of bacteria, fungi, and the like.[8] Perhaps he spoke in another sense, as well, and was characterizing the entire process of innovation.

Myth 3 - Innovation Is Product-Focused

Most discussions of innovation center on the invention of new products, such as the electric light bulb or personal computer. History books take note of the genius of Alexander Graham Bell, Benjamin Franklin, Eli Whitney, Robert Fulton, and other entrepreneurial heroes who have invented some gadget or device. Clearly they deserve attention for they have contributed greatly to our lives. Yet, they represent only one narrow band on the entire innovative spectrum.

There are other great innovators who, although not heralded in the history books, have equal significance. Few Americans would recognize the name of Rowland Hill. Yet, he is often credited with "inventing" the modern postal service in 1836. Postal systems existed since antiquity, but Hill suggested a new approach: a postage rate that was uniform across Great Britain. He also proposed that the sender pay the fee and attach a stamp to the letter, just as we do today. But it was not always that way. Previously, the cost was computed according to the weight and distance and paid by the recipient. Such service was, at the least, inconvenient and costly. Hill's proposal changed all that and was a smashing success. Yet, he invented no product or new gadget. Rather, he invented a new method that has been enjoyed by countless millions ever since.[9] Surely he deserves mention in the innovators' Hall of Fame.

Or consider a more recent example. UnitedHealth, a provider of health insurance in the United States, has revolutionized the administrative process. The title of *Fortune* Magazine's review of the company, "The HMO (Almost) Nobody Hates," reveals quite an accomplishment for a company in an industry largely disparaged by the U.S. media and public. UnitedHealth achieved its stellar reputation by challenging conventional practices and instituting many patient-friendly innovations. For example, in 1999 they abandoned the practice of requiring that physicians get permission from the company before ordering a treatment. Their analysis showed that this prior authorization policy (still used by many HMOs) consumed an enormous amount of resources and only resulted in rejecting 2% of the requests. That hardly made it worth the bother. Moreover, the old policy just made physicians and patients angry. Who benefits from this kind of innovative spirit? Consumers and shareholders: Consumers are more satisfied with service and shareholders are pleased with the company's growth and earnings.[10]

These examples demonstrate that innovation goes beyond the mere introduction of new products. There are innovative possibilities in every field of human endeavor. However, taking advantage of these possibilities requires a firm understanding of the innovative process, which we discuss next.

What Is Innovation?

Innovators need more than a good idea. The innovation process can be thought of in four stages: 1) idea generation, 2) feasibility analysis, 3) reality testing, and 4) implementation. The process winnows down the possibilities to the select few that can be really useful to the organization (see Figure 10.1).

Idea Generation

The first stage involves the generation of novel ideas. Brainstorming is an effective technique at this stage. Often done in a group setting, people are encouraged to think of wild, bold, and new ideas in a non-evaluative setting. The more far out, the better. Feasibility, logic, and practicality are *not* the guides; instead, intuition, creativity, ambiguity, and speculation reign supreme. At this stage, the quantity, not the quality, of ideas matters most. Professor of Management Science and Engineering, Robert Sutton, noted that, "Every bit of solid theory and evidence demonstrates that it is impossible to generate a few good ideas without generating a lot of bad ideas."[11]

Most employees have a wealth of creative ideas that could prove useful. Indeed, after extensive study of creative and non-creative research and design R & D employees, a group of psychologists have concluded that the greatest difference between the groups was that, "The creative people thought they were creative and the less creative people didn't think they were."[12] Or as Henry Ford said, "If you think you can, or if you think you can't, you are right." There are a variety of subtle ways that organizations stifle creativity, such as not providing a forum to make suggestions or not recognizing employees who have useful ideas. Effective managers seek to release employees' latent creativity by removing the inhibiting factors.

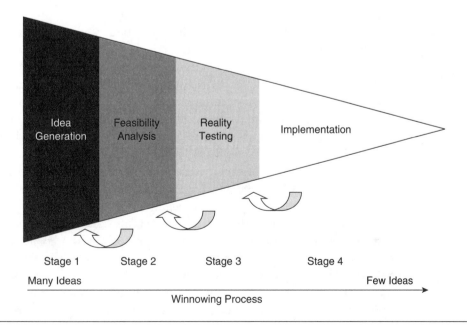

Figure 10.1   Innovation Process

Ingenuity must be cultivated in the organizational culture, much like tending a garden. With proper care and the right conditions, ideas will eventually sprout.

Feasibility Analysis

In the second stage the question becomes, "Which of the multitude of ideas generated are really feasible?" Is it actually possible to create the product or execute the idea? Experiments or test-runs are often conducted at this juncture to determine if a product can actually be made. For example, computer simulations of design changes may be created. Prototypes can be built and tested. A new advertising campaign could be test-marketed. If the results indicate that the basic idea or design needs to be rethought, the entire process can begin anew.

For example, in the early 1970s, Philips, a Dutch company, suggested that it might be possible to use lasers to play audio and video recordings. Many U.S. corporations worked for years only to abandon the project, considering it hopeless. Sony and Philips persevered, and as a result, they launched the entire compact disk revolution that made vinyl records a collector's item. For most companies the idea never got past the feasibility stage. For Philips and Sony, persistence paid off; they not only introduced an innovation, but also a revolutionary one.[13]

Reality Testing

Are resources available to produce the innovation? Can the new service be rendered with a reasonable profit? Does the new procedure reduce costs or improve productivity? These are the tough questions asked during the reality testing phase. Wisely addressing the return on investment question requires considerable expertise, intuition, and prescience. Information will be incomplete. And many innovations take a long time to be "reality tested." Consider the difficulty in assessing the economic viability of introducing a new prescription drug. The feedback loop extends over many years. Additionally, new ideas may appear more successful than objective evidence indicates because of the "placebo effect." That is, employees will often make something work simply because they thought up the idea.

Organizations also have their own idiosyncratic "reality tests" that are determined by the unique corporate culture. An idea needs to be filtered to the right people at the right time in order to succeed. Indeed, someone who develops a successful innovation not only needs a workable idea, but also the political backing in the organization to push it through to the implementation phase. An idea that might be embraced in one culture may not stand a chance in another organizational culture.

Implementation

Seemingly, if an idea has survived the feasibility and reality tests, then implementation would be a foregone conclusion. Experience does not bear out this conclusion. In one organization we found that only 60% of the ideas formally accepted were actually implemented. The frequent victims are the ideas generated at the lowest levels of the organization. The reason: Implementation frequently depends on the support at a higher level of management. For example, in an attempt to increase productivity, one paper mill employee suggested a change in the way a drum was cleaned. The idea was evaluated and deemed cost effective. Approval was given and budget allocations were made. But for some reason, the purchase was never made and the idea never implemented. Sadly, neglect, time constraints, and other priorities take their toll on new ideas and the employees who suggest them.

Implications

There are three important implications of this process view of innovation.

First, different evaluation criteria are used at each stage of the innovation process. In the first stage, judgments tend to be made in terms of novelty and creativity. But this does not mean the idea will translate into innovation. Using nuclear energy to power a space shuttle meets the novelty test but fails to meet the feasibility test. Even if an idea proves feasible, that does not guarantee workability. For example, the oceans contain billions of tons of gold. Polymers have been created that can sift the gold from ocean water. However, production costs make the process financially untenable. Hence, the idea is novel and possible, but not workable. It fails on the third criteria. Faced with a roadblock at any of the stages, innovators have two alternatives: abandon the idea, or restart the entire process until eventually the idea crosses all the hurdles.

Abandoning an idea may be the best alternative. Killing a project that many people believe in requires insight and emotional toughness. As one theorist put it, "The value of someone who is able to pull the plug on a project before it becomes a money sink hasn't generally been appreciated."[14] Innovative companies know how to stop the questionable projects without halting the innovative process.

Second, different organizational barriers crop up at each stage of the innovative process. The organizational policies or attributes that allow seeming success at one stage of the process may actually inhibit the process at another stage. Typically, organizations that are high in complexity and low in formalization and centralization provide a rich environment for innovation in the initial stages, but present difficulties at the implementation stage. This seems reasonable because complex, but loosely organized companies would allow frequent and varied communications across departmental and organizational boundaries. Thus, a great number of ideas should be spawned in such interactions. Yet, getting the employees together to do something different might prove difficult because of the very same diversity. On the other hand, a more centralized and controlled structure does not fully encourage communication across organizational boundaries and, therefore, inhibits idea formation.[15] Yet, such a structure would be able to quickly implement a new idea if one should be approved.[16] Therefore, executives need to learn how to simultaneously encourage new ideas and maintain a structure that can rapidly implement the ideas. Striking that balance requires special skills. One organizational theorist insightfully summarized the critical question,

> . . . How can complex organizations solve the problem of normal functioning (i.e., efficient operations; reduction of complexity; control; and governance), and still embody the tensions which power innovation?[17]

Managers must use different tactics at each juncture of the innovative process. Indeed, the Circuit manager tends to excel at the initial stages of the innovation process, whereas the Arrow manager excels at the latter stages. The effective manager acts like an "idea shepherd," protecting the ideas from various attacks along their journey. Flexibility and savvy are the key weapons. Table 10.1 reveals some of the more common barriers encountered at each stage. In the idea generation stage (Stage 1), the difficulties tend to revolve around developing an environment of creativity. In the feasibility analysis stage (Stage 2), managers need to get the ideas on the agenda to be tested or analyzed. In the reality testing stage (Stage 3), building commitment for the idea becomes the core challenge. In the final stage, implementation, managers need to motivate, persuade, and perhaps cajole people into doing what the organization has approved.

Third, the timeline for the innovative process is elastic. In some cases, the four stages can take a matter of days. In other cases, the process may take years. A new Web page design may take only a week from conception to implementation, whereas the design of a new microchip may take years. As J. A. Morton, a former vice president at Bell Telephone laboratories, said: "Innovation is not a single, simple act."[18] Therefore, the cost of innovation will vary greatly depending on the type of idea. The Web page, if a failure, can be easily changed, whereas an entire company's well-being may be based on a new microchip.

The length of the time line should determine resource investment at each stage. Innovations linked to longer time lines require prudence and thought. A pharmaceutical company proposing a new product must be cautious, as the failure of a new drug could seal the fate of the company. Consequently, the emphasis should be on proper research and development (Stages 2 & 3). In contrast, a marketing or advertising firm should devote most of its resources to encourage creativity (Stage 1). A single failure of an ad or marketing campaign can be relatively quickly rectified compared to a pharmaceutical's failure of a new drug. In a broader sense, wise organizational leaders ask, "Is the company investing its resources appropriately in the various stages, given the type of innovations we are seeking?" For instance,

Table 10.1   Issues in the Innovation Process

Stage	Evaluation Criteria	Critical Questions	Organizational Barriers
Idea Generation	Novelty	• Is the idea novel?	• Highly structured organizational climate • Authoritarian communication style • Too many rules and regulations • Extreme power differences
Feasibility Analysis	Possibility	• Is the idea possible?	• Lack of corporate resources dedicated to research • Lack of commitment to research
Reality Testing	Practicality	• Does the idea produce a reasonable return on investment? • Does the idea fit with organizational objectives? • Does the organization have the start-up capital for the idea?	• Short-term focus • Inadequate research on the potential return or marketability of idea • Resistance to change
Implementation	Actionable	• Has the idea been acted on?	• Too many priorities • Nobody has responsibility for the implementation • Over-consultation with involved parties • Highly unstructured organizational climate

the company may be devoting too many resources to generating new ideas and too few to Stages 2 and 3.

A Perspective on Success and Failure

Adroitly managing the innovative process requires a clear understanding of success and failure. Figure 10.2 diagrams four possible quadrants in which a given innovation might fall.

Potential Success

A potential success occurs when the results of the innovation are disappointing but the "failure" produces valuable knowledge. In every "failure,"

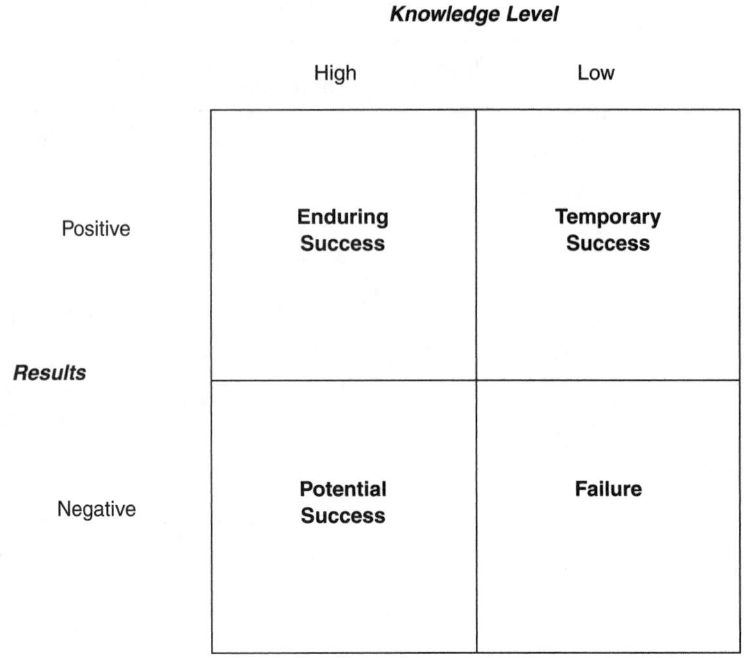

Knowledge Level

	High	Low
Positive	**Enduring Success**	**Temporary Success**
Results		
Negative	**Potential Success**	**Failure**

Figure 10.2   Innovation Successes and Failures

some knowledge can be gained. This may sound like a platitude of a motivational speaker. But the cold hard facts remain that those organizations and people who ultimately prevail learn from their "mistakes." And those who do not are at the whim of happenstance.

Consider one of the most widely hyped and anticipated inventions in recent years. Well-known investors like Jeff Bezos and Steve Jobs were sworn to secrecy during its development process. What was "IT"?[19] "IT," also known as the Segway, was an ingenuous two-wheeled scooter designed to revolutionize transportation. Yet, to date this unique "people mover" has failed to live up to expectations. A variety of reasons, such as its price and concerns about pedestrian safety, account for its less-than-stellar reception. In fact, some cities have banned them.[20] If Segway developers choose to learn lessons from the tepid consumer reactions, this may be labeled a potential success. If not, Segway will go down in the history books as a clever failure, but a failure, nevertheless.

Failure

True failure results when the organization does not learn from an innovative experiment. The movie industry, for example, has had an almost sustained rate of box office "bombs" over the years. Is this the nature of the business? Maybe. Yet, little research has been devoted to the characteristics of these box office failures other than on an individual basis. The collective knowledge yielded from such research could, at least, alter the probabilities of future box office failures. This state of affairs seems like a failure on two levels: Financial results are less than spectacular and no one seems to learn from mistakes.

Temporary Success

A temporary success occurs when the results obviously meet or exceed expectations but the organization does not understand why the success occurred. Temporarily, money—maybe lots of money—can be made, but the results are not enduring. Schwinn bicycles, for example, at one time dominated the market, but executives failed to act wisely as the market changed. "Schwinn failed to recognize that after those golden years the bicycle markets segmented, with new populations arriving to take to alternate forms of the sport."[21] Schwinn essentially missed out on the mountain biking and hybrid markets.

Enduring Success

Useful ideas, coupled with knowledge of why the ideas succeeded, produce enduring success. Certainly, people like Thomas Edison or Benjamin Franklin had this uncanny ability. Organizations, even more than individual inventors, need to understand their successes in order to pass along their knowledge to others. 3M, for example, appears to appreciate this fact of innovative life. Over the years the company has enjoyed sustained growth and development. After all, the company, now known for making Post-It® Notes among thousands of other products, was founded as Minnesota Mining and Manufacturing Company. The company continues to introduce successful products and services despite occasional and expected "failures." The company constantly conducts research, even on profitable products, seeking to understand their successes as well as their "failures."

Implications

Present success does not guarantee future success. Just because an innovation has proven successful under one set of conditions does not mean it will continue to be successful. Oscar Wilde said it best, "Consistency is the last refuge of the unimaginative." Nokia used to be in the paper business and now it makes more mobile phones than any company in the world. [22] It may seem safe to keep doing what one does well. But this reasoning can only take an organization so far. Sustaining success requires continual innovation as conditions evolve. Keeping a proper balance between the traditional successes and future potential successes may be one of the most important challenges facing management. After all, tradition is often the enemy of innovation.

The actual innovation is but the tip of the iceberg. The knowledge base underneath the idea is the key to further growth and innovation. Even "failures" can add to the knowledge base. When conditions change, a new idea can spring forth from that knowledge base.

There may not even be an awareness of all the knowledge that sustains a successful innovation. The inventor of the Ethernet and founder of 3Com, Bob Metcalfe, said, "Most successful entrepreneurs I've met have no idea about the reasons for their success."[23] The same could be said about successful innovators within organizations. To sustain success, innovators need to push for even deeper levels of understanding because that knowledge provides the basis for still further innovation. Vaccines, for example, have been used for years to prevent deadly diseases, but only in more recent years have scientists begun to understand why a vaccine actually works. As the reasons for success emerged, so have other treatment regimens. So it is with most innovations.

Fostering meaningful dialogue sparks learning and knowledge creation. The implicit rules that govern organizational discussions greatly influence the degree to which knowledge emerges from technical successes or failures. Managers who rule through intimidation induce an unwillingness to hold meaningful discussion. Paul Winch, the Senior Innovation Manager at Good Humor Breyers, adopts just the opposite approach. Perhaps his choice of diversions has something to do with it. He has written a novel, plays in a rock band, and even composed a classic local tune, "Cheesehead Girl." That's a pretty intriguing resume for a guy with a Ph.D. in Physics. He spurs on the innovative spirit of his employees by allowing discussions to veer "off the topic." As a result, light bulbs start turning on. He summed up his philosophy like this, "In the long run, a stimulating discussion beats a meticulous plan every time." In short, he engenders trust and comfort, so that employees can discuss honestly the reasons for successes or failures.

Stop and Go Signs

Stop signs regulate the flow of traffic. With too few stop signs, the streets are unsafe. With too many, drivers become irritated. Organizations may not have red, yellow, and green lights but they have other signals that have a similar impact on the flow of organizational events. The corporate policies, rules, regulations, procedures, organizational structure, the day-to-day interactions in meetings, conversations, and memoranda are all varieties of these organizational traffic signals. If there are too many stop signs, then innovative efforts come to a grinding halt. If there are too few, chaos ensues.

Effective managers then design a system that: a) does not impede the flow of innovative ideas; b) increases the probability of a safe and speedy passage for useful ideas; and c) decreases the probability that poor ideas proceed to the implementation stage. The guidelines discussed next focus on how to design a system with the appropriate organizational traffic signals.

Educate Employees About the
Organization's Innovation Philosophy and Policy

Most organizations have a philosophy or mission statement that includes a sentence or phrase about innovation. Effective leaders use these abstract commitments to develop a more thorough innovation philosophy and/or policy. The very process of developing the philosophy or policy statement encourages management to articulate goals and responsibilities. But statements of intent are not a guarantee of action; there must be mechanisms for implementation. Training provides an appropriate starting point.

The training should focus on the employee's role in the innovation process. At a minimum, the training should highlight the following issues:

- *Every employee can become an innovator.* Even "small" ideas can produce major improvements. Successful innovations are not solely the product of a few great minds in the Research and Development department.
- *Innovation is a process.* Employees should take responsibility for not only generating novel ideas, but also shepherding the best ideas through the other three stages of the innovation model.
- *"Failures" are expected and provide important learning opportunities.* When an idea gets rejected for some reason, employees can learn more about organizational standards or the marketplace.

These notions cultivate an innovative or continuous improvement mindset that can permeate the organization. The training implies that employees have some responsibility for the winnowing process, by having to set their own priorities and decide which ideas are really important to pursue.

Does it work? The joint venture of Toyota and GM, called NUMMI (New United Auto Manufacturing, Inc.), discovered the power of these notions. The "suggestion form at NUMMI makes very explicit the criteria by which the suggestion is going to be evaluated and encourages workers to evaluate their suggestions themselves using these criteria."[24] Consequently, the average employee makes about six suggestions per year and over 90% of them are adopted. Compare these statistics to the typical company. Only 8% of U.S. employees make any suggestion at all, and only 25% of these suggestions culminate into some action.[25] The lesson: Invest in the employees and they will invest in the organization. If not, opportunities will walk out of the door every day.

Develop Company Programs and
Policies That Encourage Innovation

Some companies, such as IBM, allow their employees to take sabbaticals to work in a new environment or teach in a college. By placing employees in different environments, they can meet new people, come across new ideas, and hopefully generate their own novel approaches. They can even pursue some projects on company time. For example, two IBM scientists, K. Alex Mueller and J. Georg Bednorz, toiled away on their project at their Swiss lab in-between their normal duties. They were two of the principal scientists who set off the frenzy for superconductors, which are substances that conduct electricity without resistance. At one point, Bednorz was so excited about the project that he was spending up to 30% of his time on it. In the end, they not only told management, but also the world about this revolutionary idea.[26]

Other major companies also have model programs that encourage innovation. 3M has a program that allows employees to spend up to 15% of their time working on their own innovative project with little or no direct managerial control. Indeed, the almost ubiquitous Post-It® Notes are a direct result of this rule and now account for millions of dollars of revenue. And 3M takes it one step further with its Genesis grants. Employees can apply for up to $100,000 of seed money to carry their projects past the idea state.[27]

Some companies have developed policies to open up the innovation process even further by turning to external sources. For instance, pharmaceutical giant, Merck, has a department devoted to scouring the world for useful external research. Other companies, such as Intel, have forged alliances with universities. Dow Chemical even posts nagging scientific problems on a Web site and offers up to $100,000 to any scientists who come up with useful solutions. The CEO of Procter & Gamble declared that 50% of all new ideas must come from outside sources. P & G also has 53 "technology scouts" who hunt down potentially promising ideas.[28] These policies can save money by defraying development costs, but they also combat the insular and inward looking perspective of internal innovators. In short, policies designed to extend the network of the organization may encourage innovation.

Eliminate Lengthy Proposal Procedures and Foster Informal Communication

The paperwork involved in proposing or even pursuing a project can be a major roadblock to innovation. Employees often feel stifled when asked to fully justify ideas. They may be working on a hunch. Many of the questions cannot be fully answered until later in the innovation process. In fact, many of the relevant questions cannot even be anticipated. Moreover, extensive paperwork subtly signals that employees must guarantee results and not fail. Innovative minds often resist these pressures. In fact, the National Institutes of Health recently recognized that the traditional grant process, which focuses on a particular project, inhibits some creative researchers. Thus, they decided to set up a few grants to exceptional individuals (not projects) to pursue "unconventional ideas with high potential payoff."[29]

Streamlining the documentation process may be a good start, but other procedures warrant examination. The administrative procedures for proposing, winnowing, and implementing an idea can become cumbersome. How many organizational levels does an idea have to go through to get the green light? Can any of these levels be eliminated? Can some ideas simply be approved and initiated on the spot? These questions focus attention on how to speed up the process and eliminate the natural barriers to innovation.

Why do organizations often bog down innovation with paperwork and administrative regulations? Because these barriers provide a sense of control over the process. What will be the regulative mechanism if these are scaled down? Informal communication and networks can fill the gap. Managers can keep up-to-date by informally communicating with employees about projects or new ideas. Often this kind of "checking up" proves more informative than endless reams of paperwork.

Informal networks encourage discussion across departmental boundaries and formal lines of authority. Useful ideas seem to spawn in such a free-flowing environment. Why? This is true, in part, because these discussions expose organizational problems, concerns, and needs—all of which are begging for innovative solutions.[30] Employees need to know where these gaps are before they can creatively address them. They must also have a workspace designed to encourage informal problem sharing and solving. Adding blackboards, sketchpads, and flip charts seems to do the trick.[31] These tools have one common characteristic: They enable ideas to be quickly and easily amended or deleted. A sense of informality pervades discussions. No one loses face because no one records a formal rejection. Therefore, speculation, change, and creativity are encouraged. Formal documents tend to inhibit the attributes vital for innovators. And that explains why innovative leaders favor meaningful informal communication over often meaningless paperwork.

Require and Reward Innovation

An organization or manager can make innovation a job requirement. For example, 3M sets divisional sales targets in terms of new product development with a program called 2X/3X. This means that the division sets an objective of introducing two times the number of new product innovations as the past year and three times the number of "winning" products as the past year.[32] Bonuses are also tied to this yardstick. The program works. 3M markets more than fifty thousand products worldwide, ranging from Scotch® Tape to Thinsulate™ Insulation.

Companies reward activities they value. Employees know this and react accordingly. Financial rewards have proven successful, but other rewards, such as personal recognition, are often more meaningful. 3M has a number of programs, such as the Pyramid of Excellence, designed to recognize and reward employees who make exceptional contributions. Innovators can be recognized in company newsletters, Web pages, trade publications, and the local media. For example, 3M posted "A Century of Innovation" on its Web site. This commemorates employee innovations over the company's one-hundred-year history.[33] The site sends a clear message to the public-at-large as well as employees that 3M values innovation. One can easily imagine employees locating their name in the document, copying it, and showing it to family and friends.

The initiatives and rewards cited thus far are rather mundane when compared to an award dreamed up by Jeff Bezos at Amazon.com. Employees who win the prestigious "Just Do It" award have dreamed up a useful idea and implemented it without their supervisor's blessing. This award is reminiscent of a medal David Packard of Hewlett Packard gave to an engineer who disobeyed his explicit orders and pursued a project that eventually resulted in $35 million in revenue. Packard gleefully presented the medal for "extraordinary contempt and defiance beyond the normal call of engineering duty."[34]

Regardless of the method, celebrating innovations provides recognition to innovative employees. But it is also meaningful to those who have not been recognized because it acts as a target for them. Hence, the size of the reward matters less than the meaning of the recognition.

Learn How to Properly Reject Novel Ideas

Dr. Orlando A. Battista, a research scientist, was asked to develop a fine structure of nylon fibers to be used in tires. Instead, he came up with a white powder in a crystal form. His boss wanted to fire him, but that would have been a major blunder. Other minds prevailed and he was allowed to pursue his strange substance. The result of his discovery was Avacil—a product that physicians use as a clotting agent for blood and manufacturers use in salad dressings, beauty creams, and a host of other products.[35] All of this resulted from a "bad" idea.

The art of dealing with a "bad" idea rests on a simple philosophy: An employee's idea may fail but that doesn't mean the employee is a failure. Sometimes employees who introduce ideas that do not work out are ostracized or labeled as kooks; in essence, they are treated as failures. Such practices send strong and discouraging messages to others who might have a useful idea. One wonders how many potential Battistas have been lost because a manager rejected the person along with the novel idea.

Unskilled managers evaluate a new idea in terms of whether it is good or bad, useful or useless, or effective or ineffective (see Figure 10.3). They reject problematic ideas out-of-hand, just as Dr. Battista's supervisor did. This kind of evaluation process creates a false dichotomy in which an idea either *hits* or *misses* the target. Far too many ideas go unheeded and untested because of this kind of simple-minded thinking. Even when employees receive positive feedback, they do not know what makes the idea effective (a temporary success).

In contrast, skilled managers look at an idea in terms of attributes or characteristics, some of which are useful and some not.[36] Note how in Figure 10.3, the manager more closely examines the idea by identifying key characteristics

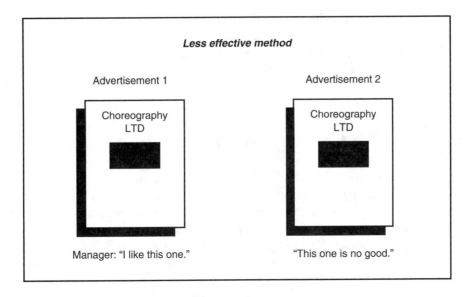

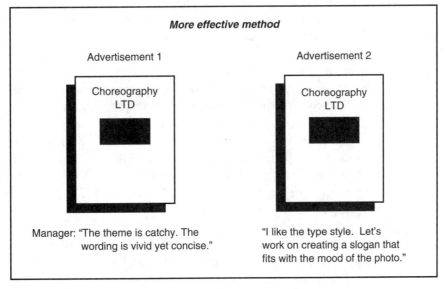

Figure 10.3   Evaluating an Idea

that can be refined. This approach fosters deeper understanding, regardless of the ultimate decision about the innovation. Inevitably, managers will have to flatly reject some ideas. Employees generally respond more positively to an honest and straightforward appraisal of the idea. Then they know precisely what criteria are being used in evaluating an idea. And they may even find some solution to the precise objection, thereby making the notion viable. In the long run, a frank appraisal may discourage pursuit of a certain idea, but it actually encourages the general pursuit of innovation.

In sum, the entire set of organizational traffic signals should be examined. When the right philosophy, policies, programs, incentives, and training are coupled with skilled managers, the organization can become an innovative superhighway allowing the best ideas to travel smoothly through all the innovation stages.

Conclusion: The Challenge of Innovation

Sir Winston Churchill is best known as a great statesman, author, or perhaps, a painter. Few know that he was also a successful innovator. His special genius led to a variety of innovations: a navigational tool used to guide pilots, the idea of dropping tin foil to confuse enemy radar, armor-plated buses, and even the artificial harbors used on D-day.[37] He was also known as the father of the modern tank. It was Churchill who, during the bloody trench warfare of World War I, thought of the tank as a practical means to end the madness. Although Churchill said that no single man could be said to have invented the tank, it was known at the time as "Winston's folly." And with good reason: He was the one who provided the idea and the money for the endeavor. But today, no one scoffs at the transformation of warfare wrought by "Winston's folly."

The invention of the tank teaches us lessons on several counts. As Churchill freely acknowledged in his memoirs, the idea was not entirely novel. H. G. Wells had speculated about such a vehicle as early as 1903. In fact, the tools used for the innovation were already well known: The technology for armor plating had been used in ships, the internal combustion engine had been proven reliable, and caterpillar tracks had been used on other vehicles. The key was to combine the various devices into a new and useful weapon. This was no easy task.

"Winston's folly" is an example of how many innovations emerge from novel combinations of already existing ideas. Moreover, his discovery provides a splendid example of the hurdles faced by most innovators. He discussed the project at length in his memoirs of the First World War:

> I thus took personal responsibility for the expenditure of the public money involved . . . . It was a serious decision to spend this large sum of money on a project so speculative, about the merits of which no high expert military or naval authority had been convinced. The matter, moreover, was entirely outside the scope of my own Department or of any normal powers which I possessed. Had the tanks proved wholly abortive or never been accepted or never used in war by the military authorities, and had I been subsequently summoned before a Parliamentary Committee, I could have offered no effective defence to the charge that I had wasted public money on a matter which was not in any way my business and in regard to which I had not received expert advice in any responsible military quarter.[38]

Churchill's narrative about his decision offers three valuable insights about the challenges facing innovators.

This Passage Illustrates the
Speculative Nature of Any Innovation

Any number of different experts and committees had rejected the idea. No one except Churchill thought it would work. In a similar fashion, disbelievers often attempt to thwart innovators in organizations. Innovators naturally seem to first run into the scoffers, then the cynics, followed by the critics, and finally, the surprised.

Churchill, like all successful innovators, recognized that there were no assurances. Someone had the courage to take a chance, albeit a calculated one. Companies that refuse to take risks, often by tying up the process with endless red tape, stifle innovation. Moreover, they are operating under the delusion that the red tape will provide certainty when, in fact, there can be no such thing. There must be room for "failure" and no amount of red tape can remove that basic risk. One theorist sums up the matter best, "The demand for predictable outcomes deprives many companies of unusual outcomes."[39]

Note That Churchill Was the First Lord of the Admiralty
at the Time When he Proposed and Authorized the Tank

Here was a man whose primary responsibility was sea warfare, backing the research and development of a land-based weapon. He obviously strayed very far afield. Organizations that believe in innovation cannot stick to rigid departmental responsibilities. Often the very best creative ideas come from the cross-fertilization that occurs between departments. Sometimes a person from another department has a totally different perspective on a problem. Ineffective managers reject ideas out-of-hand because they come from the wrong department or outside the company. They communicate this message with comments such as, "That's not really your concern." But the wise leader recognizes that innovative ideas are like wildflowers; they can crop up anywhere, even in the Admiralty.

The Tank Saga Demonstrates the Necessity
for Someone to Be the Idea Champion

Somebody must clear away the red tape, take the chance, and become an "idea shepherd." Furthermore, the person must be powerful enough and the organization flexible enough to allow this person the financial wherewithal to sponsor the endeavor.[40] There must be some slack resources to commit to the idea even when it lies clearly outside the province of one's primary concern.[41] The idea shepherd needs special skills because the task taxes even the most astute and tireless. One organizational theorist described the enormity of the job in the following way:

The product's conceptualization and development require that innovators solve complex problems to overcome surprises, work around barriers, merge processes from different functions, weave together resources from different locations. Innovators must push issues along within each function, such as setting up manufacturing processes, . . . and working through the details of design.[42]

Churchill and his team were up to the task. Innovators need this kind of tenacity to transform an idea into an innovation. Churchill did it and dedicated managers can as well.

Notes

1. Christensen, C. 1997. *The innovator's dilemma.* Boston: Harvard Business School Press.

2. Deng, A., Lev, B., & Narin, F. 1999. Science and technology as predictors of stock performance. *Association for Investment Management and Research,* May/June:20–32.

3. Larsen. P. F. 2003. Better is . . . better. *Wall Street Journal,* 22 September:R6.

4. Drucker, P. F. 1985. *Innovation and entrepreneurship.* New York: Harper & Row.

5. 1989. Nights of the garter are over. *Wall Street Journal,* 25 August:B1.

6. Daniels, C. 2003. Mr. Coffee. *Fortune,* 14 April:139–140.

7. Dubos, R. 1976. *Louis Pasteur.* New York: Scribners, p. 107.

8. Ibid., p. 45.

9. Drucker, op. cit.

10. Stires, D. 2003. The HMO (almost) nobody hates. *Fortune,* 15 September:189–191.

11. Sutton, R. I. 2001. The weird rules of creativity. *Harvard Business Review* 79 (8):94–103, p. 101.

12. See, for example, Oech, R. 1983. *A whack on the side of the head.* Menlo Park, CA: Creative Think, p. 122.

13. Browning, E. S. 1986. Sony's perseverance helped it win market for mini-CD players. *Wall Street Journal,* 27 February:A1, A11.

14. Royer, I. 2003. Why bad projects are so hard to kill. *Harvard Business Review* 81 (2):48–56, p. 50.

15. Dougherty, D., & Hardy, C. 1996. Sustained product innovation in large, mature organizations: Overcoming innovation-to-organization problems. *Academy of Management Journal* 39 (5):1120–1153.

16. See, for example, Lawrence, P. R., & Lorsch, J. W. 1969. *Organization and environment.* Homewood, IL: Irwin.

17. Dougherty, D. 1996. Organizing for innovation. In *Handbook of Organization Studies,* edited by S. R. Clegg, C. Hardy, & W. R. Nord (pp. 424–439). Thousand Oaks: Sage Publications, pp. 435–436.

18. Morton, J. A. 1971. *Organizing for innovation.* New York: McGraw-Hill, p. 49.

19. IT was the nickname used in press reports.

20. Kemper, S. 2003. *Code name Ginger.* Cambridge: Harvard Business School.

21. Sobel, R. 1999. *When giants stumble.* Paramus, NJ: Prentice Hall Press, p. 301.

22. Micklethwait, J., & Wooldridge, A. 2003. *The company: A short history of a revolutionary idea.* New York: Modern Library Chronicles Book.

23. Metcalfe, B. 1999. Invention is a flower, innovation is a weed. *Technology Review,* November/December:56–57, p. 56.

24. Adler, P. S. 1999. Building better bureaucracies. *Academy of Management Executive* 13 (4):36–49, p. 43.

25. Ibid., p. 43.

26. Hudson, R. L. 1987. Scientific saga: How 2 physicists triggered superconductor frenzy. *Wall Street Journal,* 19 August:A1, A10.

27. Studt, T. 2003. 3M—Where innovation rules. *R&D Magazine,* April: 20–24, p. 23.

28. Greene, J. 2003. Reinventing corporate R&D. *Business week,* 22 September: 74–76, p. 76.

29. Kaiser, J. 2003. NIH plans new grants for innovative minds. *Science* 301 (5635):902–904.

30. Markides, C. 1997. Strategic innovation. *Sloan Management Review* 38 (3):9–23, p. 12.

31. Peters, T. J., & Waterman, R. H., Jr. 1982. *In search of excellence.* New York: Harper & Row.

32. Studt, op. cit.

33. www.3m.com/about3m/century. Date visited: November 23, 2003.

34. Packard, D. 1995. *The HP way: How Bill Hewlett and I built our company.* New York: HarperCollins. See also Sutton, op. cit., p. 100.

35. Battista, O. A. 1984. Research for profit: The chief executive officer connection. *Accounts of Chemical Research* 17 (4):121–126.

36. Theoretically, each attribute could even have a valence attached to it. Thus, a weighted score could be computer that would allow the innovator to further work on those features that are most problematic.

37. Manchester, W. 1983. *The last lion.* Boston: Little, Brown.

38. Churchill, W. S. 1931. *The world crisis.* New York: Scribners, pp. 316–317.

39. Campbell, D. 1977. *Take the road to creativity and get off your dead end.* Allen, TX: Argus, p. 90.

40. Meyer, A. D., & Goes, J. B. 1988. Organizational assimilation of innovations: A multilevel contextual analysis. *Academy of Management Journal* 31 (4):897–923.

41. On the other hand, too many slack resources also inhibit innovation because the organization lacks the discipline to pursue only those projects likely to provide added value. See Nohria, N., & Gulati, R. 1996. Is slack good or bad for innovation? *Academy of Management Journal* 39 (5):1245–1264.

42. Dougherty, op. cit., p. 427.

11

What Is Communication Effectiveness?

Traditionally, a ship's captain was always the last person to find out that his crew intended to mutiny. Communication audits identify the symptoms of discontent, before either customers or employees storm the bridge. They are an organization's early warning system.

Dennis Tourish & Owen Hargie

The questions we ask are often more important than the answers we provide. Why? Every question implies assumptions that latently structure the answer. For instance, one executive asked, "What training package should we purchase to improve our communication?" The question assumes that a training package will provide the proper solution to the problem. As we have seen, there are many different types of communication difficulties that merit various intervention strategies, many of which may not be addressed by an off-the-shelf training program. All too often, the *perceived* communication difficulties are not the *actual* ones.

Chapter 11: By the Numbers

80%
of CEOs have a different perception of the company than employees

26%
of business executives believe that the company business strategy is "well communicated and understood"

5%
of business executives believe that their IT strategy is "well communicated and understood"

2
The minimal number of data-gathering methods recommended for conducting a communication assessment

75%
of employees identify with their organization's values

The wise executive or manager asks a more fundamental question: What is organizational communication effectiveness? In previous chapters, we have discussed the critical communication issues facing most organizations, including:

- Selecting the proper communication style (Chapters 1 & 2)
- Cultivating an energizing corporate culture (Chapter 3)
- Communicating ethically (Chapter 4)
- Selecting and using communication technologies (Chapter 5)
- Managing data, information, knowledge, and action (Chapter 6)
- Providing performance feedback (Chapter 7)
- Communicating across organizational boundaries (Chapter 8)
- Communicating about change (Chapter 9)
- Cultivating an innovative spirit (Chapter 10)

Clearly, organizations that communicate effectively would excel in all these areas. Yet, this proposition implies deeper questions: How should an organization determine its level of communication proficiency? How will enhancing communication impact the organization's strategic objectives? How should the organization start to make changes in the communication system? These are questions of assessment, communication strategy, and implementation.

I believe in a process-oriented view of effectiveness. It starts with assessment that leads to the communication strategy, and culminates in action. The process continues by returning to an assessment of the results (see Figure 11.1). Consequently, the communication strategy and plans are continually evolving as the organization changes, just as dancers adjust to a new rhythm. This chapter focuses on that process.

Assess

A communication assessment resembles a health check-up. Indeed, some organizational "patients" may find the process almost as intrusive and painful. Nevertheless, organizations that aspire to greatness willingly endure the necessary psychological discomforts in order to create a world-class

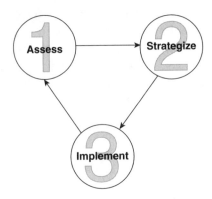

Figure 11.1   Cycle of Communication Effectiveness

communication system. Two scholars who pioneered the assessment process put it this way:

> Communication problems in the organization are not unlike the progressive development of a headache. If the initial bodily cues are ignored or not monitored, the full "throb" will hit. The result is much more time and effort lost in trying to correct the unbearable condition than would have been needed to prevent the situation in the first place. The communication audit can provide that initial sensoring or monitoring for the organization, which will allow for a preventative stance regarding communication problems rather than the typical corrective stance.[1]

An assessment reveals important facts such as employee misconceptions and reactions to current initiatives. Moreover, well-executed assessments may indicate to employees that their opinions are valued.

The assessment starts by thoroughly describing the existing communication system. All communication systems present opportunities and constraints. Some are overly dependent on written channels that may, in turn, slow down decision making. Others focus on producing and delivering elaborate oral presentations that may discourage meaningful dialogue. Consequently, assessors need to discern the impact of the existing communication system on organizational life and accomplishments. They can start by answering these base-line questions:

- *What are the existing channels of communication?* (Road Shows, quarterly meetings, newsletters, etc.)
- *What are the communication goals for each channel?* (sharing information, providing recognition, etc.)
- *What types of messages are typically transmitted in these channels?* (business results, future plans, personnel news, etc.)
- *What is the target audience for each channel?* (managers, line employees, etc.)

Communication assessors, like physicians, may conduct an extensive annual examination. Traditionally scholars use the term "communication audit" to describe this type of assessment. Or an assessor may opt for more frequent monitoring of the organization's vital signs. In either case, the assessment seeks to gauge the general health of the organization's communication system. The discussion that follows underscores the dynamics of each type of assessment.

Communication Audits

When conducting this more extensive assessment, attaining useful results depends on using proper procedures. Consider the following:

Carefully consider who should conduct the assessment. In most cases the organization can benefit from using an independent consultant. Why? Employees are often reluctant to share their true feelings with insiders because they fear identification and possible retaliation. Outside observers can be more objective in analyzing the results and are less influenced by internal politics.

Select the proper method(s) or tool(s). A variety of methods, such as questionnaires, interviews, focus groups, communication logs, and network analysis can be used to conduct an annual or biannual communication audit. Even when the organization imposes limits on data gathering, skillful auditors tend to use a combination of methods. Even as each method reveals, it conceals. So, for example, an assessor using interviews in conjunction with a survey would encounter fewer blindspots than one who relies on a single method. Using interviews in conjunction with surveys might reveal new issues. In the survey design, as well, combining traditional numeric rating scales (quantitative) and open questions (qualitative) such as, "How would you improve communication in the organization?" helps protect the integrity of the process.

Assure all employees that their comments will remain confidential. This will encourage employees to candidly respond.

Make sure that top management fully supports the assessment. This bolsters the participation rate and the likelihood that action will be taken with the findings.

Finally, carefully interpret your findings. Some managers put too much weight on one witty employee's comment. Others want to argue the meaning of a question. The assessor should expect this and be prepared to guide the discussion of the results.

The expense and time involved in collecting the information may trouble some executives. Another potential disadvantage involves building unrealistic employee expectations. If the organization does not plan to respond to the findings, then the data should not be collected in the first place. At a minimum, every employee who participates in the process should receive a summary of the results.

Even if the organization plans on responding to the audit results, the *timeliness* of the response presents one of most troublesome potential drawbacks. In our experience of conducting audits, it is not unusual for the elapsed time between the initial data gathering to the final executive response to reach six months or more. Why? Because an executive team needs time to digest the audit findings, prioritize concerns, and craft responses. By the time employees are briefed on the process, the problems or concerns have often shifted to something else. Often the snapshot taken of the organization, through the lens of an audit, merely reminds employees of a faded memory.

Pulse Process

Our frustrations with this sluggish procedure led us to develop the Pulse Process. The Pulse Process has three major objectives: 1) identify employee concerns and reactions to ongoing initiatives in a timely, reliable, and economical manner; 2) respond to these concerns; and 3) cultivate a productive dialogue between executives and employees. At the heart of this process are three items:

- A short Pulse Survey (10–15 questions), routinely administered to a rotating sample of employees on a biweekly or monthly basis. The survey includes both numerically rated, closed questions as well as one or two open questions, such as "What are the greatest challenges our organization faces?"
- The Pulse Report, a 1-page summary of the findings, presenting quantitative data for the numerically rated questions and major themes for the open questions (see Figure 11.2).
- An Executive Response, outlining senior management reactions to the issues highlighted from the current Pulse Report. In some cases, executives choose to respond to each question raised in the report.

The Pulse Report provides the organization with a timely and accurate record of the current working climate. The executive response cultivates a productive and ongoing dialogue within the organization and provides employees a way of understanding the executive thought process.

The Pulse Process requires a similar degree of attentiveness to procedural concerns as a communication audit. The survey questions should be carefully constructed and analyzed. Employee expectations about the process must be sensitively managed. They need to have a clear understanding of how the process will work, including the projected timetable for the report and executive responses. Their confidentially must be protected or they will

Pulse Report August 7

Question	Norm	Current Reading	SD (1)	D	U	A	SA (5)
I'm committed to our company.	4.3	4.7			5%	45%	50%
The company is moving in the right direction.	4.6	4.5		5%	5%	45%	45%
Safety is a high priority in my department.	4.2	4.3			15%	45%	40%
I routinely suggest ways to improve processes, procedures, or products.	4.3	4.0		5%	25%	30%	40%
I have an important role in our company's success.	3.7	3.9	5%	5%	20%	35%	35%
My supervisor provides routine updates on company issues.	3.5	3.4	10%	10%	25%	35%	20%
Our culture supports risk taking.	3.0	2.8	15%	25%	28%	22%	10%
N (Number of Respondents)	1236	56					
Response Rate	64%	68%					

Rating is on a "1 – 5" scale; "1" representing "strongly disagree,", "5" representing "strongly agree"

If you could ask the executive team one question, what would it be? (Common Themes)

Future

- Do you see any layoffs in the next few months?
- Are we still looking aggressively for acquisitions, or are we looking to grow internally?

Accountability

- How can we hold people more accountable to do things right and in a cost-efficient manner?
- People need to be more flexible and always focus on what is important to help us stay competitive. Those people who do the "wrong" things just because it is what they are used to doing have to be held accountable. Keep challenging and holding people accountable!!!

No question/Thanks and appreciation

- No question—just wanted to say that I totally respect you for the job you are doing—it can't possibly be easy to keep everyone happy.
- I have nothing but respect for you. You still make me nervous whenever you are around and I still somewhat fear you. But, you are the best managers/leaders ever! Thanks!

Figure 11.2   Sample Pulse Report

not provide candid responses. Hiring an independent firm to administer the process can be helpful with these issues. Executives must be ready to hear, share, and respond to petty, negative, rancorous, and even venal comments. Questions such as these have bubbled up in the past:

- "How can they justify giving a supervisor a $20,000 bonus and we get less than $600?"
- "Why does management treat me like a number instead of a human being?"

As Rick Fantini, an executive at Appleton Inc., warns, "If you don't have tough skin, you shouldn't get involved in this process. Honest, straight-forward answers will not always be popular, but at the very least, employees learn to trust what you say." Finally, the Pulse Process requires executives and managers to respond to the report in a timely fashion. As a result, they must be willing to admit they only have partial answers at a particular point in time.

The really tough work begins after receiving the audit results or Pulse Report. The organization must grapple with creating a strategy to address the concerns revealed in the assessment. We now turn to that issue.

Strategize

Strategy matters. Organizational leaders, such as those at FedEx, who can create passion in the workplace through consistent and energizing messages, tend to experience less employee turnover. [2] Additionally, a communication strategy can provide a hedge against employee cynicism by ensuring that dissenting opinions about decisions, practices, or policies are appropriately channeled. A well-developed communication strategy also cultivates the kind of environment that is more accepting of change and innovation.[3] 3M, for example, sows the seeds of innovation by routinely recording and telling stories about breakthrough products, processes, and ideas.[4] In short, an appropriate communication strategy enhances the probability of organiza-tional and communication effectiveness.

Crafting a communication strategy suggests three challenging questions: What exactly is a communication strategy? How do you craft the strategy? What makes a communication strategy effective?

What Is a Communication Strategy?

Communication strategy can be broadly defined as the *macro-level com-munication choices we make based on organizational goals and judgments about others' reactions, which serves as a basis for action.* The following discussion highlights the critical concepts in this definition.

Strategy involves a macro-level orientation that can be distinguished from tactical concerns. The word "strategy" is indirectly derived from the word "strategos," which denotes generalship. Generals are concerned with the big picture. Strategy occurs at higher organizational and abstraction levels than tactical issues.

Strategy involves implicit or explicit choices resulting in tradeoffs. Communicators explicitly or implicitly choose what to talk about, and what to ignore. The leader's agenda could include virtually anything from internal issues such as sexual harassment and team building to external ones such as market share or meeting customer expectations. Shaping the agenda by focusing employee attention on what executives deem important, can profoundly impact the organization.

Strategy involves goal setting. Determining communication goals is tricky. Many executives don't think about it explicitly, whereas others tend to settle for vagaries such as "keeping everyone informed." An objective of this ilk invites a host of other questions, such as "Informed about what?" "Informed in how much detail?" "Informed in what way?" "Informed how often?" These are the kinds of questions a communication strategy should answer.

Strategy involves anticipating others' reactions. Anticipating the cascade of responses proves critical. The dance between the initiative and the response and then the subsequent adjustments creates the dialogue that determines the success of the strategy. Why? Because the messages sent influence those received. If, for example, the message sent to employees is that "Mistakes will not be tolerated," then employees will often make efforts not only to *avoid* mistakes but also *not* to *tell anyone* that mistakes have been made. That dance differs greatly from one based on a theme of "learning to avoid mistakes."

Strategy naturally serves as the basis for action. Communication strategy provides the basis for structuring, executing, and evaluating communication practices. The choice of communication forums—newsletter, quarterly meetings, company-wide e-mails, and so on—naturally flow from the strategy.

How Do You Craft a Communication Strategy?

Knowing the characteristic of an extraordinary dancer does not equate with knowing *how* to become one. Likewise, knowing the attributes of a communication strategy does not guarantee that managers can craft one. Effective strategies emerge from careful assessment, thoughtful inquiry, and a deep understanding of the process. Remember, though, that successful strategists, such as choreographers, infuse the process with their artistic and intuitive sensibilities.

Select a sequence of communication goals that links to the organizational goals. Communication strategy can be viewed as reverse engineering. Organizational or unit goals provide the starting point for developing communication goals. Some companies use mass mailings of brochures and attractive publications to broadcast the organizational objectives and priorities. Once they are articulated and published, many decision makers simply assume the goals will be understood and acted on in swift order. But when

Educating

More Difficult

- Teach about executive and management thinking routines.
- Clarify links between business objectives and employees' goals.
- Shape interpretations of key organizational events.
- Make sense out of conflicting information.
- Create meaningful memories to cultivate action.

Coordinating

- Build a sense of common purpose.
- Cultivate a climate for sharing and acting on continuous improvement ideas.
- Integrate the priorities and plans of units or divisions.
- Negotiate common standards.

Inspiring

- Provide a sense of direction.
- Foster commitment to the organization's vision and values (e.g., praise examples of values in action).
- Focus attention on critical success factors.
- Frame information in meaningful ways.
- Create visual or symbolic reminders of values and/or priorities.

Relating

- Build rapport and relationships between employees.
- Provide recognition to employees.
- Clarify misperceptions between units.
- Encourage networking.

Informing

Less Difficult

- Clarify job expectations.
- Report on the organizational goals and results.
- Update employees about ongoing initiatives.
- Post press releases on the company Intranet.
- Relaying wage and benefit information.

Figure 11.3   Hierarchy of Communication Goals

questioned about these objectives, employees typically respond by saying, "I'm not sure if I completely understand them" or "I'll go to my supervisor if I have questions." The problem of poorly understood priorities plagues many organizations.

This means that executives and managers must develop a corresponding set of strategic communication goals. In one company we experimented with a hierarchy of communication goals and discovered that as the organization ascended each step, the difficulty of achieving the objective increased, but so did the corresponding payoff (see Figure 11.3). An executive who wants employees to more quickly adapt to a changing business climate might first pursue a *communication goal* of educating or teaching employees about the leadership team's thinking routines. A thinking routine describes the often complex process leaders use to make decisions, addressing such questions as,

"What factors are considered? How are they weighed? What tradeoffs are made and why?" Answering these questions suggests something deeper and more challenging than merely providing information. A variety of tactics, such as creating regular forums devoted to discussions of decision-making practices, could be used to achieve this strategic goal. Cultivating a sense of executive or managerial thinking routines helps employees better anticipate and respond to organizational changes.

Underscore and explore a few key themes or messages. Organizational leaders generally choose one of five basic message approaches that can be arranged on a continuum based on the amount of information shared with employees (see Figure 11.4). Many organizational leaders gravitate toward the "Spray & Pray" and "Tell & Sell" strategies for admirable reasons (see Table 11.1). The "Spray & Pray" strategy creates the illusion that everyone is informed because employees are showered with information. Some executives will go to meetings armed with their "deck" of one hundred PowerPoint slides, delivering the message in rapid-fire fashion. There's an inherent problem with this: Listeners can choose any card from the "deck," constructing their own novel interpretation of the message and the dealer will never know. Employees often have difficulty interpreting or making sense out of the information thrust at them and the speaker's "prayers" go unanswered.

The "Tell & Sell" strategy provides some interpretation by devoting resources to designing elaborate persuasive messages. Often leaders, or more accurately cheerleaders, enthusiastically endorse a new initiative, yet no one ever asks for employee feedback or checks to see if the message is understood.

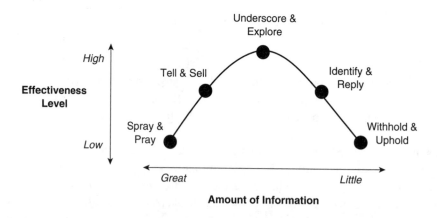

Figure 11.4   Message Strategy Continuum

Adapted from Clampitt, P. G., DeKoch, R., & Cashman, T. 2000. A Strategy for Communicating About Uncertainty. *Academy of Management Executive* 14 (4):41–57.

Table 11.1   Message Strategies

Strategy	Description	Assumption
Spray & Pray	Managers shower employees with all kinds of information, hoping that employees will be able to sort out the significant from the insignificant.	• More information = better communication and decision making.
Tell & Sell	Managers communicate a more limited set of messages, first *telling* employees about the key issues, and then *selling* employees on the wisdom of their approach.	• Employees are passive information receivers; therefore, feedback is not necessary. • Managers are in a position to know all the key organizational issues.
Underscore & Explore	Managers focus on developing a few core messages clearly linked to organizational success, while allowing employees freedom to explore the implications in a disciplined way. Managers actively listen for potential misunderstandings and unrecognized obstacles.	• Communication is not complete until managers know how employees react to the core ideas.
Identify & Reply	Managers identify key employee concerns and then reply to those issues. The strategy emphasizes the importance of listening to employees; they set the agenda, while executives respond to rumors and innuendos.	• Employees are in the best position to know the critical issues.
Withhold & Uphold	Managers withhold information until necessary; when confronted by rumors, they uphold the party line. Secrecy and control are the implicit values of those who embrace this strategy.	• Information is power. • Employees are not sophisticated enough to grasp the big picture.

The "Underscore & Explore" strategy solves that problem by addressing fewer issues and then exploring employee interpretations. It has the added benefit of shaping the agenda and creating dialogue around a few core concepts that have the greatest potential to transform the organization. The management team of a manufacturing company successfully used this strategy to create understanding of the organizational theme of "Transforming While Performing." The team identified the major challenge for the year as being able to transform the business to be more innovative and risk-taking, while, at the same time, performing their ongoing work responsibilities. The leaders weaved this theme into their communications on every possible occasion. Additionally, they focused employee attention by asking on the Pulse

Survey, "How could the company do a better job of 'transforming while performing'?" Asking this question, which was part of their "exploring strategy," encouraged all employees to think about the major success factor for the year.

Most employees want to understand the "big picture" and feel part of something bigger than themselves. They cannot internalize corporate values if they cannot see how their daily work fits into a larger structure. Executives must play an active role in translating the theme into organizational priorities and objectives, and when the opportunity presents itself, illustrate how objectives directly relate to certain work groups and individuals.

Align the communication tools and roles with the communication objectives and core messages. A well-developed strategy assigns relatively specific functions to each of the major communication channels or tools. Many organizations are tempted to use the same communication tools regardless of the core messages. In fact, those tools may subtlety undermine strategic goals.

Recall our discussion in previous chapters about selecting the proper channels. Skilled communication strategists apply these principles when designing the communication system. For example, a quarterly face-to-face meeting is better suited to sharing how a critical decision was made than it is to dumping a lot of information. In a quarterly meeting, the executive or manager can tell meaningful stories, relay nuances, and explain priorities. Broadcast e-mails simply will not cultivate a similar level of understanding or commitment. Thus, the strategist needs to specify the purpose of each channel, the usage protocol, and the rationale for the role. This macro-level view may reveal, for example, that the organization is heavy on channels that provide information to employees (Spray & Pray) but light on channels that educate employees about business dynamics.

The effective strategist also carves out relatively specific roles for key communicators. Executives have a unique inspirational and interpretative role: They are the ones who can provide a sense of direction and frame key organizational events. Typically they should *not* be charged with relaying most operating details. Others in the organization can fill different roles depending on their skills, credibility, and responsibilities. Fundamentally, the strategist seeks to *broaden* rather than *confine* responsibility for communication effectiveness; everyone has a unique role to play.

Choreographing the goals, messages, roles, and tools is the essence of a communication strategy. These choices reflect thoughtful tradeoffs between competing interests. The communication strategists must decide how communication goals link to organizational goals. Then they must determine which messages to promote and which to downplay. This involves determining the degree of message specificity as well as who has responsibility for the translating the messages. Finally, the various communication tools need to be aligned with all of these decisions.

What Makes a Communication Strategy Effective?

Communication strategies can be developed either deliberately or by happenstance. By chance, a few organizations stumble on strategies that appear to work. But generally, that is not the case. Thoughtful analysis helps an organization make the appropriate choices to incite meaningful actions. Gifted analysts can gauge their effectiveness by asking the following questions:

Does the communication strategy advance organization goals? A "one size fits all" communication strategy always disappoints because organizations have very different objectives. Researchers have linked effective communication strategies to productivity gains, efficiency improvements, cost reductions, improved morale, and decreased turnover.[5] In short, aligned strategies tend to enhance organizational performance.

On the other hand, misaligned strategies can hinder organizational performance. For instance, in one medical clinic, the executive board of physicians determined that one of its key business objectives was to increase employee accountability. Unfortunately, the board never developed a supportive communication strategy. In fact, its de facto strategy was to blame the nearest employee for any problem. The board's actions (or inaction), therefore, ran counter to its objectives. The result was that employees were simultaneously held *accountable for everything* while *not* being *responsible for anything* in particular. Inevitably this led to low morale, high turnover, disorganization, and ultimately, patient frustration. Eventually the physicians were convinced to test a strategic communication plan, which started with dialogue about employee job responsibilities. The physicians finally knew *who* to talk to about *what*. And, of course, this increased employee accountability. In sum, communication strategies that are not linked to underlying organizational goals are as effective as an aesthetically pleasing advertising campaign that fails to generate business.

Does the strategy legitimize certain issues and de-legitimize others? Teenagers popularized the phrase, "Don't go there." Although most communication strategists avoid that lingo, they should be comfortable with the underlying sentiment. Communication strategists are as concerned about what is *not* said as they are with what *is* said. By setting the agenda, leaders shape the playing field. In one case, we quite literally determined what was "in bounds" and what was "out of bounds." The culture of complaint become so debilitating in a dairy plant that the leaders drew a diagram of *what was acceptable* and *what was not acceptable* to talk about (see Figure 11.5). In an all-employee meeting, the executives introduced the diagram, discussed why it was needed, and how it was to be used. Then the diagram was posted in every supervisor's office and meeting room. "Are we talking in the circle?" became the plant mantra for several months.

Gradually the culture of complaint was transformed into a culture of confronting core concerns. Companies that promote their core values or

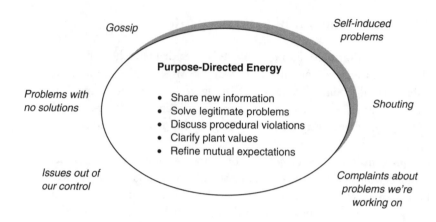

Gossip

Self-induced problems

Purpose-Directed Energy

Problems with no solutions

- Share new information
- Solve legitimate problems
- Discuss procedural violations
- Clarify plant values
- Refine mutual expectations

Shouting

Issues out of our control

Complaints about problems we're working on

Figure 11.5   Are We Talking in the Circle?

competencies are essentially doing the same thing. The values direct attention away from presumably irrelevant matters and shift attention to core issues.

Does the strategy shape an appropriate organizational memory? There are many factors that influence the interpretation of events but few are more important than memory. Brain researchers tell us that memory serves as a template that allows us to discern differences and similarities between events.

Consider the following situation. A development team spent an enormous amount of time and energy launching a new product line. Team members gave up weekends and vacation time to meet their quality standards and deadlines. Unfortunately, the product line was not well received in the marketplace. The crucial issue was, "How would this event be remembered?" The employees invested their minds and hearts in the project and it failed. But why? Unfortunately, most team members remembered this as the time that senior management did not support them, complaining that, "If only the organization would have invested a few more dollars in the marketing effort, this product would have succeeded." Consequently, the team was discouraged and less inclined to devote much energy to future projects. There was an alternative. Senior management could have created a different memory—one based on the need to learn more about the marketplace before launching a new product line. Thus, organizational memory creates a climate that can either *facilitate* or *stifle* innovation.

Many scholars have written about the "learning organization" but it is important to note that employees often learn the wrong lessons as well as the right ones. Communication strategists have a responsibility to create the right memories.

Does the strategy provide employees with a proper point of identity? An employee who thinks of himself as a "buggy whip maker" differs considerably from one who considers himself a "leather craftsman" who happens to make buggy whips. Who will more quickly adjust to changes in the marketplace? The specificity of the "buggy whip maker's" point of identity restricts his horizons as well as his employer's. This is why thoughtful organizations pay close attention to the language they use in everyday discourse. Names have consequences. Xerox, for instance, defines itself as the "document company" as opposed to a "photocopy company." The conceptual horizon of a "document company" goes beyond merely building the machinery to make photocopies. In short, increasing the variety, complexity, and subtlety of language changes the way employees think about what they do.[6]

Does the strategy help make sense of the confusing and ambiguous? One by-product of the so called "information age" is that employees often receive a vast array of information that is confusing, contradictory, and ambiguous. Karl Weick perceptively comments on this fact of corporate life:

> The problem is that there are too many meanings, not too few. The problem faced by the sensemaker is one of equivocality, not one of uncertainty. The problem is confusion, not ignorance. I emphasize this because those investigators who favor the metaphor of information processing often view sensemaking, as they do most other problems, as a setting where people need more information. That is not what people need when they are overwhelmed by equivocality.[7]

Managers must assume a number of roles: They must simultaneously play the role of a mind reader, detective, analyst, pundit, fortune-teller, and dramatist.

Consider a situation that took place during a quarterly update meeting. A maintenance employee asked an executive about the meaning of "downtime." His supervisor always pressured him to finish repair jobs in the allotted downtime slot for a piece of industrial machinery—even if the employee felt the job required an extra hour of work to "do the job right." He was perplexed and angry over the fact that the same machine could be shut down for production several days later. He inquired, "Why can't I put in an extra hour of downtime on Monday when later in the week you're going to shut down the entire machine for two days? What's the difference?" The executive responded, "It costs the company $500/hour if we don't run the machine during scheduled production time because we pay a "penalty" for not meeting customer deadlines. When we choose not to run a machine during scheduled downtime, it costs us only $150/hour." The employee's confusion was understandable, as was the executive's response. In essence there were two kinds of downtime, not one, as most people would reasonably assume.

Confusion of this sort occurs all the time. An effective strategy allows employees to ask these kinds of questions and get a sensible answer—even if they don't agree with the response. The alternative is that employees, like this one, become further confused and disenfranchised.

Does the strategy evolve? As an organization's goals and employees change, so must the communication strategy. One source of renewal comes from reassessing assumptions. Strategies can also evolve by carefully evaluating feedback about the various communication practices, initiatives, and programs. Regrettably, many executives choose to ignore the responses to their communication strategies and tactics.

Careful observers will note that the first three attributes are mainly concerned with the underlying needs of a successful organization. Advancing organizational goals, creating focus, and shaping proper memories are classic notions related to organizational effectiveness. The second set of attributes focuses more on the underlying needs of employees. Humans are sense-making creatures; we need to reduce disorder and confusion to function properly. Likewise, we need to identify with others and identify with ideas that motivate us. And finally, we all need to mature and evolve. How well an organization meets its own needs and those of its employees is intimately linked to the communication strategy.

Implement

Great strategy cannot overcome poor execution. Failure to recognize this fact may help explain why "50% of decisions never get successfully implemented."[8] Executing a communication strategy requires skill, tenacity, and insight. Over the years, my associates and I have learned many important lessons about proper implementation. We highlight these in the following section.

Use redundancy and repetition. Advertisers have long known the value of repeating commercial messages. Likewise, successful communicators learn that repetition increases the likelihood that various stakeholders will hear a similar message, remember it, and act on it. Reiterating key messages signals that the communicators are serious about the idea; reiterating serves a legitimizing function. Listeners often have clever ways of discounting or avoiding messages that conflict with their preconceived notions. Repetition helps break through those natural psychological resistance points and increases the likelihood that the message will reach listeners at a time when they are most open.

Redundancy works in a similar, if more subtle, way. Redundant messages replicate a central idea but vary the mode of expression. The value of redundancy lies in expanding the number of linkages between an idea and action. For the organization, this means thinking of clever ways to reinforce the theme by linking specific examples to the core messages. One manufacturing plant's core theme of "Performing While Transforming," was widely promoted in newsletters and broadcast e-mails. One unit that used to have long production runs started to intersperse shorter runs into its daily operations. The plant manager seized on this situation and discussed how employees from this unit were "performing while transforming" by successfully managing their regular runs while adapting to changing customer demands for smaller, more customized runs. His praise, delivered in quarterly meetings, reinforced the core message while also recognized those particular employees. It was also highly motivating for employees. Using repetition and redundancy often proves challenging for executives. It takes a degree of fortitude to recognize that even though they have reiterated a particular message a hundred times before, it may well be the first time certain employees have heard it or perhaps believed it was important.

Identify and utilize opinion leaders. Executives and senior managers often make the mistake of assuming sole responsibility for communicating core messages. Clearly they have a fundamental responsibility but the strategy cannot be sustained through their efforts alone. If executives want their initiatives to be implemented, they must engage not only managers and supervisors, but also the support of opinion leaders throughout the organization. All groups have at least one informal leader who serves a vital role in the employee social structure. The opinion leaders are clearly influential yet are often overlooked by executives. Opinion leaders are respected for their insight and expertise, are typically more outgoing, and are good at expressing their opinions as well as clarifying those of others. They help members of the group make sense of organizational life, and they set the norms for acceptable and unacceptable behavior.

Executives need to identify key opinion leaders, determine their understanding of organizational priorities, seek their input, and assess their degree of support. If opinion leaders express resistance, managers need to address their concerns and determine how to gain their endorsement. In many respects, the "buy-in" of the opinion leaders is the most important determinant of whether programs succeed or fail.[9]

Identify and attack "thought-terminating clichés." Robert Jay Clifton used this illuminating phrase to highlight how people can use language to stop further thought, discussion, and action.[10] Once someone invokes a thought-terminating cliché it becomes difficult to probe much further into the idea. In U.S. politics, for example, once a new initiative has been successfully labeled as "racist," it becomes difficult to have further dialogue. Every organizational culture creates these kinds of labels and phrases. In one Fortune 500 Company, the cliché was "Here we go again." By linking new initiatives to this phrase, employees subtly resisted change, disengaged from the process, and stopped further discussion, regardless of the merits of the proposal.

Successful leaders identify these clichés, expose them, and trigger more thoughtful discussions about their proposals. In the aforementioned case, leaders directly attacked the cliché by proactively presenting a direct counterargument—"This initiative is NOT one of these 'here-we-go-again' ideas and here's why . . . ." Then they invited employees to discuss the differences between this initiative and others. This approach sent two very strong signals: First, the leadership team understood their employees' preconceptions, and second, the leadership team wanted to quickly move beyond the prosaic and engage in serious discussions about the initiative.

Any core message worth communicating makes many employees uncomfortable because it requires them to deviate from the status quo. Consequently, it is not unusual for employees to ignore or resist the underlying objectives of the strategy by frequently using subtle thought-terminating clichés. Skillful executives learn to use the resistance as a persuasive opportunity. Instead of minimizing employee concerns, they acknowledge, legitimize, and objectify them. Often concerns are linked to some vague feelings of unease related to the perceived loss of status or fear of the unknown. Other concerns, such as fear of economic loss or disruption of routines, are more specific. In either case, effective executives *explore* the resistance as a means to *underscore* the key messages.

Assess-Strategize-Implement in Action

Effective communication strategists think like a financial analyst to properly assess, visualize like a choreographer to fashion strategy, and perform like an elite athlete to implement strategy. This unique skill set is best illustrated by the following example.

In the assessment phase at one manufacturing company, the Pulse Process revealed that many employees were confused about how the organization made major decisions. Why, for example, did one unit get funding for a project and another did not? The early detection of this concern started a dialogue in the organization about how to better communicate about decision-making practices. Our task force ascertained that, indeed, different criteria were used to make decisions in various parts of the organization. Was this a defensible position? Yes. The decisions were part of an investment strategy designed to aggressively fund projects in new and growing markets while merely maintaining funding levels for projects focused on declining markets. It was analogous to a new homeowner who fully funds home-improvement projects compared to the renter who minimizes investments, knowing that the lease will be up at the end of the year.

We made three strategic decisions. First, we developed a specific communication goal to "Educate employees about the product life cycle." This goal directly linked to the organizational goal of "Using financial resources to grow the company." Second, we developed our core message around the life cycle of their products. The company categorized their products into one of three worlds: "The Launch World," "The Growth World," or "The Decline World." The choice of the word "world" was not accidental; it was designated to convey the different set of standards, procedures, and policies that guide decision making as a product moves through the various stages in the life cycle. Third, we realigned the communication system around the core message through a number of methods including: 1) preparing special

Talking Points that were organized by "world," and 2) developing a template for company-wide meetings that was oriented around the "worlds." We also introduced a new question in the Pulse Report to measure our effectiveness. The result: Within one year there was a marked change in employee understanding of the investment strategy. And in many instances employees started using the "three world" language in their day-to-day conversations. That was when the organization knew that a significant shift had occurred.[11]

Conclusion

Business strategists have discovered that, "An organizing framework can never be right or wrong, only helpful or unhelpful. A good organizing framework is minimalist—it is as simple as is consistent with illuminating the issues under discussion—and it is memorable."[12] The "three world" framework was not the *perfect* or *only* solution, but it was helpful. Replicating success stories such as this requires that communication strategists ask the right questions, thoughtfully work through the answers, and tenaciously pursue the implications.[13] Then you will near the elusive goal of effective communication and become a choreographer of organizational effectiveness.

Notes

1. Greenbaum, H., & White, N. D. 1976. Biofeedback at the organizational level: The communication audit. *Journal of Business Communication* 13 (4):3–15, p. 5.

2. Byrne, J. 1999. The search for the young and gifted. *Business week*, 4 October:108–116.

3. Clampitt, P., & Berk, L. 1996. Strategically communicating organisational change. *Journal of Communication Management* 1:15–28.

4. Usow, J., Senior Account Representative at 3M. 2000. Personal communication. 5 January.

5. Downs, C., Clampitt, P., & Pfieffer, A. 1988. Communication and organizational outcomes. In *Handbook of organizational communication,* edited by G. Goldhaber, & G. Barnett (pp. 171–212). Norwood, NJ: Ablex Publishing.

6. Daft, R. & Wiginton, J. 1979. Language and organization. *Academy of Management Review* 4:179–191.

7. Weick, K. 1995. *Sensemaking in organizations.* Thousand Oaks, CA: Sage, p. 27.

8. Nutt, P. 1999. Surprising but true: Half the decisions in organizations fail. *Academy of Management Executive* 13 (4):75–90, p. 75. See also, Nutt, P.C. 2002. *Why decisions fail: Avoiding the blunders and traps that lead to debacles.* San Francisco: Berrett-Koehler.

9. Rogers, E. 1995. *Diffusion of innovations.* New York: Free Press.

10.   Clifton, R. J. 1961. *Reform and the psychology of totalism: A study of "brain-washing' in China*. New York: Norton.

11.   Bill VanDenBrandt, Dave Spencer, and I worked as a team at Appleton to develop this strategy.

12.   Kay, J., McKiernan, P., & Faulkner, D. 2003. The history of strategy and some thoughts about the future. In *The Oxford Handbook of Strategy*, edited by D. O. Faulker & A. Campbell (pp. 21–46). New York: Oxford University Press, p. 37.

13.   This chapter is based on the following: Clampitt, P. G., DeKoch, R. J., & Cashman, T. 2000. A strategy for communicating about uncertainty. *Academy of Management Executive* 14 (4):41–57; Clampitt, P. G., Berk, L., & William, M. L. 2002. Leaders as strategic communications. *Ivey Business Journal* May–June:51–55.

Index

Note: Page numbers in *italic* type indicate a table or figure.

About the Author

Phillip G. Clampitt is the Hendrickson Professor of Business at the University of Wisconsin-Green Bay, where he teaches in the Information Sciences program. He is the co-author of *Embracing Uncertainty: The Essence of Leadership* (see www.imetacomm.com/eu). His work has been published in a variety of journals including the *Academy of Management Executive, Management Communication Quarterly, Journal of Business Communication, Communication World, Journal of Broadcasting, Journal of Communication Management, Ivey Business Journal,* and *Journal of Change Management.* Additionally, his research on uncertainty management was profiled in the *Sloan Management Review.* Professor Clampitt is a recognized expert on communication assessments. He has conducted over one hundred communication audits and has written chapters for two books on the subject in the *Handbook of Communication Audits for Organisations* (edited by Owen Hargie and Dennis Tourish) and *Communication Audits* by Cal Downs. In addition, Professor Clampitt founded MetaComm, a communication consulting firm that specializes in assessing, analyzing, and resolving communication problems in organizations. He has worked with many companies, including PepsiCo, Appleton, Schneider National, American Medical Security, Dean Foods, and The Boldt Company (see www.imetacomm.com).